Dictionaries of Civilization

Egypt

Pharaonic Period

Alessia Fassone
Enrico Ferraris

Translated by Jay Hyams

University of California Press
Berkeley   Los Angeles   London

Dictionaries of Civilization
Series edited by Ada Gabucci

University of California Press, one of the most distinguished university presses in the United States, enriches lives around the world by advancing scholarship in the humanities, social sciences, and natural sciences. Its activities are supported by the UC Press Foundation and by philanthropic contributions from individuals and institutions. For more information, visit www.ucpress.edu.

University of California Press
Berkeley and Los Angeles, California

University of California Press, Ltd.
London, England

ISBN-13: 978-0-520-25648-4 (pbk.: alk. paper)

Manufactured in Spain

16   15   14   13   12   11   10   09   08
10   9   8   7   6   5   4   3   2   1

Art direction
Dario Tagliabue

Graphic design
Anna Piccarreta

Layouts
Morena De Filippo

Editorial direction
Caterina Giavotto

Editing
Fabrizio Begossi

Picture research
Simona Bartolena
Chiara Franchini

Technical coordination
Andrea Panozzo

Quality control
Giancarlo Berti

English-language translation
Jay Hyams

English-language typesetting
Michael Shaw

Cover
Portrait bust of Tutankhamen, 1346–1337 BC, Egyptian Museum, Cairo.
Page 2
Colossus of Ramses II (detail),
19th dynasty, alabaster, Museum of Mit Rahina, Memphis.

Contents

Introduction

Without question, one of the most intriguing aspects of the civilization of ancient Egypt is how long it has held its fascination. By the time of the classical Greek civilization, Egypt was already looked back upon as a "sacred" time and place from which knowledge could be drawn and with which the present could be compared; even then, Egypt was a place to visit and to explore. In the description of Egypt that Herodotus handed down in Book Two of his History one senses the same mixture of astonishment and admiration that the visitor to Egypt experiences today with undiminished intensity. The powerful attraction that Egyptian civilization has exercised over the centuries constitutes a kind of golden thread that unites our modern sensibility to that of the ancients, and it is in light of such considerations that we have sought to concentrate on the "travel-guide" aspect of the books that are part of the Dictionaries of Civilization series. By no means does this volume try to exhaust the subject of Egyptology, seeking instead to be a useful study tool, a helpful guide to some of the principal historical and social phenomena of so-called pharaonic Egypt. The chronological period covered by this work includes the thirty dynasties of pharaohs that reigned over the country from the 4th millennium BC to the middle of the 4th century BC. Given the enormous span of time involved, we have decided to exclude from this book the historical period following the conquest of the country by Alexander the Great, meaning the Ptolemaic Period, which of course merits a book of its own.

The subjects covered in this book have been divided into seven broad categories, each of which is in turn divided into separate entries composed of an introductory text, an in-depth sidebar or chronology, and illustrations with informative captions with callouts to explain details. In many cases, the title of the entry is accompanied by a quotation, most of which have been drawn from ancient Egyptian literature. The dating used in the texts is based on the chronology given by Nicolas Grimal in his History of Ancient Egypt *(Oxford–Cambridge, 1992)*. In those cases where doing so seemed more useful to the reader, the literary citation has been replaced with the original hieroglyphic form of the name of the historical person, the locality, or the Egyptian divinity, also giving the reader the phonetic pronunciation and translation. It should be remembered that the ancient Egyptian language was consonantal (as are the Semitic languages), and that the indications for the reading of vowels appeared only in the postpharaonic period; in truth, there is no solid agreement on what the pronunciation of ancient Egyptian sounded like.

Each entry also includes bibliographic references to facilitate further study; the works referred to are listed in the bibliography in the back of the book. The books given were selected on the basis of two categories of use. To ease further access to information about the subject in general, we have indicated readily available texts of which there has been a recent edition; to assist those readers who wish to study the subject at a more in-depth level, space was also given to publications that, although old and perhaps in a foreign language, are still considered to be of fundamental importance in their field.

Also in the back of the book are maps of ancient Egypt, a chronology of ancient Egypt's dynasties, a glossary of the special terms used in the book, a museum guide, and a general index.

As a fitting conclusion to this exciting project, we would like to express our sincere thanks to Ada Gabucci, Valentina Lindon, Caterina Giavotto, Simona Bartolena, Chiara Franchini, Fabrizio Begossi, Sara Salvi, and to the entire staff of Electa for their extraordinary professionalism and for the encouragement and support they gave us.

People

◀ Colossal sarcophagus of Queen Meritamon, from the cachette at Deir el-Bahri, painted cedarwood, h 314 cm, Egyptian Museum, Cairo, CG 53140.

Menes and Narmer

Hieroglyph
Men-i
(meaning uncertain)

Chronology
3150–3125 BC,
1st dynasty

Bibliography
Grimal 1988, Chap. I-
III. Midant-Reynes
1992. Shaw 2000,
Chap. 1-4.

Egyptian historical tradition attributed the foundation of the kingdom of Egypt, and the consequent installation of royal power, to the
acts of a legendary figure named Menes. He was the first pharaoh of
Egypt and the mythical founder of the administrative, economic, and
cultural styles that later became characteristic of Egyptian civilization. According to legend, Menes founded the capital of the country,
Memphis, established the division of the territories of Lower and
Upper Egypt into provinces, organized a central bureaucracy based
on written documents, and created an efficient large-scale system of
irrigation. Despite various attempts to attribute an identity to him,
Menes remains a legendary figure. The first ruler whose existence is
attested to by concrete evidence, both in the south and the north of
the country, is Narmer, who lived around 3000 BC. This sovereign is
usually credited with carrying out the process of unification of the
country and beginning the so-called Thinite dynasties, meaning the
first two historical dynasties, which according to both ancient
sources and archaeological finds were originally from the city of Thinis, in Upper Egypt. However, recent excavations near Umm el-
Qaab, in the area of Abydos, have brought to light the burial sites of
at least a dozen rulers who may have carried out the unification of
the country as much as 200 years before Narmer's reign. This line of
predynastic rulers, of whom Narmer may have been the last member, is conventionally called dynasty o.

▶ Plaquette perhaps
bearing a
representation of the
name of King Scorpion
of the dynasty o,
Predynastic Period,
carved ivory, Egyptian
Museum, Cairo.

Found toward the end of the 19th century, this decorated macehead bears Narmer's name. The central motif of the scene depicted is a procession in front of the ruler, but the precise meaning has not been established and is the subject of ongoing debate. The most widely shared opinion today holds that this is a depiction of the sed *festival, the royal jubilee celebration. According to another theory, the scene depicts the presentation of the spoils taken by Narmer in his victories in the Delta.*

Above the canopy, the dynastic goddess of Hierakonpolis, Nekhbet, appears in the form of a vulture, spreading her wings over the pharaoh in a sign of divine protection.

The principal figure of the scene is the ruler. He wears the crown of Lower Egypt and sits beneath a canopy erected on a high, stepped dais.

Below can be seen the two figures of the king's "fan bearers."

▲ Macehead of King Narmer, from Hierakonpolis, dynasty 0, limestone, h 19.8 cm, Ashmolean Museum, Oxford, E. 3631.

Palettes were used for crushing and mixing pigments for use in ornamentation and usually had hollow areas to hold the material to be worked. Such palettes were also put to ceremonial uses during the Predynastic Period, with examples made in precious materials bearing relief decoration. The Palette of King Narmer belongs to this category, for it celebrates the king's victory over the Egyptian populations of the Delta.

The pharaoh is assured protection by the celestial goddess Hathor, whose half-human half-bovine head appears to the sides of the king's name.

Narmer's name appears within the protection of a palace-façade motif (serekh), in keeping with the magical practices behind the use of the cartouche.

The king is depicted with all the attributes typical of an Egyptian sovereign: the white crown of Upper Egypt, the bull tail, the short skirt called a shendyt, and the false beard. He is presented in the imperious gesture of striking down an enemy with a mace.

The pharaoh is accompanied by a "sandal bearer," a servant in his personal service.

The pharaoh is here assimilated to the astral divinity Horus. The people of the Delta are presented through the symbol of a papyrus thicket from which a human head emerges, while Horus holds their "breath," and thus their life, with a rope.

▲ Palette of King Narmer, front, from Hierakonpolis, dynasty 0, schist, h 64 cm, Egyptian Museum, Cairo, CG 14716.

The awkward poses of the defeated enemies indicate that they are dead, following a style that was still being used in reliefs during the Ramessid period.

The back of the palette is divided in three levels, the central theme of which is Narmer's triumph and the unification of the country under his rule.

Beneath the celestial boat of Horus, the cadavers of fallen enemies are arranged in orderly rows, ritually mutilated by decapitation, their heads placed between their legs.

The pharaoh is far larger than everyone else. Unlike the image on the front, he now wears the red crown of Lower Egypt, meaning the Delta. He advances holding his scepter preceded by standardbearers with the cult emblems of the provinces of the south.

The Two Lands, the designation of Egypt in use until the Arab conquest, are represented here by two fabulous long-necked animals. They are symbolically intertwined, indicating the unity of the two regions of Upper and Lower Egypt.

Here the pharaoh is presented in the guise of a powerful animal, a bull. The scene shows the king's fury as he knocks down the wall of an enemy fortress and tramples its occupants.

▲ Palette of King Narmer, back, from Hierakonpolis, dynasty 0, schist, h 64 cm, Egyptian Museum, Cairo, CG 14716.

Djoser and Imhotep

Hieroglyph
Djoser–Netjerikhet
("Divine of body")

Chronology
2700–2650 BC
3rd dynasty

Sources
The Famine stela,
(Lichtheim 1980,
Vol.III, p.94)

Bibliography
Grimal 1988, chap. IV.
Shaw 2000, chap. 5.

The Papyrus Westcar attributes the foundation of the 3rd dynasty (2700–2625 BC) to a king named Nebka; even so, the period was dominated by the figure of his successor, Djoser, who ruled Egypt for nineteen years under his "Horus name," Netjerikhet. Little information exists about him or his reign, but his noble stature and illuminated outlook left an indelible mark on Egypt's historical tradition, such that during the Ptolemaic Period, 2,500 years after his death, he was still fondly remembered on a famous (if spurious; see page 18) relic. This is the Famine Stele, which presents a vivid image of a pious ruler dedicated to caring for his people, struggling to find a way to save them from famine. This pharaoh's importance in the history of Egypt is also tied to the fundamental contribution he made to the evolution of funerary architecture and to the promotion of stone as a symbol of monumentality. Djoser entrusted the construction of his own funerary complex, at Saqqara, to the high priest of Heliopolis, Imhotep. This priest began with the traditional royal burial—the mastaba—and worked it into the Step Pyramid, which he made the center of an articulated architectural space entirely made in stone and surrounded by a powerful wall. Later tradition elevated the figure of Imhotep; he was made the patron of scribes and physicians and was venerated as the very personification itself of wisdom.

▶ Panel of Djoser from the funerary complex of Djoser at Saqqara, northern tomb, faience, h 181 cm, Egyptian Museum, Cairo, JE 68921.

This statue of Djoser was found in the serdab *of the Saqqara funerary complex in 1924–25. Within the sphere of mortuary architecture, the Arabic term* serdab *refers to a room used for a statue of the deceased. Such rooms most often cannot be entered and communicate with the mortuary temple by way of narrow slits in a wall.*

Djoser is the first ruler of whom there exists a fully round and life-size statue. He is presented dressed in the ceremonial costume for the jubilee festival (in Egyptian, heb sed*). He wears a massive wig and the royal headdress with horizontal bands known as the* nemes.

The statue of the deceased was placed in the serdab *to permit the soul of the deceased to dwell there when it so desired so as to receive the offerings placed in the mortuary temple, to hear the prayers of his family, and to see them while remaining hidden, a presence both invisible and inscrutable to humans.*

An inscription on the back of the plinth bears the ruler's Horus name, Netjerikhet. This is the only name for this pharaoh handed down from the Old Kingdom; the identification of Netjerikhet with the legendary Djoser is based on sources from the Middle Kingdom.

▶ Statue of Djoser, from the funerary complex of Djoser at Saqqara, painted limestone, h 142 cm, Egyptian Museum, Cairo, JE 49158.

Imhotep's fame among the ancients was only partially based on his role as chief architect in the design and construction of Djoser's funerary complex. The image that Egyptian tradition preserved of him shows that after his death Imhotep was soon accorded the highest honors, in consideration of his notable cultural and moral stature. During the New Kingdom, he was deified and looked upon as the patron of scribes and a personification of wisdom. This last characteristic emerges in particular in the Ramessid papyrus known as the Turin Canon, in which Imhotep is presented as the "son of Ptah," the Memphite god of wisdom and knowledge.

Details of the statue reflect aspects of Imhotep's character. The skullcap he wears is a clear iconographic reference to the tight headband worn by Ptah, while the papyrus open on his knees refers to the immense knowledge attributed to Imhotep as well as to his role as the patron of scribes.

▲ Seated statuette of Imhotep, Late Period, Musée du Louvre, Paris.

Djoser's funerary complex represents a milestone in the history of Egyptian architecture. It can be considered a sort of experimental laboratory in which the new stylistic and formal elements of royal mortuary architecture were first established. It also marks the truly revolutionary replacement of perishable mud bricks with construction in stone. From both symbolic and realistic points of view, stone was better suited than bricks to immortalize the memory of the pharaoh, preserving him from the slow erosion of time.

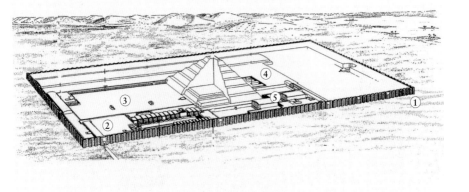

Legend

1. The outer walls are exceptionally large: the perimeter wall is 544.9 x 277.6 m with a height that reached 10.5 m.
2. The monumental entrance led to a covered corridor 54 m long with fascicled semicolumns set into the walls.
3. The large open court in front of the Step Pyramid symbolically recalled the large area in which the pharaoh celebrated, with a race, the *sed* festival, the royal jubilee that marked the renewal of the pharaoh's power and authority after 30 years of reign.
4. The mortuary temple built next to the Step Pyramid is the first of its kind and became a constant element in pyramid complexes from the 4th dynasty on. A small room, called the *serdab*, flanked the mortuary temple and held the seated statue of the ruler.
5. The so-called House of the North represented the throne of Lower Egypt, while the House of the South represented the throne of Upper Egypt.

▲ Perspective reconstruction of the funerary complex of Djoser at Saqqara.

During the period of Ptolemy V Epiphanes, the priests of the temple of the local god Khnum at Elephantine exploited the reverence and authority inspired by the figure of Djoser to create a forgery to serve their purposes. They had a stone stele made and set up at Gebel Silsila, backdating it to the period of Djoser, in which the pharaoh decrees the donation of the entire Nubian region of the Dodecaschoinos (from Aswan to Tacompsos) to Khnum as protector of the Nile, for having intervened to end the famine that had raged in Egypt for seven years.

The pharaoh Djoser is depicted in the gesture of offering the lands mentioned in "his decree" to the Elephantine triad composed of Khnum, Sati, and Anukis.

"I was in mourning on my throne, those of the palace were in grief . . . because the Nile had failed to come in time. In a period of seven years grain was scant, kernels were dried up, every man was without resources . . . children cried, temples were shut . . . I consulted one of the staff of the Ibis, the chief lector-priest of Imhotep, son of Ptah . . . Then I was asleep, my heart was in life and happiness. I found the god standing before me . . . He said, 'I am Khnum, your creator . . . I will make the Nile swell for you . . . the plants will flourish, bending under their fruit . . . the land of Egypt will stir again, the shores shining wonderfully.' Then I awoke happy . . . and made this decree."

▲ Famine Stele, Gebel Silsila, reign of Ptolemy V Epiphanes (205–180 BC).

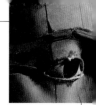

4th dynasty

The 4th dynasty marked the apogee of Old Kingdom pharaonic absolutism. Indeed, the most eloquent and suitable symbols for this period are the magnificent pyramid complexes built at Meidum, Dahshur, and most of all Giza. Literary sources describe the founder of the dynasty, Snefru, as a good-natured king, but the historical tradition preserved in the Palermo Stone (a 5th-dynasty stele inscribed with royal annals) indicates that he did everything in his power to expand the area of Egypt's commercial interests by way of periodic military expeditions in the nearby territories of Libya, the Sinai, and Nubia, bringing back to Egypt such spoils of war as cattle, prisoners, exotic goods (panther hides, spices, ebony), and precious stones and minerals (turquoise, granite, copper, gold). Snefru also strengthened Egypt's contacts, begun at the beginning of the 3rd dynasty, with the regions of Syria and Lebanon, sources of precious cedarwood, a building material that was scarce in Egypt. The availability of these human and material resources and the needs of an increasingly centralized administration based on the person of the pharaoh explain the vast building programs of Snefru and his immediate successors (Khufu, Khafre, and Menkure). This situation also led to the maturation of sculpture and relief carving in Egypt, which in this period reached formal and expressive fullness, leading to some of the greatest masterpieces of Egyptian art.

Hieroglyph
S-nefru
("He who brings
perfection")

Chronology
2625–2510 BC
4th dynasty

Sources
*The annals of the
Palermo Stone,*
(Wilkinson 2000a)

Bibliography
Malek 1986.
Grimal 1988, chap. IV.
Shaw 2000, chap. 6.

◀ Inscription on rock
celebrating Snefru's
victory over the
Bedouins, 4th dynasty,
Wadi Maghara, Sinai.

This small statuette is the only known portrait of Khufu, builder of the most impressive pyramid at Giza. It was found, missing its head, in 1903 by several workers on the excavations directed by Flinders Petrie near the temple of Osiris of Abydos. Aware of the importance of the discovery, Petrie had the entire area where the statuette had been found sifted, but without finding the head. Not long after this, however, the statuette's head showed up at an antiquities market, making it possible for Petrie to reassemble the only known portrait of Khufu.

Khufu is depicted seated on a throne. He wears the red crown of Lower Egypt and a shendyt, a sort of short, pleated skirt. He holds the traditional flail in his right hand, his left resting on his knee.

Enclosed within the serekh is the engraved name of Khufu, which is how Flinders Petrie was able to identify the pharaoh portrayed in the statuette.

▲ Statuette of Khufu from the temple of Osiris at Abydos, 4th dynasty, ivory, h 7.5 cm, Egyptian Museum, Cairo, JE 36143.

*Aside from its great artistic value, this statue of Khafre constitutes an extraordinary
synthesis of the "mystery" of Egyptian royalty, which was based on the identification of
the pharaoh with the god Horus. This supernatural relationship explains the presence,
behind the ruler's head, of the divine falcon Horus, who spreads his wings as a sign of
protection, confirming the celestial origin of the power and authority of the pharaoh.*

*The statue reveals
the high level of
technical skill
reached by Egypt's
artists during the 4th
dynasty. Its notable
aspects include the
plastic rendering of
the ruler's muscles
and facial features,
the fine polishing of
the hard-to-work
surface, and finally
the skillful
exploitation of the
veining of the dark
stone to achieve
surprising chromatic
and luminous effects.*

▲ Statue of Khafre, from Khafre's
valley temple at Giza, 4th dynasty,
black diorite, h 168 cm, Egyptian
Museum, Cairo, CG 14.

The position of Menkure within the group, in the center and slightly ahead of the others, is a compositional expedient that serves to concentrate perspective focus on him, giving him preeminence and expressive force.

The inscription at the feet of the figure to the pharaoh's right identifies her as the goddess Hathor. Throughout all of Egyptian history, Hathor was seen as strongly tied to Egypt's royalty, a result of both her great antiquity and her strong connection to the god Horus, of whom the pharaoh was the incarnation, as indicated by her name (in Egyptian, Hut-Hor), which means "the house of Horus."

Menkure may have had a triad like this made for each of the administrative provinces (the nomes) of Egypt's Old Kingdom, of which there were then probably 38 or 39.

▲ Triad of King Menkure with Hathor and a nome, from Menkure's valley temple at Giza, 4th dynasty, graywacke, h 96 cm, Egyptian Museum, Cairo, JE 46499.

The figure to the left of the pharaoh is a personification of the seventh nome of Upper Egypt with its capital at Diospolis Parva, as indicated by the standard she bears on her head, which presents the face of the goddess Bat.

Pyramid of Khafre.
Egyptian name: "Great is Khafre."
Length of base: 215.25 m; h 143.50 m.

Pyramid of Menkure.
Egyptian name:
"Divine is Menkure."
Length of base:
104.6 m; h 66.45 m.

Great Pyramid of Khufu.
Egyptian name: "Horizon of Khufu."
Length of base: 230.38 m; h 146.50 m.

To the west of the pyramids are
the mastaba tombs of dignitaries.
Outstanding in terms of importance
and size is that of Hemiunu, who
served as vizier during the period of
Khufu. Hemiunu was a member of
the royal family, probably a nephew
of Khufu, and he supervised work on
construction of the Great Pyramid.

▲ Photograph of Giza taken from
a U.S. military aircraft in 1943.

Mentuhotep II

Hieroglyphic
Nebhepet-Ra Sa-Ra
Mentju-hetep
("Pleased is the Lord
Ra. The Son of Ra.
Montuhotep"
["Montu is
satisfied"])

Chronology
2061–2009 BC
11th dynasty

Important events
Year 30 of reign:
conclusion of the
reunification of
Egyptian territory
under a single
crown.
Movement of the
capital of the
country to Thebes.
Restoration of the
roles of vizier and
chancellor.

Bibliography
Arnold 1979.
Grimal 1988, chap.
VII. Shaw 2000,
chap. 7.

▶ Bas-relief
depicting
Mentuhotep II
striking down an
enemy, 11th dynasty.

With the end of the 6th dynasty, and with it the Old Kingdom, Egypt entered a period of history marked by the disintegration of central power, resulting in a multiplicity of local autonomies governed by magnates known as nomarchs. This historical period is conventionally known as the First Intermediate Period and corresponds to the 7th, 8th, 9th, 10th, and part of the 11th dynasties. Various factors led to this phenomenon: the increasing power given by the pharaohs to the nomarchs in the administration of their territories; the progressive weakening of the royal house; the effects of an ongoing phase of arid weather that may have created drought conditions and created difficulties in the maintenance and functioning of the canal system. At the end of the period various families of nomarchs united around two large factions: the 10th dynasty of Heracleopolis, which controlled Lower Egypt, and the 11th dynasty of Thebes in Upper Egypt. The victor in the clash between these two zones of influence was Thebes, which under Mentuhotep II undertook a new process of unifying the country. By the time of the thirty-ninth year of his reign, pharaonic authority had been restored, and he assumed the

important Horus name of "He who unifies the Two Lands." After strengthening the borders, he rewarded the nomarchs that had remained faithful to him and placed Theban overseers in all the other territories, promoted the restoration of the temples of Upper Egypt, and resumed the exploitation of Nubian quarries and the Syrian-Lebanese markets for exotic goods.

This statue of Mentuhotep II was found in an underground room accessible through an entrance located at the center of the large court of the king's mortuary temple at Deir el-Bahri. The entrance is called Bab el-Hosan ("Gate of the Horse") in memory of how it was found: Howard Carter (discoverer of Tutankhamen) was taking a ride in the court when his horse tripped, bringing to light a deep shaft that turned out to be the entrance to a subterranean corridor.

When found, the statue was wrapped in linen, which permitted the excellent preservation of its colors. Mentuhotep wears the red crown of Lower Egypt and is wearing the short white garment typical of the royal jubilee.

The narrow garment the king wears, similar to that worn by Djoser, is his costume used in celebration of the royal jubilee (in Egyptian the heb sed, *"sed festival") that marked a sovereign's first thirty years of rule and served to renew and celebrate his power. After the first jubilee, the* sed *festival was repeated every three years.*

The sovereign's skin is black, a color often used to depict Osiris and thus probably an indication of the ruler's coming resurrection in the afterlife.

▲ Jubilee statue of Mentuhotep II, from the mortuary temple of Mentuhotep II at Deir el-Bahri, 11th dynasty, ca. 2020 BC, painted sandstone, h 138 cm, Egyptian Museum, Cairo, JE 36195.

The strong ties between the Theban dynasty and its territory of origin is reflected in Mentuhotep II's decision to build his funerary monument at Deir el-Bahri on the western bank of the Nile at Thebes. The diagram of the mortuary temple, arranged on overlapping levels modulated by porticos and columns, was repeated five centuries later by Queen Hatshepsut, who built her sanctuary to the side of that of Mentuhotep II.

Legend

1. Access ramp
2. Portico with two rows of columns decorated with reliefs of hunting and war
3. Terrace with porticoes on three sides
4. Hypostyle portico dominated at the center by a raised, square architectural form, today destroyed, that may have been both a mastaba and a pyramid
5. "Pit" tombs, each with an independent shrine, belonging to the queens of Mentuhotep II
6. Peristyle court
7. Hypostyle hall
8. Sanctuary
9. Rock chapel

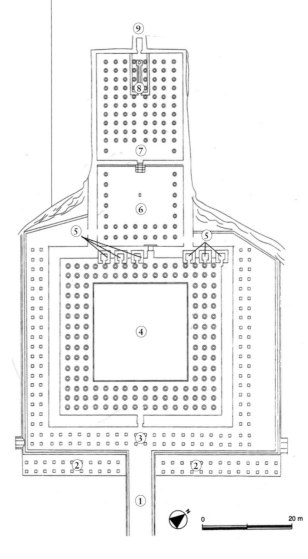

▶ Diagram of the mortuary temple of Mentuhotep II at Deir el-Bahri, 11th dynasty.

Amenemhet I

The unification of the territory carried out by Mentuhotep II had restored peace, but it was peace guaranteed only by the force of arms, and he had not resolved the internal divisions that, despite his efforts, still spread because of local aristocracies. Twenty years after unification, during the reign of Mentuhotep IV, the country erupted in a state of civil war that was brought to an end by the vizier Amenemhet, who seems to have taken power in a peaceful way, leading to the dynastic change that led to the 12th dynasty. Beginning with his Horus name, "He who renews the births," Amenemhet I sought to bring about the beginning of a new era, distinguished by important changes in the arrangement of the state, including movement of the capital to Itjet-Tauy (today's Lisht). He had to face challenges to the legitimacy of his rule. Various narrative works intended to establish proof of his right to the throne date to his period, and he took exceptional measures to guarantee the succession of his son Sesostris I, even making him coregent. Amenemhet I's fears were justified: he was

assassinated in a palace plot, but the provisions he had made permitted his son and his descendents to maintain power. For its power and sobriety, the 12th dynasty became an example of regality followed by later dynasties. The period also created an artistic model distinguished by harmonious and elegant classicism.

Hieroglyph
Sehetep-ib-Ra Imen-em-hat ("Satisfied is the heart of Ra. Amenemhet" ["Amon leads")]

Chronology
1991–1962 BC
12th dynasty

Important events
Movement of the capital from Thebes to Lisht, near the Faiyum oasis
Year 20 of reign: his son Sesostris I joins in rule as coregent
23 and 29: military expeditions in Nubia, with construction of a series of powerful forts.

Sources
The Instruction of King Amenemhet I for his son Sesostris I, (Lichtheim 1973, Vol.I, p.135). *The Story of Sinuhe,* (Lichtheim 1973, Vol.I, p.222). *The Shipwreck sailor,* (Lichtheim 1973, Vol.I, p.211).

Bibliography
Wildung 1984.

◀ Portrait of Sesostris I (detail) in the White Chapel, 12th dynasty, Open Air Museum, Karnak.

On the occasion of his first jubilee (sed festival),
marking the first thirty years of his reign, Sesostris I
dedicated to the god Amon the so-called White
Chapel, a monument rightly considered one of the
most elegant and harmonious of ancient Egypt.

The White Chapel, which belongs to
the architectural genre of the kiosk,
was made to store the sacred boat of
Amon. During the most important
Theban religious processions, the statue
of the god Amon was taken out of his
sanctuary in a structure shaped like a
boat. Since these processions sometimes
covered long distances, special
buildings were made along the route in
which the sacred boat could be stored
and where the rites involved in the
god's worship could be performed and
the bearers could stop and rest.

The stone roof with its projecting
cornice is supported by piers on all
four sides set atop a platform. At
the center of the building stood a
podium probably made to hold the
sacred boat of the god Amon.

▲ White Chapel, 12th dynasty,
limestone, 6.54 x 6.45 m,
Open Air Museum, Karnak.

The White Chapel, reconstructed almost entirely with original material, is decorated with hieroglyphs and figurative religious themes engraved on the entryways and on the walls of the balustrade; the rest of the building is decorated with more delicate bas-reliefs.

The decorative program involves 60 scenes in which the pharaoh appears with the Theban god Amon, to whom the chapel was dedicated, and various other divinities. The northern and southern faces of the chapel bear a list of the Egyptian nomes, including the name of each province's capital and the names of the local divinities, along with information of a geographical-economic nature, such as the physical size and the value of the lands of each nome.

▲ Decorative pilasters (detail), White Chapel, 12th dynasty, limestone, Open air Museum, Karnak.

Statues had been made in copper as early as the Old Kingdom, such a those of Pepi II at Hierakonpolis, proof that even in the earliest epochs Egyptian artists were able to make portraits of their rulers in metal. Unfortunately, they are very rare since over time most were melted down so the metal they were made of could be reused. This bust is usually thought to depict Amenemhet III on the basis of comparison with stone portraits made of that king.

One of the most extraordinary aspects of this bust is the skilled rendering of the eyes with their deep expressivity, obtained through the application of such precious materials as silver and rock crystal.

The large nemes headdress was made separately and was attached to the head by a frontal strip that is today lost, although the groove into which it fitted is visible immediately above the king's forehead.

▶ Bust thought to depict Amenemhet III, from the temple of Sobek at Medinet el-Faiyum, 12th dynasty, copper alloy with inlaid gold, silver, electrum, and rock crystal, h 46.5 cm, private collection, Switzerland.

Hyksos kings

One consequence of Egypt's increasingly close relationship with Syria and Lebanon during the 12th dynasty was the progressive infiltration of peoples from the eastern border. Over time, these merchants and artisans settled in Egypt and came to constitute a large minority, most of all in the eastern Delta area. The gradual weakening of pharaonic authority during the 13th and 14th dynasties resulted in a power vacuum, and the tribal leaders of these peoples succeeded in imposing their rule, giving life to the 15th dynasty, with its capital at Avaris. Thus Egypt entered its Second Intermediate Period. In Egyptian, these rulers were called *Heqau khasot*, meaning "rulers of foreign lands," a name that, by way of its sound when vocalized by Greeks, became *Hyksos*, the term still in use today. Although Egyptian tradition has codified these foreign rulers (who cover the 15th and 16th dynasties) as wicked and infamous, dedicated to the cruelest barbarities, history presents a picture composed of reciprocal exchanges, most of all of a cultural nature, that brought to Egypt not only the technology of bronze working, but also the use of the wheel as an instrument of locomotion, as in war chariots. For their part, the Hyksos kings adapted to Egyptian culture, assuming royal titles, dedicating monuments in temples, and integrating their religious views with those of the Egyptians, as indicated in the adoption by the Hyksos of the cult of Set, associated with the eastern god Baal.

Hieroglyph
Heqau khasot
("Rulers of foreign lands")

Chronology
ca. 1730–1530 BC
15th and 16th dynasties

Important events
1730–1720 BC: Avaris falls to the Hyksos.
1720–1674 BC: Progressive expansion of the Hyksos in the Delta.
Year 33 of the reign of Auserre Apopi I: compilation of the Rhind Mathematical Papyrus.

Sources
The Quarrel of Apophis and Seqenenre', (Goedicke 1986)

Bibliography
Grimal 1988, chap. VIII. Oren 1997. Shaw 2000, chap. 8.

◄ Hyksos scarab seals, 15th–16th dynasties, Israel Museum, Jerusalem.

Kamose and Ahmose

Hieroglyph
Wadjkheper-Ra Ka-mes
("Flourishing is the
transformation of Ra.
Kamose" ["generated by
the Ka"])

Chronology
Kamose: 1555–1552 BC
17th dynasty
Ahmose: 1552–1526 BC
18th dynasty

Important events
Year 1 of the reign
of Kamose: naval
expedition against
the Hyksos.
Year 11 of the reign of
Ahmose: renewal of
hostilities against the
Hyksos and conquest of
Memphis and Avaris.
12: expedition to Syria-
Palestine.
16: destruction of the
last Hyksos fortress,
at Sharuhen.

Sources
*The Autobiography of
Ahmose son of Abana,*
(Lichtheim 1976, Vol.II,
p.12). *The stela of
Kamose,* (Habachi
1972).

Bibliography
Vandersleyen 1971.
Grimal 1988, chap. VIII-
IX. Shaw 2000, chap. 9.

Toward the end of the Second Intermediate Period, the local dynasty in Thebes, the 17th, began to contend with the Hyksos kings for rule of Egypt. This political friction became increasingly heated, finally exploding in armed conflict, as indicated by the mummy of the Theban king Seqenenra Taa II, today exhibited in Cairo, which bears visible wounds that were probably received in battle. His son, Kamose, carried on his father's struggle, taking the throne with the bellicose Horus name of "He who bends the Two Towers." Against the advice of his councilors, Kamose undertook a crusade against the Hyksos king Apopi. Kamose's advance along the Nile proved unstoppable, and his victories in the field took him to the very walls of Avaris, but he did not succeed in taking the city. To the south, the Theban rear guard found itself threatened by the king of Nubia, who had allied himself with Apopi. On his return to Thebes, Kamose had the story of his undertakings engraved on a large stele dedicated in the local temple of Amon. He then under-

took the conquest of the desert caravan routes, communication lines between the north and Nubia. At Kamose's death, the crown passed to his brother Ahmose, who was probably only ten. The struggle against the Hyksos was carried forward first under the regency of the queen mother Ahhotep and then, when he came of age, by Ahmose, who destroyed Avaris and then the fortress of Sharuhen, in south-western Palestine, the last base of operations for the Hyksos.

When he returned from his expedition against the Hyksos rulers of the Delta, Kamose had his glories engraved on this large stele.

"Bad news is in your city. You are driven back together with your army. Your mouth is clamped shut because I have become great . . . I see your cowardly back when my soldiers follow you. Look behind you! The mistresses of Avaris shall not conceive, their hearts no longer beat when they hear the war cry of my soldiers . . . I saw your women on the roofs, peering out the windows toward the port: they no longer moved when they heard me, but stuck their noses out between their loopholes like young owls looking out of their nest."

"I destroyed their towns and burned their homes to reddened ash-heaps forever . . . Thebes was festive, women and men had come out to see me, every woman hugged her neighbor, no one was tearful . . . I commanded: have all that my majesty has done in war put upon a stele and have it set in Karnak in Thebes forever and ever."

◄ Ceremonial ax of Ahmose (detail), from the tomb of Ahhotep at Dra Abu el-Naga, Western Thebes, 18th dynasty, gold, lapis lazuli, enamel, h 47.5 cm, Egyptian Museum, Cairo, CG 52645.

▲ Kamose victory stele, from the temple of Amon-Ra at Karnak, 17th dynasty, limestone, h 224 cm, Museum of Ancient Egyptian Art, Luxor.

The corneas of the eyes are made of alabaster, the pupils of obsidian, and they are inserted in cavities opened directly in the wood.

The tomb of Queen Ahhotep I, mother of Kamose and Ahmose, was found in 1859 by the Egyptian Antiquities Service. The objects uncovered (a knife with gold sheaf, ritual ax, ship models in silver, bracelets in gold and lapis lazuli, necklaces in gold, turquoise, and carnelian) amounted to an important treasure that is today preserved in the Egyptian Museum in Cairo. The treasure's splendor reflects Egypt's renewed ability to acquire raw materials from distant lands.

The surface of the sarcophagus is completely dressed in thin sheets of gold fixed to the wood with resin. The cover was carved so as to frame the minute and delicate face of the queen with her thick Hathoric wig; the cover is worked with narrow undulations that reproduce curls and give the surface a sense of constant movement.

▲ Sarcophagus of Queen Ahhotep, from Dra Abu el-Naga, Western Thebes, 18th dynasty, wood, gold leaf, obsidian, alabaster, Egyptian Museum, Cairo.

Amenhotep I

After expelling the Hyksos, Ahmose restored Egypt to its ancient unity, and with the foundation of the 18th dynasty the country entered the New Kingdom, the historical phase of its greatest expansion and wealth. Following Ahmose's death, the regency of the country passed to Queen Ahmose-Nefertari since the direct heir to the throne, Amenhotep I, was still a child. The queen most probably began assuming political power during the period when the pharaoh was away from Thebes, involved in the continuous clashes with the Hyksos in the Delta; it is not surprising to find that she actively participated in the rule of the country, as indicated by the numerous inscriptions bearing her name. The twenty-one years of Amenhotep I's reign were relatively peaceful, and the internal and external tranquility of the country permitted the flowering of the arts and sciences, which Amenhotep I supported by way of the revival of ancient traditional texts and promoted through the compilation of new scientific and religious works. Amenhotep I carried out an important innovation, separating for the first time the royal tomb from the mortuary temple, and he assembled a special group of craftsmen involved in mortuary construction and decoration and had a village built to house them at Deir el-Medina, near the royal necropolis on the West Bank at Thebes. After their deaths, both Amenhotep I and his mother were deified and worshipped as protectors of the royal necropolis.

Hieroglyph
Djeser-ka-Ra Imenhetep ("Sacred is the Ka of Ra. Amenhotep" ["Amon is satisfied"])

Chronology
1526–1506 BC
18th dynasty

Important events
Composition of the Ebers Medical Papyrus, primary source of Egyptian medicine. Definition of the canonical version of the *Amduat*. Division of royal burials into two parts, tomb and mortuary temple.

Bibliography
Grimal 1988, chap. IX.
Shaw 2000, chap. 9.

◄ Statuette of Ahmose-Nefertari, from Deir el-Medina, 18th dynasty, wood, h 43 cm, Fondazione Museo Antichità Egizie, Turin, S. 6128.

The state of preservation of the statue's colors is surprising, in particular the chromatic contrast between the pallor of the sovereign's skin and the alternating black and gold bands of his nemes. On the basis of the statue's style, in particular the treatment of the modeling of the king's face, some scholars date the statue to the 19th dynasty; other scholars see the face as the departure point for a dynamic style of portraiture that was to become especially lively during the period of Queen Hatshepsut and Thutmose III.

Like the architect Imhotep, Amenhotep I and his mother, Ahmose-Nefertari, were worshipped as deities, revered as the founders and protectors of the village of Deir el-Medina, created to house the artists and craftsmen who made the tombs in the Valley of the Kings for rulers of the 18th, 19th, and 20th dynasties. This worship was also expressed on certain festive occasions when statues of the pharaoh were carried in processions.

▲ Statue of Amenhotep I, from Thebes, 18th dynasty, painted limestone, h 65 cm, Fondazione Museo Antichità Egizie, Turin, C. 1372.

Worship of Amenhotep I and his mother, Queen Ahmose-Nefertari, was centered at Deir el-Medina, the village made to house the artists and craftsmen who made the tombs in the Valley of the Kings. Amenhotep I had his tomb built in the rock of the Theban mountain, probably at Dra Abu el-Naga. After his death, he was deified as the patron of the necropolis of Thebes, together with his mother. The veneration of the two rulers by the inhabitants of Deir el-Medina was also manifested through the dedication of numerous votive chapels, a sanctuary, and ex-votos, such as the small stele shown here.

Amenhotep I is depicted together with his mother. In front of his effigy is his praenomen: "Djeser-ka-Ra."

The two dedicators of the stele are father and son, Amenemope and Amennakht; both bear the title of sedjem ash em set Maat, *meaning "servants in the place of truth," a title applied to all those who worked on the tombs in the Valley of the Kings.*

▲ Stele of Amenemope and Amennakht, from Deir el-Medina, 19th dynasty, painted limestone, h 30 cm, Fondazione Museo Antichità Egizie, Turin, C. 1452.

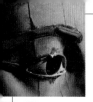

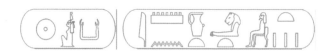

Hatshepsut

Hieroglyph
Maat-ka-Ra Khenemet–Imen
Hat-shepesut ("Maat is the
ka of Ra. She that Amon
embraces Hatshepsut" ["first
of the noble women"])

Chronology
1478–1458 BC
18th dynasty

Important events
Year 7 of the reign of
Thutmose III: Hatshepsut
abandons the form of
government of the regency
to have herself crowned
"pharaoh."
Departure of the trade
mission to Punt, which
provides the subject for
reliefs in the funerary
complex at Deir el-Bahri.
22: Death of Hatshepsut.

Sources
*The obelisk inscriptions
of queen Hatshepsut,*
(Lichtheim 1976, Vol.II,
p. 25)

Bibliography
Grimal 1988, chap. IX.
Shaw 2000, chap. 9.
Roehrig 2005.

► Head of Osirian colossus of
Hatshepsut, from the mortuary
temple of Hatshepsut at Deir
el-Bahri, 18th dynasty, painted
limestone, h 61 cm, Egyptian
Museum, Cairo, CG 56262.

Hatshepsut was the daughter of Thutmose I and wife of Thutmose
II, with whom she had a daughter, Nefrura. When Thutmose II
died, the succession favored Thutmose III, a son the pharaoh had
had with a concubine named Isis. However, Thutmose was still a
child when he was crowned, so Hatshepsut assumed the regency
until the legitimate heir reached adulthood. Around the seventh
year of Thutmose III's reign, Hatshepsut went further, assuming
the titles and epithets usually reserved to a king and becoming in
all effects the first female pharaoh. Events were still formally dated
according to the years in the reign of Thutmose III, but increasingly in association with the queen, who had the valuable support
of the clergy of Amon as well as the powerful councilor Senenmut,
architect and chief steward. As assistant she had Princess Nefrura.
The queen dealt with the problem of getting people to accept this
infraction of tradition in a decidedly audacious way, claiming that
she had already been a coregent with her father, Thutmose I, who
had proclaimed her as his heir, and that hers had been a miraculous birth through the direct intervention of Amon. This justifica-

tion, at once political and
religious, was expressed in the
reliefs that decorate the
queen's temple at Deir el-
Bahri. Hatshepsut died under
mysterious circumstances
during the twenty-second year
of the reign of Thutmose III,
who soon ordered the queen's
name expunged from all monuments. Her mummy, found
by Howard Carter in 1903,
was not identified until 2007.

The statue reveals obvious changes in royal portraiture: the quadrangular face typical of the first rulers of the dynasty has grown narrow, the chin smaller, revealing the cheekbones and giving the bony structure of the face a delicate triangular form. The expression is firm, with an intense and brilliant aspect.

A recurrent aspect in the iconography adopted by Hatshepsut is the concealment, most of all in the more traditional contexts, of all indications of her gender. Such is not the case with this statue, today in New York's Metropolitan Museum of Art, which dates to the initial period of her reign. While it presents her in the canonical form of the enthroned pharaoh wearing the nemes *headdress, it does not hide the young Hatshepsut's female body, including her small bone structure and the soft modeling of her body.*

At least three key elements of the statue reveal Hatshepsut's intention to have herself presented as a legitimate pharaoh: the nemes *headdress, the throne she sits on, and most of all the royal title engraved on the throne.*

▶ Seated statue of Hatshepsut, from the mortuary temple at Deir el-Bahri, Western Thebes, 18th dynasty, red granite, h 195 cm, Metropolitan Museum of Art, New York, 29.3.2.

Hatshepsut is here depicted with unmistakably male features. This subject may have called for greater caution on the part of the queen, since it deals with a ritual intimately connected to the foundation of Egypt's royalty and was thus worthy of the most conservative restraint.

Hatshepsut performs the ritual race of the sed *festival alongside an Apis bull, god of the flooding of the Nile. The* sed *festival celebrated the thirtieth year of a pharaoh's reign, but Hatshepsut probably decided to celebrate her own ahead of time, perhaps as early as the sixteenth year of her coregency with Thutmose III, probably for reasons of political propaganda.*

The queen's delicate, recognizable face emerges from the thick lion's mane, creating a pleasant artistic contrast.

The desire to establish legitimacy is also behind this exceptional sphinx, which bears the deliberately recognizable features of Hatshepsut. In this way the queen joined herself to her predecessors, having herself presented as the incarnation of one of the most traditional and ancient symbols of pharaonic power.

▲ Relief of the ritual race of Hatshepsut, from the Red Chapel in the temple of Amon-Ra at Karnak, 18th dynasty, quartzarenite, h 60 cm, Open Air Museum, Karnak.

▶ Sphinx of Hatshepsut (detail), from the mortuary temple of Hatshepsut at Deir el-Bahri, Western Thebes, 18th dynasty, painted limestone, h 59.5 cm, Egyptian Museum, Cairo, JE 53113.

Senenmut

Senenmut played a key role in the historical events related to Hatshepsut's assumption of the title of pharaoh. Born into a modest family in Armant, he had a highly successful career as administrator, councilor, and probably also lover of the queen. He held the highly influential position of director of the property of the temple of Amon at Karnak and of the royal family and was director of the works the queen commissioned in Thebes, the most important of which included the quarrying, transportation, and erection of the high obelisks of the temple of Amon and most of all the original design and construction of Hatshepsut's mortuary temple at Deir el-Bahri. Aside from his presumed relationship with Hatshepsut, the important positions Senenmut assumed made him an intimate of the royal family, with the role of protector of the queen's daughter, Nefrura, with whom he is depicted in several statues that have survived to modern times. Aside from being a skilled functionary, Senenmut was a true intellectual, as indicated by his architectural creations and the objects found inside the two tombs he had built at Sheik Abd el-Qurna and at Deir el-Bahri, opposite the queen's mortuary temple. The first tomb was found to contain around 150 ostraca bearing literary, mortuary, and religious works, while the second tomb bears Egypt's first documented astronomical ceiling.

Hieroglyph
Sen-en-Mut
("Companion of Mut")

Chronology
Reign of Hatshepsut
1478–1458 BC
18th dynasty

Important events
Design and construction of the funerary complex of Hatshepsut at Deir el-Bahri.
Year 11 of the reign of Thutmose III: death of Nefrura, daughter of Hatshepsut; Senenmut attempts a reconciliation with Thutmose III.
19: Hatshepsut abandons Senenmut.

Bibliography
Grimal 1988, chap. IX. Dorman 1991. Shaw 2000, chap. 9.

◀ Kneeling statue of Senenmut with the goddess Renenutet, 18th dynasty, gray green schist, h 41 cm, Kimbell Art Museum, Fort Worth.

Legend

1. First court
2. Access ramp
3. First portico
4. Second court
5. Second portico with relief

decoration
6. Third portico with Osirian pillars
7. Hypostyle hall
8. Sanctuary of Hatshepsut and Thutmose I
9. Shrine of Anubis

10. Temple of Hathor cut into rock
11. Shrine dedicated to solar cults
12. Sanctuary cut into rock

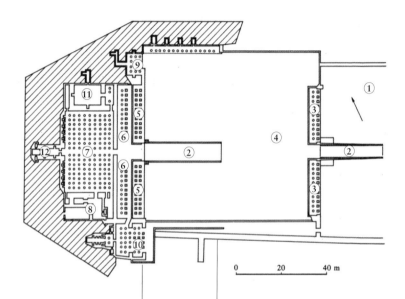

The rear wall of the second portico was decorated with elegantly expressive bas-reliefs presenting two figurative cycles: The Divine Birth of Hatshepsut (north colonnade) and The Expedition to the Land of Punt (south colonnade). The first is little more than blatant propaganda, using the relief for political-ideological ends; the other is an honest narrative that takes joy in things foreign and exotic.

Constructed alongside the funerary complex of Mentuhotep II, the mortuary temple of Hatshepsut united, in its choice of site, both cultural and logistical values. The temple is located at the feet of the el-Qurn massif and is composed of two large overlapping courts, the back of each of which is porticoed with square-sectioned columns. From the courts one enters the building itself, first by way of yet a third portico, dominated by 26 pillars representing the queen as Osiris, and then through a hypostyle hall that leads to the inner sanctuary, cut into the rock.

▲ Diagram of the mortuary chapel of Hatshepsut at Deir el-Bahri.

This famous statue of Senenmut is an example of what is called, because of its shape, a block statue. Block statues were first used by various high officials in the 12th dynasty's administration. The learned Senenmut probably chose to have himself portrayed in this type of statue as a kind of intellectual citation, looking back fondly on a period, the Middle Kingdom, that by the 18th dynasty was considered a model of harmony and perfection, both in the exercise of royal power and in the development of the arts.

The head of Hatshepsut's daughter, Nefrura, rises out of the flat surface directly in front of Senenmut's face and is depicted as a child, as indicated by the typical sidelock that distinguished Egyptian children. Thus Senenmut seems to embrace Nefrura in affirmation of his close and affectionate protection of her; it is also true, as some scholars have noted, that the "emersion" of the princess's head may allude to the myth of the daily rebirth of the sun over the primordial hill.

▲ Block statue of Senenmut, from the cachette of the temple of Amon-Ra at Karnak, granite, h 130 cm, Egyptian Museum, Cairo, CG 42114.

Block statues were used a great deal from the 18th dynasty on. The surfaces created by their shape made possible the display of long inscriptions, and they could easily be placed inside the sacred areas of sanctuaries and in the mortuary temples of rulers, thereby locating the subjects of the statues in a place where they could hope to earn credit in the eyes of the gods and dead kings.

Thutmose III

Hieroglyph
Men-kheper-Ra Djehuty-
mes nefer-skeperu
("Stable is the future of
Ra. Thutmose ["Thoth is
born"] Perfect in form")

Chronology
1458–1425 BC
18th dynasty

Important events
Year 22 of reign:
Thutmose acquires full
power.
23–42: sixteen military
campaigns against the
coalition of Syrian-
Palestinian princes
supported by the
kingdom of Mitanni.
26: conquest of Megiddo
after a seven-month siege.
25: construction of the
Akh-menu ("Festival
Hall") and the room
known as the Botanical
Garden because of its
decoration.

Sources
Annals of Thutmose III,
(Lichtheim 1976, Vol.II,
p.29). *The poetical stela
of Thutmose III,*
(Lichtheim 1976, Vol.II,
p.35).

Bibliography
Grimal 1988, chap. IX.
Della Monica 1991.
Shaw 2000, chap. 9.

Beginning only in the twenty-second year of his reign, after the death of Hatshepsut, was Thutmose III completely free to exercise his sovereignty. His first major undertaking was to put down a rebellion of Syrian princes who had united under the leadership of the prince of Kadesh. Thutmose I had extended Egypt's sphere of influence into Syria, but the relationship had become increasingly unstable during the reign of Hatshepsut, in part because of interference from the kingdom of Mitanni, which was located in today's northern Iraq and was contending with Egypt for control of the territory of Syria and Palestine. Over roughly twenty years of his reign, Thutmose III had to lead sixteen military campaigns before finally crushing opposition and putting in place a system of territorial control based on the creation of garrisons at strategic points to support local administrations that collected tribute from the cities in their area. He also arranged for the sons of foreign leaders to be sent to Egypt, where they could be educated in the royal palace. In that way he raised the future generation of vassals, sending them home when they were "Egyptianized" to succeed their fathers. With his fifty-three-year reign (including the years of Hatshepsut), Thutmose III is considered one of the most glorious rulers of ancient Egypt, recalled by his successors as a skilled military commander and an erudite connoisseur of culture and art.

Thutmose III was renowned for his glorious victories, his image being that of a fearless "warrior pharaoh." Even so, his exceptional personality found expression off the battlefield as well. He is known to have worked as a potter and was a refined man of letters, interested in the study of ancient texts and in the preservation of the monuments of the sovereigns who had preceded him.

◄ Statue of Thutmose III, from the cachette of the temple of Amon-Ra at Karnak, 18th dynasty, green graywacke, h 200 cm, Egyptian Museum, Cairo, CG 42053.

▲ Statue of Thutmose III, from the cachette of the temple of Amon-Ra at Karnak, 18th dynasty, green graywacke, h 90.5 cm, Museum of Ancient Egyptian Art, Luxor, J2.

Because of the long campaigns, captured cities, and great victories of Thutmose III, most of all in the regions of Syria and Palestine, he has been considered the "warrior pharaoh" par excellence since antiquity. His deeds were made eternal in monumental reliefs, such as those shown here, which inaugurated a new way of celebrating a sovereign.

The scene depicts Thutmose III conquering Asiatic populations of the north. He is shown wearing the red crown of Lower Egypt while delivering a blow with a weapon that is no longer visible but that was probably a mace.

With his left hand Thutmose grasps a rod to which a confused mass of Asiatic prisoners is tied; they are recognizable, on the basis of Egyptian iconography, by their characteristic pointed beards. Some of the faces are presented from an unusual angle that serves to increase the tragic impact of the scene because of the deformations and inclinations it gives the faces of the prisoners.

▲ Monumental relief of Thutmose III striking down Asiatics, from the temple of Amon-Ra at Karnak, southern wall of the 7th pylon, 18th dynasty.

The long row of square pillars provided the interior area of the temple with exceptional luminosity, most of all in comparison to the dark recesses of the sanctuary of the temple of Amon-Ra. Being airy and pleasant, the space thus transferred to stone not only the shape but also the pleasurable aspects of the ceremonial tent.

Among the largest architectural undertakings of the reign of Thutmose III was construction of the Festival Hall against the eastern side of the temple of Amon-Ra at Karnak. The layout of the building included a large hall at its center, measuring 78.76 x 38.84 m, that may have been a reproduction in stone of the tent normally used for the rites of the renewal of power, such as the sed festival.

Thutmose III's many interests included botany, as indicated by the cycle of reliefs in a room in the Festival Hall at Karnak conventionally known as the Botanical Garden, made around the twenty-fifth year of his reign, meaning in the middle of his campaigns in Syria. In this work, made on the pharaoh's instructions, Egyptian artists reproduced the exotic plants and animals encountered during the pharaoh's operations in the Near East.

▲ Western façade of the Festival Hall of Thutmose III in the temple of Amon-Ra at Karnak, 18th dynasty, sandstone.

▲ Cycle of reliefs from the Botanical Garden (detail), Festival Hall of Thutmose III, temple of Amon-Ra at Karnak, 18th dynasty.

Amenhotep III

Hieroglyph
Neb-Maat-Ra Imen-hetep
Heqa-Uaset ("Ra is lord of
the Maat. Amenhotep
["Amon is satisfied"], lord
of Thebes")

Chronology
1390–1352 BC 18th dynasty

Sources
Stela of Amenhotep III,
(Lichtheim 1976, Vol.II,
p.43). *The Amarna Letters,*
(Moran 1987)

Bibliography
Grimal 1988, chap. IX.
Moran 1992. Berman L.M.,
Bryan B.M., Delange E.,
Kozloff A.P. 1993. Shaw
2000, chap. 9.

▼ Colossi of Amenhotep III,
called "of Memnon,"
Western Thebes, 18th
dynasty, quartzite, h 18 m.

The thirty-nine years of Amenhotep III's reign marked the apogee of the 18th dynasty. Egypt's prosperity was reflected in its relations with the Near East, with Egyptian influence spreading into Asia and throughout the Mediterranean basin. The expansionist policies of Thutmose III in the Syria-Palestine territories gave way to the flowering of peaceful diplomatic relations that consolidated Egyptian preeminence in the Near East and drew in even the Mitanni kingdom, until then an enemy but now threatened by the emergence of a new power in Anatolia, that of the Hittites. Modern understanding of this vast network of political relationships received an enormous boost with the discovery at Amarna of 379 tablets written in Akkadian cuneiform, the diplomatic language of the period, containing the correspondence between the courts of Amenhoteps III and IV and Egypt's consuls and allies in the Near East. Known as the Amarna Letters, this correspondence reveals Egypt as the true "center of the world," a country in which wealth and cultural influence of every kind flowed together and stimulated the formation of a refined artistic style drawn to luxury, a style characteristic of the period. Another result of these contacts was the assimilation of oriental divinities and the resurgence of solar cults, factors that the king exploited to distance the crown from the cumbersome and also powerful Theban clergy of Amon, a religious policy, probably begun by his father, Thutmose IV, that was taken to extreme consequences by his son, Amenhotep IV.

The period of Amenhotep III saw the maturation of extremely refined aesthetic ideas that affected the rendering of the ruler's face. This portrait of the king follows canonical rules and is easily recognizable by such obvious characteristics as the narrowing of the outline of the eye sockets, which become increasingly elongated, and the fleshy lips that form a youthful smile.

This statue was found in 1989 together with another twenty-five dating to the New Kingdom and the Late Period. These had been put in a ditch dug in the colonnaded court of Amenhotep III in the temple of Luxor. This so-called cachette was probably made around AD 300 when the Romans restored the rear areas of the temple to make them suitable for imperial worship. Both the statue of Amenhotep III and the other works of art are today preserved in the Museum of Ancient Egyptian Art in Luxor.

The pharaoh is portrayed standing atop a processional sledge, the structure usually used to carry the statue of a divinity or of the sovereign in a procession. In the strictest sense, this means that the statue does not portray Amenhotep III, but rather a statue of the deified pharaoh set upon a sledge to be carried in the midst of the festive throng. Because of its very special character, this statue is truly unique in the history of Egyptian art.

▶ Statue of Amenhotep III on a processional sledge, from the cachette of the temple of Amon-Ra at Luxor, 18th dynasty, sandstone, h 210 cm, Museum of Ancient Egyptian Art, Luxor, J 838.

In terms of the arts, the age of Amenhotep III represented the apogee of elegance and aesthetic refinement both in terms of figurative arts and artisan crafts. This stele was originally located in the court of the mortuary temple of Amenhotep III, Western Thebes, and its dense scene of triumph celebrates the ruler's function as protector of the ordered cosmos.

The vulture-goddess Nekhbet, protector of the royal house, projects a complex series of symbols toward the nose of the sovereign: a shen (protection), an usas scepter (power), a djed pillar (stability), and an ankh cross (life).

The power of the ruler is immediately perceptible in the energy with which he personally drives his war chariot, which is drawn by a spirited pair. Amenhotep III controls his horses with long reins while also grasping his bow in his right hand and a whip in the left.

The defeated enemy prisoners have Negroid features and feathers on their heads, characteristic Egyptian iconography for the indication of Nubian peoples, although in this case they are being used to represent all foreign populations. They are depicted as smaller than the ruler, some of them arranged atop the pharaoh's horses, others on the axle of his chariot.

▲ Stele of Amenhotep III, from the mortuary temple of Amenhotep III, Western Thebes, 18th dynasty, circa 1360 BC, painted limestone, h 206 cm, Egyptian Museum, Cairo, CG 34026.

Queen Tiy had a forceful personality and took an active part in guiding the affairs of state during her husband's reign. On his death, she assumed the regency during the first years of the reign of her son Amenhotep IV, still too young to rule, administering the country with great skill.

When he was around fourteen Amenhotep III married the equally young Tiy, daughter of a noble from Akhmim named Yuya. Tiy was associated with her husband in divine honors and was worshiped as a personification of the Maat of the king. Amenhotep III let her accompany him in the performance of royal activities that until then had never been shared with a queen, such as the major cultural festivals connected to pharaonic power, including the jubilee festivals. Having been elevated to the level of a divinity, she was depicted as a sphinx, and the king even dedicated a temple to her, at Sedeinga in Nubia.

This portrait is an outstanding masterpiece of Egyptian woodworking. The artist captured the face of the queen on the brown surface of the precious yew wood, showing her somewhat advanced in years but with an expression that reveals her determination.

The possibilities offered by wood are exploited to the maximum in this piece, giving the queen's face expressive accents and great realism, such as the line of her cheekbones and the slight indication of wrinkles around her pouting lips. The portrait has an almost astonishing sense of naturalness and energy, which is truly amazing considering the small size of the work.

▲ Portrait head of Queen Tiy, from Medinet Gurob, Faiyum, 18th dynasty, yew wood, gold, silver, glass, h 9.5 cm, Ägyptisches Museum, Berlin, N 2312.

Amenhotep, son of Hapu

Hieroglyph
Imen-hetep Sa Hepu
("Amon is satisfied.
Son of Hapu")

Chronology
1440–1359 BC
18th dynasty

The figure of the royal scribe Amenhotep can be taken as iconic of the meritocracy that regulated Egypt's social and professional world. Amenhotep was the son of Hapu, a modest provincial scribe of Athribis during the period of Thutmose III. When he came of age, he followed his father in the profession of scribe; his talents soon revealed themselves, and Amenhotep III made him his royal scribe. His began his career with religious writings, but was soon moved into increasingly important positions, such as overseeing the movement of the troops that patrolled the coasts of the Delta and the western and eastern borders and organizing a military operation in Nubia. The true leap in an already rewarding career came when he was made director of works of the many constructions commissioned by Amenhotep III in Thebes; after this came the position of organizer of the pharaoh's jubilee, marking his thirty years of reign. For all the services rendered and for the esteem earned, he had the honor—never conceded to anyone else of his position—of seeing a mortuary temple built for him beside that of his ruler, fulfilling one of the most felicitous destinies that an Egyptian

▶ Copies of statues of
Amenhotep, son of
Hapu, and Paramessu
(the future Ramses I),
temple of Amon-Ra at
Karnak, 10th pylon,
18th–19th dynasties.

subject could have hoped for. More than eighty when he died, he was deified and considered a son of the god Apis; oratories and sanctuaries were erected in his honor, a custom that was still very common in the Greco-Roman age.

Engraved on the right side of the chest is the
cartouche of Amenhotep III, the ruler for
whom Amenhotep, son of Hapu, occupied
positions of enormous responsibility.

After his death,
Amenhotep was
deified and during the
Ptolemaic Period was
worshiped as a healing
god, taking on the
function of intermediary
between humans and
gods. For this reason
the faithful attributed
special powers to his
statues. The many
statues of Amenhotep
thus performed a very
precise function in the
temple of Amon-Ra;
in this example, the
central part of the
papyrus open in
Amenhotep's lap shows
signs of great wear,
probably the result of
religious practices.

The hair dressed in
braids behind the head
is a style characteristic
of the 18th dynasty.

Hanging from his
left shoulder is the
scribe's tablet that
held the black and
red pigments used
in writing.

Amenhotep is portrayed in the flower of his
years. His pose is that typical of a scribe, with
his legs crossed and the scroll of papyrus open
on his lap. With his left hand he holds the scroll;
his right held a reed pen that is today lost.

▲ Statue of Amenhotep, son of Hapu,
as scribe, from the temple of Amon-Ra
at Karnak, 10th pylon, 18th dynasty,
circa 1370 BC, granodiorite, h 128 cm,
Egyptian Museum, Cairo, JE 44861.

Amenhotep IV/Akhenaten

Hieroglyph
Nefer-kheperu-Ra Ua-
en-Ra Imen-hetep-netjer-
heqa-Uaset Akh-en-Iten
("Perfect are the
transformations of Ra.
Only son of Ra.
Amenhotep, divine ruler
of Thebes. Splendor of
Aten")

Chronology
1352–1338 BC
18th dynasty

Important events
Years 1–2 of reign:
Amenhotep IV marries
his cousin Nefertiti.
2: he gives religious
primacy to the worship
of Aten.
5–6: foundation of
Akhetaten.
14: death of Nefertiti
and, a little later, of the
ruler himself.

Sources
*The Later Boundary
Stelae of Amenhotep
IV/Akhenaton,*
(Lichtheim 1976, Vol.II,
p.48). *The Great Hymn
to the Aten,* (Lichtheim
1976, Vol.II, p.96).

Bibliography
Aldred 1988. Grimal
1988, chap. X. Shaw
2000, chap. 10.

The period of Amenhotep IV's reign represents a true historical rupture in terms of both Egypt's political and administrative structure and its religious and cultural organization. The son of Amenhotep III took to extreme consequences the process, begun under his grandfather Thutmose IV, of popularizing the solar cults of Heliopolis, holy city of the ancient capital Memphis. Out of respect for his father, he passed the first two years of his reign continuing that man's policies, but he then suddenly and quite unexpectedly proclaimed the god Aten (the solar disk) the supreme divinity of the country, replacing Amon, and promoted a movement of religious intolerance of almost all other cults. Around the fifth year of his reign he changed his name from Amenhotep ("Amon is satisfied") to Akhenaten ("Splendor of Aten") and decided to distance the capital from Thebes, seat of the worship of Amon. Significantly, he chose an "uncontaminated" site in Middle Egypt, known today as Amarna, where he began construc-

tion on empty ground of a city that he named Akhetaten ("The Horizon of the Aten"). The new settlement was intended to present a new model of royalty and civilization, as incarnated by Akhenaten himself and by his royal consort, Nefertiti. Following Akhenaten's death, which took place in a climate of political and social instability, the new city was hurriedly abandoned, soon becoming a stone quarry for nearby Hermopolis. Akhenaten's name and his "heresy" were condemned to a *damnatio memoriae:* they were obliterated from memory.

Akhenaten is here portrayed kissing Princess Meritaten. His form shows the principal elements of the new stylistic canon formed at Amarna: fleshy lips, protruding belly, slender limbs and thin body, elongated head, angular features. He wears the blue crown called the khepresh *while streamers at his neck flutter as though carried by a gentle breeze.*

Aten was the personification of the solar disk. Signs related to its worship trace back to the period of Akhenaten's grandfather Thutmose IV.

Inscriptions identify the two princesses clambering on Nefertiti: Maketaten (to the left) and Ankhesenpaaten (to the right), future wife of Tutankhamen.

One of the great innovations brought by Akhenaten within the sphere of the royal relief was the introduction of scenes presenting the intimate life of the royal family, presented as models of the values of peace and love connected to the new religion. Images of the sacred family appear in place of the usual domestic divinities in the gardens and homes of Amarna, as intermediaries between humans and Aten.

Nerertiti wears a delicate robe with tight pleating, probably a stylized representation of the rays of the sun. The elements of the Amarna style were to have a great influence on much of the art of the later Ramessid period, and this despite the damnatio memoriae *hurled against Akhenaten by his successors, enraged by the heresy of Amarna and all its symbols.*

◄Dyad of Akhenaten and Nefertiti, from Amarna, 18th dynasty, painted limestone, h 22.5 cm, Musée du Louvre, Paris, E 15593.

▲Relief of the royal family, from Amarna, 18th dynasty, limestone, h 32.5 cm, Ägyptisches Museum, Berlin, 14145.

The most important religious area of Amarna is the sanctuary of the god Aten, the sacred precinct of which reached the astonishing size of 760 x 270 m. The sacred area, in its entirety, was called the Per-Aten ("home of Aten"). It has been possible to identify at least two large structures inside the Per-Aten, the Pa-hut-Aten ("sanctuary of Aten"; 191 x 108 m) and the Gem-pa-Aten ("Aten has been found"; 210 x 32 m).

The Gem-pa-Aten extends over a length of 210 m and is divided in two sections: the Per-Huyt ("house of happiness") and the true sanctuary. Past the 1st pylon one enters a hypostyle hall with an opening in the roof along the central axis to let in the sun's rays.

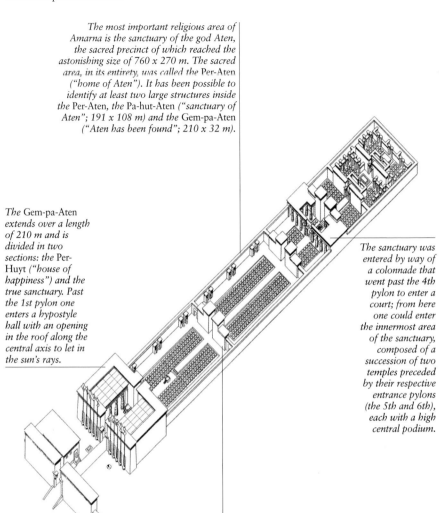

The sanctuary was entered by way of a colonnade that went past the 4th pylon to enter a court; from here one could enter the innermost area of the sanctuary, composed of a succession of two temples preceded by their respective entrance pylons (the 5th and 6th), each with a high central podium.

Behind the hypostyle hall, two pylons (the 2nd and 3rd) divided a large area open to the sky into two courts, one larger and one smaller, in which 554 small altars were arranged for offerings to Aten.

▲ Reconstruction of the Great Temple of Aten (*Gem-pa-Aten*) at Amarna.

Here is the Amarna art canon: the figure of the king is substantially androgynous, with a thin body, slender arms and legs, narrow shoulders, prominent belly. The head is elongated, the face has fleshy lips and long, almond-shaped eyes.

The chief sculptor Bak claimed he had been given precise instructions from Akhenaten in person concerning the new stylistic canon of Amarna. It was certainly the figure of the ruler that most drastically reflected the stylistic changes, arriving at an erosion, even a deformation, of the rock-solid age-old image of the powerful authoritarian pharaoh. Many theories have been put forward to explain the reasons for this change: the physical effects of an hereditary disease, such as Marfan's syndrome; the attempt to depict a compilation of solar symbols; or the desire to make an ideological break with the past. The last explanation is the one most widely accepted.

Despite other changes, the symbols of royal power remained the same, including the heqa *crook scepter the king holds in his left hand and the* nekhakha *flail in his right.*

▲ Colossus of Akhenaten, from Amarna, 18th dynasty, sandstone, h 185 cm, Egyptian Museum, JE 49528.

Nefertiti remains one of the most famous queens in Egyptian history. Some of this fame results from her extraordinary beauty, but there is also the fact that together with Akhenaten she was a leading participant in a brief historical break that was full of consequences for Egyptian civilization.

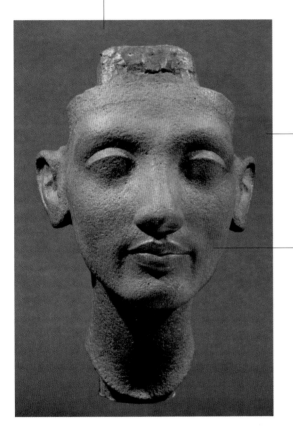

Toward the end of Akhenaten's reign, the Amarna style was slightly modified, resulting in a more tempered version. The relaxation of the initial ideological fervor and the softening of the style are especially evident in this sandstone head found in the ruins of the workshop of Akhenaten's chief sculptor, Thutmose.

The face, probably a youthful portrait of Nefertiti, emanates a soft and uncommon sensuality. The yellow-brown porous surface of the stone captures light, making the treatment of the queen's skin seem realistic and lifelike. The lips, painted red, form a sensuous smile that exalts the sweetness of her expression, apparently lost in a quiet ecstasy.

▲ Unfinished portrait of Nefertiti, from Amarna, 18th dynasty, limestone, h 30 cm, Ägyptisches Museum, Berlin, 21.220.

▶ Pectoral in the shape of a vulture, an image of the goddess Nekhbet, from the tomb of Tutankhamen in the Valley of the Kings, Western Thebes, 18th dynasty, gold, coral limestone, vitreous paste, width 48 cm, Egyptian Museum, Cairo, JE 61876.

Tutankhamen

Tutankhamen's fame is tied primarily to the exceptional discovery of his tomb and its fabulous contents, but his history is also of special interest because it involved the restoration of religious orthodoxy following Akhenaten's Amarnian scandal. Tutankhamen was most probably related to the royal family, and his original name was Tutankhaten, "living image of Aten." The traumatic conclusion of the Amarnian heresy elevated him to the royal throne together with his wife, Ankhesenpaaten, at the tender age of nine, and for the first nine years of his reign he was guided by the "divine father" Ay, an obscure character in that delicate phase of transition. The *damnatio memoriae* to which Akhenaten had been condemned led to the inevitable revival of the worship of Amon, and his clergy returned to the upper echelon of religious power. Tutankhamen, who did not return the government to Thebes and instead moved his residence to Memphis, issued an edict of restoration in the fourth year of his reign that restored the ancient cults and ordered the reopening of the temples closed during the Akhenaten period; it was on this occasion that he changed his own name to Tutankhamen, "living image of Amon." This decree was engraved on the so-called Restoration Stele set up in the temple of Amon at Karnak and today preserved in the Museum of Cairo, by far the most important document related to the historical events of Tutankhamen.

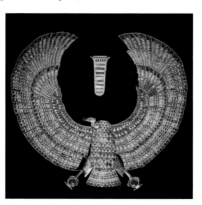

Hieroglyph
Tut-ankh-Imen
Heqa-Iunu-resut
("Tutankhamen
["living image of
Amon"] ruler of
Heliopolis of
the south")

Chronology
1336–1327 BC
18th dynasty

Important events
Year 1 of reign:
Tutankhamen takes
power at the age of
nine and moves the
seat of government
to Memphis.
4: the king
promulgates an edict
that restores the
primacy of Amon
and his clergy. In
this edict the king
changes his name to
Tutankhamen.
9: Tutankhamen dies.

Bibliography
Grimal 1988, chap. X.
Reeves 1990. James
1991, 1992, 2000.
Shaw 2000, chap. 10.

The eyes are encrusted with quartz and obsidian, materials that gave the face luster and depth; a thick line extends the highlighting around the eyes to the temples.

The mask's protective value is expressed in the long inscription on its back, inspired by Chapter 151 of the Book of the Dead: *the various parts of the body of the dead are identified with the limbs of various divinities, invoked for their protection.*

With its weight of about 11 kg, Tutankhamen's gold mask is one of the most impressive funerary ornaments from antiquity.

▲ Gold mask placed on the mummy of Tutankhamen, from the tomb of Tutankhamen in the Valley of the Kings, Western Thebes, 18th dynasty, gold, lapis lazuli, precious stones, vitreous paste, h 54 cm, Egyptian Museum, Cairo, JE 60672.

The sides of the nemes, ruled off by elegant stripes in gold and blue vitreous paste, drape onto a wide usekh necklace composed of twelve strands of beads made of colored vitreous paste connected at the king's shoulders by two falcon heads.

Above the royal couple is a radiant solar disk, each ray of which ends with a hand offering life to the ruler, symbolized by the hieroglyphic sign ankh.

The entire composition strongly resembles the Amarna style. The figures are fleshy, the facial features are marked, and the heads are elongated. Even the setting of the scene closely resembles the family images of Akhenaten and Nefertiti.

This famous ceremonial throne is one of the most renowned examples of Egyptian artisan work. The back attracts particular attention because of its rich decoration and for the intimacy with which it portrays the ruling couple.

The figures of Tutankhamen and Ankhesenamen (the new name of Ankhesenpaaten) stand out against an elegant gold background; their figures were created through the delicate use of bas-relief, intaglio, and intarsia. The clothes of the king and queen are made in silver, while intarsia of red vitreous paste was used in the bare-skin areas, and blue faience was used for the headdresses.

▲ Back of ceremonial throne, from the tomb of Tutankhamen in the Valley of the Kings, Western Thebes, 18th dynasty, gold, precious stones, vitreous paste, h 102 cm, Egyptian Museum, Cairo, JE 62028.

In his left hand the king holds a cord, while with his right he throws a harpoon: with these gestures the king vanquishes the forces of evil, affirming the domination of order over chaos.

The bust of the figure is depicted leaning forward slightly; this is one of the rare examples of the realistic depiction of physical movement in Egyptian art.

The statue was found together with a companion piece and another three figures of the king in a tabernacle in the "treasure chamber" annexed to the king's burial chamber.

Tutankhamen wears a pleated skirt held up by a sash and a wide necklace; on his head he wears the red crown of Lower Egypt topped by a uraeus.

The pharaoh, or better his ka, stands atop a light papyrus boat and steps forward; the weight of his body rests on his left leg, while his right arm draws back, preparing to throw the harpoon.

▲ Statue of Tutankhamen with harpoon, from the tomb of Tutankhamen in the Valley of the Kings, Western Thebes, 18th dynasty, stuccoed and gilded wood, bronze, h 69.5 cm, Egyptian Museum, Cairo, JE 60709.

Seti I

Tutankhamen's premature death also meant the end of the 18th dynasty, leaving Egypt in a highly unstable situation in terms of both internal and external politics. In this climate of disorder Horemheb, commander of an Egyptian army and a powerful court figure, managed to secure the throne. He began a program to eliminate the corruption that had taken hold in the administration of Egypt's territory and in its legal system and sought to extend Egypt's borders toward Nubia and the Near East. Horemheb chose as his successor one of his army companions, Ramses I, with whom the 19th dynasty began. After only two years of reign, the throne passed to his son, Seti I, who continued the policies of Horemheb and reorganized the government. As a military man, his primary object was the reconquest of Syria and Palestine, which had been lost during the difficult post-Amarna years. He dedicated himself to this from the first year of his reign, and in four victorious campaigns completed the reconquest, ending with a treaty with the Hittite king Muwatalli. Seti I was also a great builder, his works including reliefs of his military campaigns carved in the Great Hypostyle Hall in the temple at Karnak; the mortuary temple and Osireion (at Abydos); and the stupendous decorative program of his tomb in the Valley of the Kings, which expresses artistic heights never surpassed.

Hieroglyph
Man-Maat-Ra
Seti-mer-en-Ptah
("Stable is the Maat of Ra, Seti ["that of Seti"], beloved of Ptah")

Chronology
1294–1279 BC
19th dynasty

Important events
Years 1–4 of reign: submission of Palestine and Syria.

Sources
Dedication Inscription of Seti I, (Lichtheim 1976, Vol.II, p.52).

Bibliography
Grimal 1988, chap. XI.
Shaw 2000, chap. 10.

◄ Statuette of Seti I as standardbearer, from Abydos, 19th dynasty, schist, h 22 cm, Egyptian Museum, Cairo, CG 751.

The usekh *necklace and bracelet in the foreground embellish the portrait without disturbing its compositional harmony.*

This portrait of Seti makes clear his youthful beauty through the soft treatment of the lips and the elegant dark outlining of the eyes. The curling form of the uraeus, which extends straight up from the wig, repeats the tonalities of the skin and the outlining, creating a balanced and warm chromatic composition.

The skin color shows through the delicate folds of the ruler's clothes. Pleats and elbow-length sleeves were typical of the age of Amarna and remained a constant style feature through the Ramessid age.

The art of Egyptian bas-relief reached its greatest and most surprising results in the age of Seti I. The decorative program of the temple of Osiris at Abydos, begun by Seti I and completed by his son Ramses II, along with the reliefs made for the tomb of Seti I in the Valley of the Kings, represent an unsurpassed high point in the history of Egyptian art in terms of both style and execution.

▲ Portrait of Seti I, from the tomb of Seti I in the Valley of the Kings, Western Thebes, 19th dynasty, Musée du Louvre, Paris, B7.

The upper level presents the expedition Seti I led against the Libyan tribes. The scene is divided in two parts: to the right the pharaoh attacks his enemies with a spear; to the left he celebrates his triumph on a war chariot while leading row upon row of Libyan prisoners to the temple of Amon.

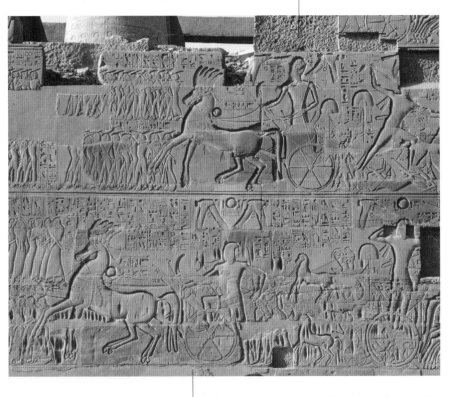

The lower level presents the conflict with the Hittites, which was resolved with the treaty established between Seti I and Muwatalli. The scene is again divided in two "episodes": to the right Seti is partially visible as he unleashes an attack against the Hittites; to the left is the scene of the king's triumph. He climbs onto his chariot while turning back, all around him two long lines of prisoners.

▲ Relief of the Asiatic and Libyan campaigns of Seti I, from the Great Hypostyle Hall, exterior face of northern wall, temple of Amon-Ra at Karnak, 19th dynasty.

The temple of Seti I at Abydos is an excellent example of the religious significance of a so-called mortuary temple. The structure combines worship of the dead ruler with that of the local divinity. Thus assimilated to the city's god, the pharaoh can eternally enjoy the offerings presented to the god.

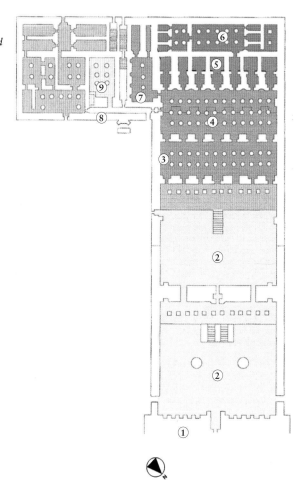

Legend

1. Pylon in sandstone erected by Ramses II, today destroyed
2. Open court with pillared portico along the rear
3. First hypostyle hall
4. Second hypostyle hall
5. Main chapels dedicated to Seti I, Ptah, Ra-Horakhty, Amon, Osiris, Isis-Horus (from left to right)
6. Sanctuary dedicated to the mysteries of Osiris
7. Hall dedicated to the Memphite gods Ptah-Sokor and Nefertum
8. Corridor of the *Annals of Abydos*
9. Hall of solar boats

0   50 m

▲ Diagram of the mortuary temple of Seti I at Abydos, 19th dynasty.

The Oseireon was located directly behind the mortuary temple of Seti at Abydos and in line with it. This cenotaph temple was made for the mortuary worship of the dead king transfigured as Osiris.

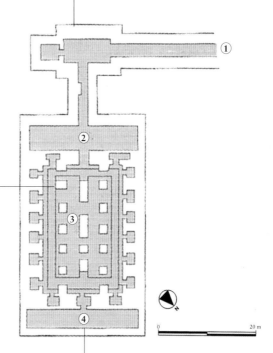

The central area of the structure was a pillared hall open to the sky. At its center was a small mound that was once surrounded by water and that was meant to recall the hill that rose from the primordial waters.

0   20 m

Legend

1. Access corridor
2. Atrium
3. Pillared hall
4. Mortuary chamber with barrel-vaulted ceiling

A long crosswise passage at the far end of the complex has a barrel-vaulted ceiling that reproduces the shape of a sarcophagus and is decorated with low reliefs that depict astronomical themes: the sky goddess Nut raised by Shu, the decans, the nocturnal route of the sun. It was meant to represent the mythical tomb of Osiris and, symbolically, that of the pharaoh arisen in the afterlife.

▲ Cenotaph temple to the southwest of the mortuary temple of Seti I at Abydos, 19th dynasty.

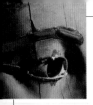

Ramses II

Hieroglyph
User-Maat-Ra Setep-en-
Ra Mery-Imen Ra-mes-su
("Powerful is the Maat of
Ra. Elect of Ra. Ramesse
["Ra has generated
him"])"

Chronology
1279–1213 BC
19th dynasty

Important events
Year 2 of reign: naval
expedition against the
Shardana sea pirates.
4: military campaign
against the Syrian prince
Benteshina of Amurru.
5: battle of Kadesh.
21: peace treaty between
Egyptians and Hittites.

Sources
*The Kadesh battle
inscriptions of Ramses II*,
(Lichtheim 1976, Vol.II,
p.57).

Bibliography
Kitchen 1982. Grimal
1988, chap. XI. Shaw
2000, chap. 10.

Ramses II is certainly the most famous pharaoh in Egyptian history and is the symbol itself of Egyptian civilization. He brought Egypt to the height of its power and left an indelible mark on the Near East as well, ruling during a period of continuous confrontations among great empires. Egypt's clash with the Hittites was of central importance to his foreign policy, and in the fifth year of his reign this clash culminated in the famous battle of Kadesh. The Egyptian army was taken by surprise by a skilled maneuver by the Hittites that isolated the pharaoh from the larger portion of his troops, putting him in danger for his life. The strenuous defense put up by Ramses himself, the arrival of auxiliary troops stationed nearby, and the approach of the bulk of the army made it possible for the Egyptians to beat back the Hittite attack, but by the end of the encounter both armies were badly shattered, and Ramses decided to put an end to that year's operations in Syria. On his return home, Ramses had reliefs made in the major temples of the country celebrating what he described as a great victory, thus

using monumental architecture in a shrewd and audacious act of propaganda. He was an active builder and covered the Nile Valley with his monuments, including the temples at Abu Simbel, Karnak, Luxor, and the Ramesseum. In the following years the conflict with the Hittites continued until, in the twenty-first year of his reign, Ramses II signed history's first recorded peace treaty between two states, guaranteeing a prosperous and lasting peace.

▶ Relief of Ramses II
striking down Libyans,
from the Small Temple at
Abu Simbel, 19th dynasty.

The ruler's crown, called the blue crown (khepresh) or war crown, is a round leather or cloth helmet with wings decorated with hundreds of copper disks with a characteristic green-blue color; on the front is the coiled uraeus cobra, ready to protect the king from enemies.

The statue of Ramses II in the Museo Egizio in Turin was found at Thebes in 1818 by J.J. Rifaud, who at the time was acting for Bernardino Drovetti, the French consul in Egypt. It was later acquired by the house of Savoy, eventually becoming part of the Turin collection. The young Ramses is depicted with his face slightly lowered toward his subjects, as though he were giving an audience, and the entire composition is a translation in stone of royal power and authority.

The long, pleated white linen gown is a ceremonial costume that is also a reminder that the ruler is also the high priest, a kind of living god and an intermediary between humans and the divine. The decorative band that runs down the front of the gown lists the constructions commissioned by the king in the great sanctuary of Amon-Ra at Karnak, where this statue was located.

In his hands Ramses bears symbols of his power: at his chest he holds the curved heqa (an Egyptian word for "prince") crook, while in his left, resting on his knees, he holds a small cylinder instead of the other regal scepter, the flail (nekhakha).

To the sides of the king, but in reduced size for reasons of hierarchical respect, are the ruler's son Amonherkepsehf and (not visible here) his wife Nefertari.

▶ Statue of Ramses II, from Thebes, 19th dynasty, diorite, h 190 cm, Fondazione Museo Antichità Egizie, Turin, C. 1380.

Hieroglyphic writing is the most important and complex manifestation of the close relationship between image and sound that is characteristic of Egyptian culture. This relationship was also expressed in so-called rebus statues, which were particularly widespread during the Ramessid period. The example shown here, from Tanis in the northeastern Delta, portrays Ramses in the guise of an infant protected by an imposing figure of the sun-god Hurun depicted as a falcon.

This rebus statue can be read in two ways. The first is related to the idea expressed by the image itself, the second is based on the sounds that elements in the image create, forming a kind of rebus. Thus the ruler wears a sun disk (Ra), is positioned as a child (mes, "child"), and with one hand grasps a reed (su), together forming Ra-mes-su, the ruler's name, here positioned under the protection of the god Hurun as though this were a three-dimensional hieroglyphic inscription.

▲ Rebus statue of Ramses II with the god Hurun, from Tanis, 19th dynasty, gray granite, h 231 cm, Egyptian Museum, Cairo, JE 64735.

The arrangement of spaces (entrance pylon, courts, hypostyle hall, and naos, or inner sanctuary) that was typical of temples during the 18th dynasty was regulated by a somewhat rigid formula that usually created a route, both symbolic and visual, that was both direct and unambiguous. This direct system was discarded during the Ramessid period in favor of an architectural design involving a multiplication of perspectives. This made it possible for the visitor to enter the building, and thus also to experience it, through an infinite number of angles and intimate viewpoints.

During the Ramessid period, architects had numerous means at their disposal for the creation of variations in perspective and composition. In the Ramesseum, for example, the overall shape of the temple is slightly trapezoidal, which helps break the axial alignment of the whole, leading to slight overlapping in the perspective views between columns, entrances, causeways, and Osirian pillars.

▲ Colonnade of the second court in the mortuary temple of Ramses II, Western Thebes (Ramesseum), 19th dynasty.

Legend

1. Entry pylon, 69 m wide. Its inner side bears reliefs depicting the Asiatic campaigns of Ramses II, in particular the battle of Kadesh.

2. The first court was dominated by a formidable sculptural row composed of 11 Osirian pillars on the eastern side with two colossi of the seated king flanking the access ramp to the temple. The head of one of these is still in the second court, while the bust and head of the other were taken away in 1816 by G. B. Belzoni, working for the British consul Henry Salt, who then sold them to the British Museum in London, where they are still preserved.

3. The second court had porticoes to the east and west supported by Osirian pillars; to the north and south were papyriform columns. Three ramps gave access to three entrances to the hypostyle hall.

4. Great Hypostyle Hall supported by 48 columns

5. Small hypostyle hall, also called the Astronomical Hall because of the ceiling decoration, which reproduced part of a star clock, along with depictions of several constellations.

6. Vestibules

7. Solar temple

Three halls each with eight columns led to the sanctuary of the boat. The first of these antechambers is called the Astronomical Hall because of its ceiling decoration, which reproduced part of a star clock along with depictions of several constellations.

▲ Diagram of the mortuary temple of Ramses II, Western Thebes, 19th dynasty.

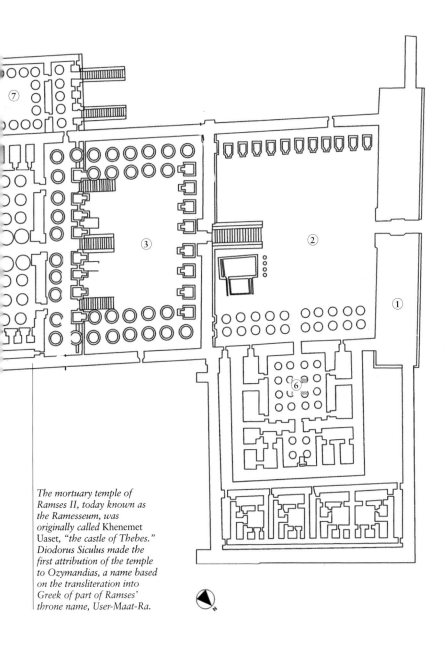

The mortuary temple of Ramses II, today known as the Ramesseum, was originally called Khenemet Uaset, *"the castle of Thebes." Diodorus Siculus made the first attribution of the temple to Ozymandias, a name based on the transliteration into Greek of part of Ramses' throne name, User-Maat-Ra.*

The Great Temple at Abu Simbel is one of the best-known architectural creations of ancient Egypt and also one of the most extraordinary monuments of Ramses II. It was built in honor of Amon-Ra, Ptah, Horus of Mehu, and the deified form of Ramses himself. The detail presented here, including this statue of Ra-Horakhty, is an example of the plurality of levels that the royal propaganda had available to convey its message to the people.

The diffusion of rebus statues during the Ramessid period is truly impressive. At Abu Simbel, the statue of Ra-Horakhty to which the relief of Ramses seems to be making the offering of Maat is in fact a rebus. The god wears the solar disk of Ra on his head, has a statue of the goddess Maat on his left, and the hieroglyphic symbol User is on his right, thus forming User-Maat-Ra, the throne name of Ramses. To whom, then, goes the offering of Maat? If one looks only at the statue, the answer is Ra-Horakhty; but if one "reads" the image, it becomes clear that Ramses is making his offering to himself as a divinity, and such scenes are repeated in various places on the internal decoration of the temple.

▲ Façade of the Great Temple at Abu Simbel, 19th dynasty, reign of Ramses II.

The four seated colossi at Abu Simbel reach 22 meters in height, roughly equal to a seven-story building. They were conceived as living statues of the ruler, for which reason each was given its own name. The temple was completed around year 34 in Ramses' reign, but a few year later, around year 42, an earthquake collapsed part of the second colossus from the left. The remains were never removed, and even after the relocation of the temple by UNESCO the fallen remains were not repaired since they bear unique witness to the ancient earthquake.

An engraved relief depicts Ramses in the act of performing the ritual offering of Maat to the god Ra-Horakhty. With this the pharaoh symbolically makes an offering of the order he has brought to the world.

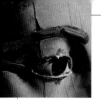

Ramses III

Hieroglyph
User-Maat-Ra Mery-Imen
Ra-mes-su Heqa Iunu
("Powerful is the Maat
of Ra. Beloved of Amon.
Ramesse ["Ra has
generated him"] ruler
of Heliopolis")

Chronology
1186–1154 BC
20th dynasty

Important events
Year 5 of reign: first
Libyan war.
8: war against the Sea
Peoples.
11: second Libyan war.
12: completion of the
mortuary temple at
Medinet Habu.
End of reign: first
documented strike in
history; the workers at
Deir el-Medina stop work
because of repeated
delays in the payment of
their salaries; a palace
plot organized by a wife
of the pharaoh and
several members of the
military cadres is
uncovered.

Bibliography
Grimal 1988, chap. XI.
Grandet 1993. Shaw
2000, chap. 10.

None of the successors to Ramses II ever matched the level of their great ancestor, and over the span of twenty years following his death the 19th dynasty came to an end. The most authoritative and representative personality of the 20th dynasty was Ramses III, who deliberately took Ramses II as his model, adopting his titles and having a magnificent mortuary temple built at Medinet Habu inspired by the layout of the Ramesseum. As early as the period of Ramses II and his successor, Merenptah, a new threat had appeared in the west, a result of the continuous pressure of the Libyan peoples. This had forced Ramses II to build a chain of coastal forts between Rakotis and Mersa Matruh. Ramses III victoriously confronted these confederated tribes in two great battles, in years 5 and 11 of his reign, integrating some of their forces into his armies as mercenaries and reducing many of them to slaves. Even so, the country was entering a difficult political and economic situation, and after year 12 he tried in vain to remedy the weakening of his authority in the face of a clergy that had become too powerful and that possessed, in the name of the gods, extensive property. Despite the difficulties of his reign, Ramses III stands as the last great pharaoh of the New Kingdom: with him, in fact, Egypt returned to its ancient splendor and for the last time exercised its traditional political weight in the Near East.

The "standardbearer" is a statuary type that appeared around the end of the 18th dynasty and spread most of all beginning in the Ramessid dynasties. The subject (originally only the ruler, but later also private citizens) sought to display his reverence for a divinity by having himself depicted as a bearer of the divinity's sacred standard during a sacred procession. The statue shown here refers to one of the ritual processions periodically held in the temple of Karnak in honor of Amon-Ra, whose usual insignia, with its ram's head, Ramses proudly bears at his side.

The wig divided in two reflects the style in vogue during the 19th and 20th dynasties.

On the pharaoh's right shoulder and also on the band of the skirt appears a cartouche bearing the king's Horus name and his name as king of Upper and Lower Egypt: User-Maat-Ra Mery-Imen.

The shendyt skirt with it delicate pleating is a creation of the Amarnian period. Dominating its center is a composition made up of several vertical stripes and a pendant (such pendants were usually made of gold). The pendant is in the shape of a the head of a panther, an animal associated with rituals and magic; attached to it are five uraei.

Standards were composed of a long wooden shaft topped by an aegis bearing a symbol of the god. In the case of Amon, the symbol is a ram's head, the animal sacred to that god; during the Late Period, the god Sekhmet was modeled with the features of a lioness. On the statue, the shaft of the standard is engraved with all of Ramses III's titles.

◀Ramses III offers incense to the god Ptah, from the tomb of Ramses III in the Valley of the Kings, Western Thebes.

▲ Statue of Ramses III as standardbearer of Amon, from Karnak, 20th dynasty, granodiorite, h 140 cm, Egyptian Museum, Cairo, CG 42150.

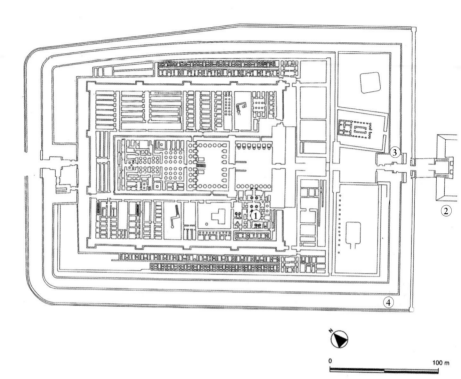

Legend

1. The cult center faces the first court and is accessible from that area by three open entrances. Since the temple is a symbolic palace, each space represents a precise purpose: a throne room, a bedroom, a bathroom. A false door located in the throne room symbolically permitted the spirit of the pharaoh to move from his tomb to the palace to receive offerings.

2. Originally, the temple was reached by way of a canal leading to the Nile, making it possible for religious processions to arrive at the temple by river; they docked at a monumental wharf that was located just outside the wall.

3. The fortified entrance was protected by a high tower based on a Syrian type of military architecture called a *migdol*.

4. The walls are 18 m high and surround an area of 205 x 315 m, making the temple a true divine fortress.

▲ Layout of the mortuary temple of Ramses III at Medinet Habu, 20th dynasty.

Storehouses and
service quarters.

First court.

Second court.

Entrance
pylon.

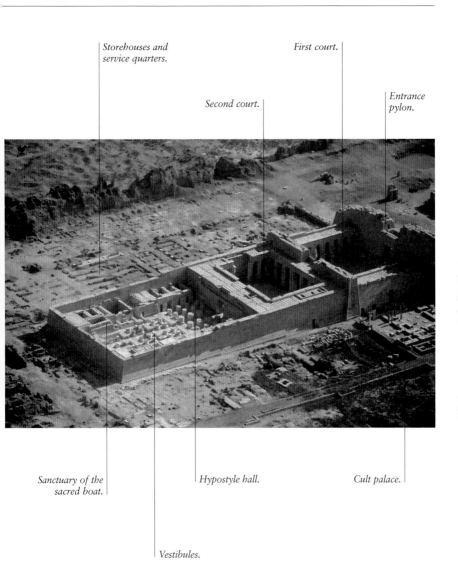

Sanctuary of the
sacred boat.

Hypostyle hall.

Cult palace.

Vestibules.

▲ Aerial view of the mortuary
temple of Ramses III at Medinet
Habu, 20th dynasty.

The art of the monumental relief reached the apogee of its expressive power during the period of Ramses III. This large relief, made on the pylon of the mortuary temple at Medinet Habu, depicts the ruler riding his war chariot while chasing, together with massed ranks of hunters, three bulls that seek to escape in a marsh. The composition is full of expressive details that make this hunting scene one of the most mature creations in the history of Egyptian monumental reliefs.

On the formal plane, the rendering of the bodies of living things is here enriched with a new realism. The animals are presented with respect given their proportions, a factor that contributes to giving the scene its lifelike feel and its intense dynamism.

▲ Monumental relief with Ramses III hunting bulls, temple of Amon-Ra, Karnak, rear of the south tower of the 1st pylon, 20th dynasty.

The technical-expressive advances presented in the relief include a more attentive division of time, established by the representations of the three bulls, superimposed and inserted in different times of the narration: the central bull is in flight, the one above is in its death throes on the ground, the third below is about to fall prey to the king.

The artists' awareness of new expressive methods is indicated by various truly original solutions applied in this composition, beginning with the clearer definition of the natural space in which the scene takes place. Other examples are the line drawn beneath the hooves of the bulls to indicate the ground and the use of the superimposition of plant stalks or animals to create different levels of depth.

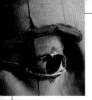
 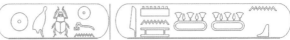

Sheshonk I

Hieroglyphic
Hedj-kheper-Ra
Setep-en-Ra Mery-Imen
Sha-sha-n-q
("Luminous is the
transformation of Ra.
Elected by Ra. Loved by
Amon, Sheshonk")

Chronology
945–924 BC
22nd dynasty

Important events
Gives sons leading roles in
the state: Iuput, great
priest of Amon at Karnak;
Gedptahiuefankh, third
prophet of Amon at
Karnak; Nimlot, military
chief of Heracleopolis.
Year 18 of reign:
Sheshonk I gives political
asylum to a pretender to
the throne of Israel,
Jeroboam I.
20: campaign in Palestine
and taking of Jerusalem.
21: works enlarging the
temple of Karnak.

Bibliography
Kitchen 1972. Grimal
1988, chap. XIII. Shaw
2000, chap. 12.

▶ Sarcophagus of
Sheshonk II, from
Tanis, 22nd dynasty,
silver, h 10 cm,
Egyptian Museum,
Cairo, JE 72154.

The forced assimilation of the Libyans, defeated by Ramses III, resulted in a phenomenon similar to what had occurred at the time of the Hyksos invasions. Over time, the "Egyptianized" descendents of the defeated Libyans formed their own local dynasties inside Egypt, and they rose to power during the so-called Third Intermediate Period when, at the end of the 20th dynasty, the Egyptian state again collapsed into anarchy. Sheshonk I (called Shishak in the Bible), founder of the 22nd dynasty, was the son of a Libyan noble family long established at Bubastis, in the eastern Delta. When he took power he was already head of the army and a councilor of the king, of whom he was also son-in-law. With the strong internal divisions tearing apart the 21st dynasty, he had no great difficulty in assuming power and, with the pharaonic titles, beginning a new age, that of the Libyan chiefs. Over the long period of just over 250 years, the 22nd dynasty restored Egypt's authority in terms of international affairs; various masterpieces of goldworking from the period testify to the artistic diversity and skills available to these rulers.

New divisions soon led to the formation of at least two collateral Libyan dynasties, the 23rd and the 24th, with their respective capitals of Leontopolis and Sais, which ruled their territories alongside the 22nd dynasty, dividing the Delta and putting all of Egypt at risk of the dangers that were beginning to take shape from Assyria.

Piankhi

When Nubia broke from Egypt at the end of the 20th dynasty, an independent kingdom known as Kush arose at Napata, near the Fourth Cataract. On the basis of the prestige of the local temple of Amon, at Gebel Barkal, a dynasty came into being, the 25th, and around the middle of the 8th century BC it rose against the Libyan princedoms of the Delta, fighting in defense of the more traditional values of Egyptian culture, in particular those of Thebes. When Piankhi was crowned, he organized a crusade on the model of Kamose's against the Libyan chiefs who decided to unite to form a common front against the growing power of the 25th dynasty. Piankhi's army conquered one city after another, forcing all the rulers of the Delta to submit, and many of them were left to rule their territories as vassals. Far from having resolved the situation with the rebellious Libyans, Piankhi returned to Napata. The last pharaohs of the dynasty (Shabaka, Taharqa, and Tanutamani) found themselves involved in continuous clashes with Assyria for control of the Delta and of Palestine, and rather than submit to a Nubian ruler, the Libyan princes opened their doors to the Assyrian army of Ashurbanipal as soon as doing so was possible. In 667 BC the Assyrian army conquered Memphis, and three years later Thebes was sacked; by then powerless, the 25th dynasty retreated to Nubia.

Hieroglyph
Men-kheper-Ra P-Ankhy
("Stable is the
transformation of Ra.
Piankhi ["the living"])"

Chronology
747–716 BC
25th dynasty

Important events
Year 12 of reign:
Piankhi's sister
Amenirdis I is adopted
by Shepenupet I to
succeed her as God's
Wife of Amon.
21: victorious "crusade"
against a coalition of
Delta princes led by
Tefnakht.

Sources
*The victory stela of king
Piye*, (Lichtheim 1980,
Vol. III, p.66).

Bibliography
Kitchen 1972. Grimal
1988, chap. XIV. Shaw
2000, chap. 12.

◀ Head from a statue of
Taharqa, from Karnak (?),
25th dynasty, black
granite, h 36.5 cm, Nubia
Museum, Aswan.

Amenirdis I was the sister of the Nubian ruler Piankhi. When he took the throne, Amenirdis was formally adopted by the current God's Wife of Amon, Shepenupet I, giving her the right to exercise a great deal of power based on the influence of the temple of Amon at Karnak. When she became the God's Wife, Amenirdis led the political life of Thebes during the early troubled years of the clashes between the rulers of the 25th dynasty and the Assyrians, demonstrating diplomatic skills and excellent organizational abilities.

This life-size standing statue of Amenirdis I, made of precious alabaster, is a true masterpiece for its period. The broad features and sinuous lines of the chest and hips reflect the style adopted in the rendering of the female body by Nubian artists; here it is toned down somewhat by the smooth surface of the alabaster, which shades the forms, creating an effect of soft lightness.

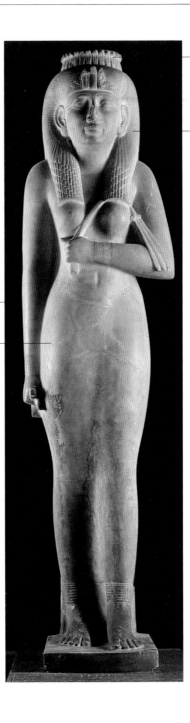

▶ Statue of Amenirdis, from Karnak, 25th dynasty, alabaster, h 170 cm, Egyptian Museum, Cairo, CG 565.

The statue is given a greater sense of balance by the round headdress composed of bunched uraei.

The face with its youthful vitality is framed by voluminous locks of hair.

Mentuemhat

During the difficult transition between the Ethiopian and the Saite periods, Thebes remained relatively stable both politically and economically because of the rule of the great priests of Amon. Among these, the personality of Mentuemhat—fourth prophet of Amon, mayor of the city, and governor of Upper Egypt—stands out. His figure takes form after the death of Taharqa, when the Assyrians pressed on the borders, and the prince of Sais Psamtik I established the 26th dynasty in Lower Egypt. Descendent of an ancient family of Theban priests, Mentuemhat ruled the south of the country with almost royal power, and his tomb at Assasif (West Bank at Thebes) must have been the largest and most monumental of its period. It consists of a large open court and numerous sub-terranean shrines covered by a structure similar to a palace. In his rule of the city Mentuemhat profited from the support of Shepenupet II, daughter of the Nubian king Shabaka. As a female priest she performed the role of Divine Adoratrice of Amon, which gave her a great deal of political and temporal power. When Psamtik I consolidated his power in the north, he made his daughter Nitocris Divine Adoratrice; in accepting this, Mentuemhat and Shepenupet recognized the domination of the Saite dynasty over the south, but they continued to govern the territory, albeit in accordance with the new priestess of Amon.

Hieroglyphic
Mentju-em-hat
("Montu is in the lead")

Chronology
First half 7th century BC
25th–26th dynasty

Bibliography
Kitchen 1972.

◀ Statue of Mentuemhat, from the cachette of Karnak, end 25th–beginning 26th dynasty, gray granite, h 137 cm, Egyptian Museum, Cairo, CG 42236.

Psamtik I

Hieroglyph
Uah-ib-Ra P-s-m-tj-k
("Benevolent is the heart of
Ra. Psamtik")

Chronology
664–610 BC
26th dynasty

Important events
Introduction of Carian and
Ionian mercenaries in the
Egyptian army.
Nationalistic exaltation of
classical Egyptian culture.
Diffusion of demotic
writing.
Construction of the "Great
Galleries" in the Serapeum
of Memphis.
Year 8 of reign: as regent
under the Assyrians,
Psamtik retakes the Delta
and Thebes.
11: Psamtik renounces
allegiance to Assyria and
drives the Assyrian
garrisons out of Egypt.
52: enlargement of the
Serapeum of Memphis.

Bibliography
Grimal 1988, chap. XIV.
Shaw 2000, chap. 12.

▶ Ahmose II portrayed as
a sphinx, 26th dynasty,
basanite, 90 cm, Museo
Gregoriano Egizio,
Vatican City, MC0035.

Having successfully eliminated opposition from the 25th dynasty,
the Assyrians found themselves facing the problem of the continuous
rebellions of the principalities of the Delta, so they entrusted control
of the area to the local ruler of Sais, Necho I, for he had distinguished
himself in their eyes by his loyalty: with him begins the Saite 26th
dynasty. At his death, the Assyrians recognized his son Psamtik I as
the only king of Egypt and entrusted him with control of the country
provided he put down any attempts at revolt. After winning complete control of the Delta by force of arms, Psamtik decided to take
the next step and turned against the Assyrians, driving them out of
Egypt and becoming the national champion of the reunification of
the country and the revival of Egyptian royalty after many years of
foreign domination. With Psamtik I, Carian and Ionian mercenaries
made their first appearance in the Egyptian army. Facing a new
geopolitical reality, Egypt started along a course destined to enrich it
with new cultural influences, most of all from Greece. This opening
out to foreigners was counterbalanced, however, by the great attention Psamtik paid to traditional Egyptian culture, with a revival of
artistic, literary, and religious models based on the classical style of
the Middle Kingdom and the glories of the New Kingdom.

Only a few portraits remain of the rulers of the Saite period, but they offer a sense of that dynasty's basic style and aesthetic ideals: smoothly polished surfaces, accurate and gentle modeling of features, and a benign "Saite" smile, emblematic of the ruler's inner peace.

▲ Head of a statue of the pharaoh Ahmose II, from Sais, 26th dynasty, green schist, h 24 cm. Ägyptisches Museum, Berlin, 11864.

This famous portrait head, thought to represent Ahmose II on the basis of stylistic aspects, is noteworthy for its brilliance and for the areas of shading that contrast the areas of skin with the almost metallic clarity of the nemes. The uraeus with its double S-coils is a stylistic element introduced by the Saite rulers.

Udjahorresnet

Hieroglyphic
Udja-hor-resnet
(meaning uncertain)

Chronology
circa 600–520 BC
26th–27th dynasty

Important events
Composition of
pharaonic titles for
Cambyses II, king
of Persia.
Liberation from
Persian troops of the
sacred precinct of
Neith at Sais.
Restoration of the
center of priestly
studies annexed to the
temple of Neith at Sais.

Sources
*Statue inscription of
Udjahorresne,*
(Lichtheim 1980,Vol.
III, p.36).

Bibliography
Grimal 1988, chap.
XIV. Shaw 2000,
chap. 13.

▶ Naophorus of
Udjahorresnet, called the
"Vatican Naophorus,"
from Sais, 27th dynasty,
green basalt, h 70 cm,
Museo Gregoriano Egizio,
Vatican City, 196.

Udjahorresnet is an extremely interesting figure because of the role of mediator he played during a highly difficult period for his country, the first period of Persian domination, between 525 and 404 BC. What is known about his life and work comes from texts engraved on a statue of him today in the Vatican Museums. He was a priest of Sais and a high dignitary, learned and refined, who had performed various administrative tasks, including for the royal fleet, under the last two rulers of the 26th dynasty, Ahmose II and Psamtik III. In 525 BC, the defeat of the Egyptian army at Pelusium left the field open to the Persian king Cambyses II, who turned Egypt into a satrapy. It was under these circumstances that Udjahorresnet thought it would be wisest, for his country and for

its traditions, to pass into the service of the new rulers, seeking a means of collaboration that would prove beneficial to both sides. Thus he came to serve as the chief physician for Cambyses II, for whom he composed a royal titulary following the pharaonic model; in return, the king agreed to remove the Persian garrison that had been installed in the sacred precinct of the temple of Neith at Sais. Udjahorresnet traveled to Susa, in Persia, and was recalled to Egypt by Darius I to reconstruct the school of scribal and priestly studies and to instruct the new rulers of Egypt in the theology and the ritual duties of the pharaoh, in that way safeguarding the culture and traditions of his country.

Nectanebo I

The political events that led to the last dynasty of native pharaohs, the 30th, are directly related to the war between Greeks and Persians that afflicted the Mediterranean at the beginning of the 4th century BC. Under Achoris, last ruler of the 29th dynasty, Egypt joined an alliance composed of Athens and Cyprus against the king of Persia, but they were defeated, and the Persian army prepared to march on Egypt, by then politically isolated. In 380 BC, a general from Sebennytus, Nectanebo I, usurped the throne from the successor of Achoris, Nepherites II, and proclaimed himself king and began to organize the defense of the country against the Persian attack, which came in 373 BC. The Persians came by land and sea with an army that included Athenian components, obtained through negotiations following the defeat of Greece's alliance with Cyprus. The operation was commanded by the satrap Pharnabazus and the Athenian general Iphikrates. The Greek naval forces succeeded in breaking through the Egyptian defenses near the Mendes branch of the Nile and were about to march on the capital Memphis, but the Persian satrap's distrust of his allies led him to await the arrival of the bulk of his forces. This decision proved fatal, for it permitted Nectanebo to reorganize his army. It was the end of July, and the pharaoh, profiting from the flooding of the Nile, which transformed the Delta into a swamp, inflicted a crushing defeat on the forces of the Persian king.

Hieroglyph
Kheper-ka-Ra
Nekhet-neb-ef
("The ka of Ra comes
into existence.
Powerful is his lord")

Chronology
380–362 BC
30th dynasty

Important events
Spring of year 7 of his
reign: a Persian army
invades Egypt, taking
control of Memphis.
July: Nectanebo defeats
the Persians, exploiting
the Nile flood, which
transforms the Delta
into a swamp.

Sources
*The Naucratis Stela of
King Nectanebo I,*
(Lichtheim 1980, Vol.
III, p.86)

Bibliography
Grimal 1988, chap.
XIV. Shaw 2000,
chap. 13.

◄Head thought to be
of Nectanebo I, 30th
dynasty, basalt, h 6.5
cm, Musée du Louvre,
Paris, E 8061.

This basalt slab was probably an architectural element composed of several other parts, as indicated by both the inscription and the decoration, which covers both sides. The slab was found at Alexandria, but like many other pharaonic relics from the Hellenistic capital, it comes from Heliopolis.

The tight cap with the uraeus that Nectanebo wears is a characteristic trait of this iconography.

The better-preserved side presents a palace façade upon which appears the kneeling figure of Nectanebo, making an offering. This is one of the few portraits of the pharaoh to have survived; he has been identified on the basis of his small chin and slightly hooked nose.

▲ Slab with portrait of Nectanebo I, from Alexandria, 30th dynasty, basalt, British Museum, London, EA 22.

This statuette represents an interesting stage in the evolution of the relationship between ruler and divinity in Egyptian art over the course of about two thousand years. In the earliest times, when pharaonic authority was absolute, the ruler was perceived as the personification itself of supernatural and invisible divine power. Sculptors of the period paid more attention to the depiction of the monarch than to that of the divinity. An example of this can be seen in the reduced size of the falcon Horus, hidden by the head of Khafre, in a famous statue in Cairo. By the time of Nectanebo II the relationship had reversed, as indicated by this statue, in which the tiny figure of the pharaoh is enclosed between the massive legs of Horus.

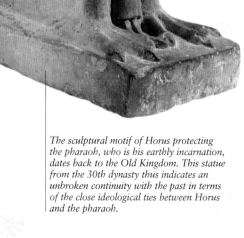

▲ Statue of Horus protecting Nectanebo II, 30th dynasty, painted limestone, Musée du Louvre, Paris, E 11152.

The sculptural motif of Horus protecting the pharaoh, who is his earthly incarnation, dates back to the Old Kingdom. This statue from the 30th dynasty thus indicates an unbroken continuity with the past in terms of the close ideological ties between Horus and the pharaoh.

State and society

Pharaoh
Names of the king
Symbols of power
Priesthood
Scribes and officials
Soldiers and the army
Foreigners
Court artists

◄ Statue of chief lector priest, or
Kaaper, from the mastaba of Kaaper
at Saqqara, 4th dynasty, sycamore
wood with inlays, h 112 cm,
Egyptian Museum, Cairo, CG 34.

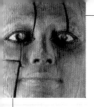

"His majesty at the head of his army attacked his enemies . . . when they saw he was overwhelming them they broke and fled to Megiddo in panic" (Annals of Thutmose III)

Pharaoh

In depth
The vizier (in Egyptian *tjaty*) was a high official who performed administrative functions for the pharaoh; his role consisted of the supervision of all the government departments: justice, agriculture, irrigation, public safety, finance, foreign relations. During the New Kingdom the position was doubled, with separate officials in charge of Upper and Lower Egypt.

Bibliography
Ziegler 2002.

Related entries
Names of the king, Symbols of power, Humans and gods, Maat, The Osirian drama, Historical sources

From the religious point of view, the function of the sovereign in Egyptian society was that of maintaining the universal harmony that had come into being at the moment of the creation of the cosmos, expressed in the concept of Maat. The pharaoh's temporal power was expressed in the exercise of his functions as ruler, administrator, high priest, supreme judge, and commander in chief of the army; put simply, he was truly the master of the world in the eyes of his subjects. The fact that he represented a direct intermediary between the divine and the human made the pharaoh virtually infallible and omnipotent. In accordance with the myth according to which the gods reigned on the earth before the coming of humans, Egypt's king was the physical incarnation of the god Horus, son of Osiris and vanquisher of the forces of evil; when dead, he became Osiris, and his successor perpetuated the cycle by again personifying Horus. Because of his divine nature, the sovereign received a "son of Ra" name at birth and

became the "king of Upper and Lower Egypt" when he took the throne; the complex titulary of the monarch was composed in reality of five names, the meanings of which reflected his political and religious roles. The word *pharaoh* is the biblical Hebrew rendering of the Egyptian phrase *per-aa*, "the big house," meaning the royal house. The word is encountered somewhat rarely, having come into common use only in the Late Period.

▶ Panel depicting the goddess Hathor and Seti I, from the tomb of Seti I in the Valley of the Kings, Western Thebes, 19th dynasty, painted plaster, h 226 cm, Musée du Louvre, Paris, B7.

This work is of interest in part because all three figures reach the same height. This goes against the general rule of Egyptian art: the hierarchically most important person is usually presented larger than the others. Furthermore, divinities are usually depicted as taller than royal figures.

The bride of Amon-Ra, the goddess Mut, wears a long tunic and the classic Hathoric crown reserved for female divinities: between the bovine horns is the solar disk.

Amon-Ra is depicted anthropomorphically, wearing the typical crown topped by a double feather.

The composition's central figure is Ramses II. He is seated between the divine couple of the religious capital of Thebes. He wears the skirt and the nemes topped by the ram's-head crown completed by a solar disk and two feathers.

▲ Triad composed of Amon-Ra, Ramses II, and Mut, from the temple of Karnak at Thebes, 19th dynasty, pink granite, h 174 cm, Fondazione Museo Antichità Egizie, Turin, C. 767.

The pharaoh's military deeds, as presented in this image, were of symbolic importance. The king's victories over enemies had propaganda value not simply as a demonstration of his excellence or his unerring strategic skills, but as support for his role as guarantor of cosmic and social harmony.

To the side of the figure of the pharaoh are two columns of partially mutilated inscriptions. Opposite his face are cartouches that enclose the names of Ra-messu Mery-Imen ("Ra has generated him, beloved of Amon") and User-Maat-Ra-Setep-en-Ra ("Powerful is the Maat of Ra, the chosen of Ra"); behind the king's body is the phrase "the protection is over him, as Ra."

One of the three prisoners is Nubian, with dark skin and curly hair; another is Libyan, with brown flesh tones; the third is Syrian, with pale skin and a pointed beard.

The pharaoh presented here is Ramses II, dressed in a ceremonial skirt with a parade headdress, in the act of grasping three enemies by the hair before striking them with an ax.

▲ Decorated block with Ramses II striking down enemies, from Memphis, 19th dynasty, painted limestone, h 110 cm, Egyptian Museum, Cairo, JE 46189.

The inscription recounts that the god Harmakhis ("Horus is on the horizon"), depicted in the form of a lion with a human head, appeared to the prince in a dream, asking him to free the monument that represented him from the sand and to undertake certain works of restoration. At the same time the god recognized Thutmose as his son and foretold his ascension to the throne.

The stele narrates a miraculous dream Thutmose IV had when still a young prince, while resting in the shadow at the foot of the monument after a hunt in the desert.

▲ Dream Stele of Thutmose IV between the paws of the Sphinx at Giza.

As guarantor of cosmic harmony, the pharaoh had to make clear that he was a continuation of the unbroken line formed by his illustrious predecessors. It was thus important to maintain or restore monuments from earlier epochs.

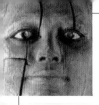

"His majesty assigned to me the office of chief physician . . . I composed his titulary, to wit his name as king of Upper and Lower Egypt" (Naophorus of Udjahorresnet)

Names of the king

In depth
In Egyptian, the sovereign was called *nesut* ("king"), *heqa* ("chief, prince"), *ity* ("sovereign"), or *hemef* ("his majesty"). The pharaoh also bore the names of *neb-tauy* ("Lord of the Two Lands"), *neb-khau* ("Lord of the apparitions"), and *netjer-nefer* ("Perfect god"). The name of the king is followed by the auspicious formula *ankh-udja-seneb* ("life, prosperity, health").

Related entries
Pharaoh, Symbols of power, The Osirian drama, Magic

The complex so-called fivefold titulary assumed by the king as the earthly incarnation of the god Horus and protector of regality reflected a specific political and religious program. At birth, the prince received a birth name (*nomen*), often the same as that of other members of his family, such as Mentuhotep, Sesostris, Amenhotep, Ramses. This was called his *sa-Ra* ("son of Ra") name to emphasize his divine lineage; this name is always written inside a cartouche, an oval area created by a loop that magically encircles the name. Upon taking the throne, the pharaoh assumed power over all of Egypt, North and South unified, so was given the name *nesu-bit* ("king of Upper and Lower Egypt"). This title, written in a cartouche, was preceded by the symbols for the Two Lands, the sedge (*nesu*) for the South and the bee (*bit*) for the North, and was full of political significance. The coronation brought another three names. One is the Horus name, since that god protected the pharaoh; this name was written in the *serekh*, a rectangular space decorated with a "palace-façade" motif; another is the "Horus of Gold" name, probably tied to the legend of the falcon-god, son of Osiris, victorious over Set and the forces of evil; the last was the "Two Ladies" name, referring to the protector goddesses of Egypt: Nekhbet for the South (the vulture) and Uadjet for the North (the serpent).

► Statue bearing a double cartouche with the names of the god Aten accompanied by those of the pharaoh Akhenaten, from Amarna, 18th dynasty, limestone, h 108 cm, Fondazione Museo Antichità Egizie, Turin, C. 1378.

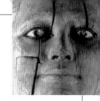

"Risen as king upon the great throne, the double crown of Upper and Lower Egypt clings to his head . . . the nemes embraces his shoulders" (Stele of the Sphinx of Amenhotep II)

Symbols of power

The pharaoh performed many roles in society, each one visibly expressed by an easily distinguishable detail; his crowns, robes, scepters, and other attributes were visual depictions of his functions. Various symbols referred to his dominion over both Upper and Lower Egypt: the bee for the North and the sedge for the South, placed before the royal titles written in a cartouche. In the same way, the sides of his throne were decorated by the plants characteristic of the Two Lands, the lotus and the papyrus. For the same reason, the king wore the "double crown" composed of a low headdress with a high back of a red color, emblematic of the goddesses Neith and Uadjet, protectors of the Delta, and a white tiara ending in a bulbous shape, carried by the goddess Nekhbet of el-Kab, near Thebes. The area atop the royal crown could be occupied by personifications of these protective goddesses, the serpent and the vulture. The two scepters, the *heqa* crook and *nekhakha* flail, are also emblems of Egypt's unification. As the chief of the clergy, the pharaoh was often depicted in ceremonial robes wearing sandals in the act of performing rituals and offerings to the gods. The pharaoh's military role was indicated by his clothing, such as a breastplate made of metal scales or the blue "war crown," decorated with copper disks, and weapons, such as a stone-headed mace or a bow and arrows. He was often depicted while striking down enemies at his feet.

Bibliography
Frankfort 1948.

Related entries
Pharaoh, Names of the king, The Osirian drama

▼ Frieze composed of the words *ankh*, *djed*, and *uas nb* ("all the life, stability, and power"), temple of Karnak, New Kingdom.

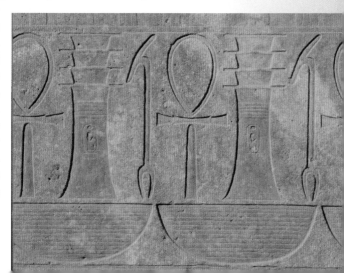

The scarab's legs support a sacred boat that bears a udjat eye flanked by two uraei cobras; this is a symbol of health and physical soundness, connected with the lunar god Thoth. Above the eye is a golden crescent and a silver lunar disk in which are depicted Thoth (the moon) and Ra (the sun) to the side of the figure of the king.

The jewel is a pendant with compound decorations that blend symbols of royalty. The center is dominated by a scarab, emblematic of the god Khepri, the rising sun; it has wings, feet, and a falcon tail. To the sides of the scarab are two uraei with solar disks.

The scarab, symbol of the sun and thus of the king's divine nature, grasps a shen ring in each of its rear legs. One bears a lily flower, the other a lotus, these being heraldic plants of the North and South of Egypt.

The base of the composition is decorated with pendants shaped like flowers of lotus, papyrus, and poppy.

▲ Pectoral of Tutankhamen, from the tomb of Tutankhamen in the Valley of the Kings, Western Thebes, 18th dynasty, gold, silver, semiprecious stones, and vitreous paste, h 14.9 cm, Egyptian Museum, Cairo, JE 61884.

The central scene of the pectoral is framed by a trapezoidal architectural cornice topped by a flared molding decorated with palm leaves.

The oval space between the vulture's wings is occupied by a cartouche of Ramses II, beneath which is a second vulture with a ram's head and spread wings, emblem of regality. The jewel was found in the Serapeum of Memphis on the mummy of a noble, perhaps Prince Khaemwaset, son of Ramses II.

In the empty space created between the wings and the base are located two djed amulets, stylizations of the backbone of Osiris and symbols of stability.

The central space is almost entirely occupied by a vulture with spread wings that represents the goddess Nekhbet flanked by the cobra of the goddess Uadjet. Together they are symbolic of the unification of Egypt. The nearly circular shape of the wings enlivens the rigidity of the frame.

▲ Pectoral of Ramses II, from the Serapeum of Memphis, 19th dynasty, gold and semiprecious stones, Musée du Louvre, Paris, 767.

The front face of the back of Tutankhamen's ceremonial throne is decorated with a scene of family life. The pharaoh sits on the throne in ceremonial dress with his wife Ankhesenamen in front of him.

The rear face of the throne is decorated by an embossed gold sheet decorated with papyrus reeds spreading to form a fan shape across which several birds can be seen flying.

Standing between the support bars are four uraeus cobras, their hoods flared in the position of attack, their heads topped by solar disks.

The back is supported by wooden bars covered in gold; the two on the sides bear the pharaoh's titles and coronation names: "the king of Upper and Lower Egypt Nebkheperu-Ra, the Son of Ra Tutankhaten, who lives as Ra in eternity."

The central bar bears the queen's title, "the great royal wife Ankhesenpaaten." The fact that the royal names include that of the god Aten indicates that the throne was made before the restoration of the worship of Amon.

▲ Rear face of the back of the throne of Tutankhamen, from the tomb of Tutankhamen in the Valley of the Kings, Western Thebes, 18th dynasty, wood, gold, semiprecious stones, vitreous paste, h 102 cm, Egyptian Museum, Cairo, JE 62028.

"It is in the name and place of the reigning sovereign that the priests of Egypt daily and throughout the land maintain the practice of the divine religion" (Serge Sauneron)

Priesthood

Each god of the Egyptian pantheon had at least one place of worship in the care of priests whose number depended on the importance of the divinity. A temple constituted an autonomous microcosm, with living quarters for the personnel, storehouses for provisions, sometimes also artisan workshops, ovens, and kitchens. In a theocratic state such as pharaonic Egypt, the leading families of priests came into possession of great economic and temporal power. Important positions within the priestly hierarchy were usually handed down from father to son, and it was possible to be promoted from position to position all the way to the level of the most important officials. Various hierarchical levels existed within the priesthood itself, and in particular there were differences between the priests involved in the actual worship and those serving administrative functions. Those involved in the worship had to maintain themselves in a state of ritual purity, shaving their hair, making ablutions, and abstaining from all contamination. Each priesthood had its own rules concerning prohibited foods and the sex lives of its priests. The daily worship of the divine simulacrum was performed by a high-ranking priest who opened the tabernacle accompanied by chants and prayers, made food offerings to the statue, washed it, and dressed it in new clothes. The statue was taken out of the temple only during festivities, when it was carried out in a procession and could be seen by the faithful.

In depth
Herodotus reports that Egyptian priests kept themselves ritually clean. They were circumcised, washed twice daily in cold water and twice every night, wore linen garments and papyrus shoes. These hardships were offset by the benefits of their position: they were completely supported by the state and enjoyed great wealth.

Bibliography
Sauneron 1988.

Related entries
Humans and gods, Temple, Priests

◀ Offering tablet with the depiction of food and drink and a carved groove for liquids, New Kingdom, sandstone, Fondazione Museo Antichità Egizie, Turin.

The role of the sem priest, who performed libations and aspersions, could be performed by a son of the deceased. The sidelock indicates the youth of this sem priest.

In front of the priest is a divinity's standard, topped by the image of a ram crowned with a double plume. Under this effigy of the god are another two gods in attitudes of jubilation.

Sem priests performed elaborate rituals at mummifications; the characteristic dress of such priests was composed of a spotted leopard skin.

The tomb of Ramses IX is decorated with scenes drawn from several important funerary texts from the New Kingdom, including the Litanies of Ra, the Book of the Day, and the Book of the Night. The texts recount the nocturnal journey of the sun and its constant struggle against the forces of evil.

▲ *Sem* priest performing a funerary rite, from the tomb of Ramses IX in the Valley of the Kings, Western Thebes, 20th dynasty.

The storehouses of the funerary temple of Ramses II in Western Thebes, the Ramesseum, were quite extensive, surrounding the religious complex on three sides. They were long, rectangular rooms covered by a barrel vault, built on inclined planes set into a rear wall.

Temples were self-sufficient, supported by their possessions and by income provided to the clergy by the state administration. The surplus from a temple's agricultural production was put in storehouses located near the places of worship.

Aside from holding food reserves, a temple's storehouse could be used as its treasury, the place to store the wealth from the donations and offerings of the faithful.

The secular structures of the Ramesseum included the royal palace, the "house of life" (scriptorium, school, and archives), and the living quarters for the administrative and religious personnel.

▲ Storehouses of the funerary temple of Ramses II, Western Thebes, 19th dynasty.

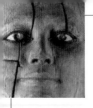

"Egyptians write from right to left. They use two different kinds of writing, one called sacred and the other common"
(Herodotus)

Scribes and officials

In depth
Writing instruments
included a wooden case,
sometimes with sliding
cover, for the storage of
pens and tablets of dry
ink. The pens were
reeds cut crosswise to
form a point. Black and
red inks were used, the
first made of lampblack
or charcoal, the second
from red ocher, both
mixed with a glue
solution and dissolved
in water.

Bibliography
Chadefaud 1993.

Related entries
Amenhotep, son of
Hapu, Priests, Humans
and gods, Thoth,
Literature, Writing

The temple was the place in which priests received their religious training; it was also the place where state officials were trained. Sanctuaries had spaces reserved for the copying, preservation, and teaching of sacred texts and also classics of literature. Called "houses of life," these spaces were often used to store the temple's archives. The craft of scribe was particularly popular, looked upon as the noblest work a man could perform; the extreme specialization of scribes in the various spheres of state administration made them equal in status to state officials. Many figures of great importance in the direction of the country began their careers as scribes. Among these was Amenhotep, son of Hapu, who lived during the period of Amenhotep III. So important did he become that he was the right hand of the king and after his death was venerated as a divinity. Egypt's officials were the cornerstones of its bureaucracy, seeing to the efficient management of the country's economy. The most important immortalized their achievements, always undertaken on orders from the pharaoh, in autobiographical inscriptions on their sumptuous tombs. Some were charged with embassies to foreign lands, others directed the construction of temples or palaces or concluded political and commercial treaties.

▶ Statue of seated scribe, from Saqqara, 5th dynasty, painted limestone, glass eyes, h 51 cm, Egyptian Museum, Cairo, CG 36.

The slab is decorated with four figures of young scribes. All of them bear a roll of papyrus and a reed pen with which to write; the ink tablets and pan of water in which to dilute them were kept in a case tied to a cord that was usually draped over one shoulder.

The scribes received their instruction in a temple, in the area set aside for the teaching of writing. The sons of the nobles and officials destined to become integral parts of Egypt's administration studied in such "houses of life."

Surviving scholastic texts and fragments of rough copies indicate that the Egyptian educational system was based on the rote learning of texts, which were copied over and over by the students.

Since it was costly and highly valued, papyrus was used almost exclusively for religious, accounting, and administrative texts. Nonofficial texts as well as those not destined to be preserved in archives were written on more ordinary materials, such as the stone chips and pottery fragments known today as ostraca, from a Greek word meaning "potsherd."

▲ Relief with figures of scribes, from the tomb of Horemheb at Saqqara, 18th dynasty, carved limestone, h 24 cm, Museo Archeologico Nazionale, Florence, 2566.

The administrative organization of the Egyptian state was a complex machine divided into departments responsible for the proper functioning of different sectors, among them agriculture, justice, transportation, and foreign relations.

The smooth wig falls behind the back, leaving the ears visible.

Little is known about the Egyptian legal system, for no texts containing civil laws have been recovered. There were codes covering generic behavior based on a religious concept of ethics. Indeed, justice was administered in temples in a space called the djadjat, and the most problematic controversies were sometimes settled by consulting the oracle of the temple's god.

The pendant the man wears around his neck presents the goddess Maat seated with her characteristic feather on her head. The fact that the noble bears an image of the goddess of law, truth, and justice suggests that he may have been a judge.

▲ Bust of an official, 26th dynasty, graywacke, h 36 cm, Fondazione Museo Antichità Egizie, Turin, C. 3075.

The wooden panels that decorated the burial chamber of the mastaba of Hesyra represent an excellent example of sculptural art. Their perfect state of preservation makes them unique within their genre.

Hesyra was chief of the court's dental physicians as well as a royal scribe. The role of scribe is emphasized by the strong presence of writing instruments, both held in his hand and draped over his shoulder.

Symbols of Hesyra's noble status include the long walking stick and the kherep scepter, which clearly indicate his official role in society. The deceased wears a simple skirt and a short but densely worked wig.

Hesyra is seated on a backless stool at an offering table bearing elongated loaves; other funerary offerings are listed in the inscription above the table: libations and other drinks, beef and goat meat, wine, and incense.

▲ Panel of Hesyra, from the tomb of Hesyra at Saqqara, 4th dynasty, wood, h 114 cm, Egyptian Museum, Cairo, CG 1426.

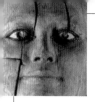

"I journeyed to Elephantine, I returned to the Delta. Having stood on the land's borders, I observed its interior" (Teaching of Amenemhet I)

Soldiers and the army

In depth
Between the Middle and New Kingdoms fortresses were built to control conquered territories and to protect caravan routes and strategic points. In Nubia, there were forts at Buhen and Semna; during the Middle Kingdom, the "Wall of the Prince" was erected along the Syrian border, and a system of forts protected the western coast of the Mediterranean Sea.

Bibliography
Faulkner 1953.

Related entries
Foreigners

▼ Wall painting with scenes of wrestling and training, tomb of Khety III at Beni Hasan, Middle Kingdom.

Among the pharaoh's functions as protector of cosmic harmony was that of dominating the enemies forever pressing against Egypt's borders, threatening to invade. The most frequent depictions of the pharaoh include that of a warrior smiting enemies or standing above them victorious. In the beginning, the Egyptian army's duties were primarily logistical, providing support to commercial expeditions and maintaining order. Since no specific skills were required for serving in the army, military service was one of the many jobs that Egyptians performed for the state. There were also various elite corps, such as the famous Nubian archers, or the fearsome Medjau (an African population) frontier police, or the Libyan mercenaries. During periods of weakened central power, it often happened that the nomarchs—provincial chiefs—formed personal armies to control and enlarge their territories. When Egypt became an imperialist country during the New Kingdom, a permanent standing army came into being, and the career of soldier became hereditary, with related social and financial advantages. This led to the formation of a rigid and codified military hierarchy controlled by a solid administrative network. By the Late Period, however, it was more customary for Egyptians to hire mercenaries, drawing them from throughout the Mediterranean to fill the ranks of Egypt's various local armies.

Nubians were used in the Egyptian army as archers or frontier police; in both cases, they were part of elite corps with specific functions.

The forty statues are arranged in four rows of ten and are attached to a single flat base. Their black skin identifies them as Africans.

The archers wear a short wig held in place by a band and wear brightly colored loincloths tied around their waists. They are barefoot but wear anklets and march with their left foot forward.

The tomb of the noble Mesehti at Asyut, dating to the early Middle Kingdom, was furnished with models of two army groups, one of archers and one of spearmen (next page). The models reflect the period of tension and clashes between the provinces of Middle and Upper Egypt during the First Intermediate Period.

Each soldier bears a bow in his left hand and holds a bunch of arrows in his right.

▲ Models of Nubian archers, from the tomb of Mesehti at Asyut, 11th dynasty, painted wood, h 55 cm, Egyptian Museum, Cairo, CG 257.

The skin of the soldiers is brown, typical for representation of people who work in the open; they wear black helmet-shaped wigs and a simple pale-color skirt.

The figures are of different heights, lending the group a sense of great realism.

The second group of models found in the tomb of Mesehti presents another forty soldiers arranged in four rows of ten, these armed with spears. They are a companion piece to the group of Nubian archers.

The forty soldiers march with their left foot forward. Each bears a shield covered with cowhide on his left arm and carries a spear in his right.

▲ Models of Egyptian spearmen from the tomb of Mesehti at Asyut, 11th dynasty, painted wood, h 59 cm, Egyptian Museum, Cairo, CG 258.

"Thou didst create the earth according to thy desire the foreign countries, Syria and Nubia, the land of Egypt. Thou settest every man in his place and his days are reckoned" (Hymn to Aten)

Foreigners

To the Egyptian mentality, the ordered cosmos was under constant threat from the chaos surrounding it. In the same way, Egypt was exposed to the assaults of foreigners. In royal propaganda, the pharaoh, at least symbolically, crushed the "Nine Bows" (an expression that encompassed all foreign peoples) beneath his sandals. Of course, foreigners were present in Egypt from the earliest period, first as prisoners, then as citizens; very often they brought the customs, foods, products, and even divinities of their homeland, and such elements were easily assimilated into Egyptian social life. The children of the principal royal families of the Near East, destined to become ambassadors, attended Egyptian schools; in their service were often interpreters who were of fundamental importance to the maintenance of political and commercial contacts with the outside world. Alliances between the pharaoh and foreign rulers were sealed by political marriages as well as by the exchange of gifts. A state of subjugation is indicated by the parades of Africans, Libyans, and Orientals with their typical dress and hairstyles, bringing the products of their lands to the Egyptian sovereign.

The history of Egypt's Late Period was dominated by foreign dynasties, first the Libyans in the Delta, then the Ethiopians in the South, and finally the conquest of the country by the Assyrians, by the Persians, and then by the Greeks of Alexander the Great.

In depth
In royal propaganda, all foreign peoples were grouped under the denomination "Nine Bows," trampled under the king's sandals. They are the *Khastiu*, who inhabit the deserts. The Nubians were called *Nehesu* or *Medjau*, the Syrians *Shasu* and *Aamu*, the Libyans *Tjehenu*. To exorcise the danger of invasion, statuettes representing prisoners were ritually broken. Such statuettes bore inscriptions to ward off evil and were called "heads of abomination."

Bibliography
Valbelle 1990.

Related entries
Hyksos kings, Soldiers and the army, Commerce

◄ Enameled tiles with figures of foreigners, from the royal palace of Ramses III at Medinet Habu, 20th dynasty, glazed polychrome terracotta, h 25 cm, Egyptian Museum, Cairo, JE 38682.

The stele is shaped like a small shrine with a central picture. The stele is from the tomb of a private citizen, a Syrian soldier accompanied by his wife.

The soldier is seated on a folding stool. Standing in front of him is a servant who offers him a drinking straw inserted in a vase of wine or beer resting on a support.

The inscription above the scene, divided in five columns, bears the names of the figures. The man's name is Tura; his wife is "the lady of the Arbura house."

The wife, dressed in a white tunic draped according to the style of the period, sits on a lower stool opposite her husband.

The man wears a richly decorated skirt secured at his waist and wears a large necklace in the Egyptian style. There must have been a massive number of foreigners in Egypt during the New Kingdom, and a great many became fully integrated in the social fabric.

The soldier's hair is held back by a band, perhaps forming a chignon at the back. His thick, dark beard, pointed on his chin, indicates he is a Semite. His profession is indicated by the spear against the wall behind him.

▲ Stele of a Syrian soldier, perhaps from Amarna, 18th dynasty, painted limestone, h 29.5 cm, Ägyptisches Museum, Berlin, 14122.

The scene located under the curve has a symmetrical composition; the central axis is represented by the figure of the Syrian goddess Qadesh ("saint" in Semitic), presented frontally. The nude goddess stands on the back of a lion and bears a serpent in one hand and a bunch of lotus flowers in the other. The goddess had a twofold nature, being connected to both sensuality and eroticism and to war.

To the left of the goddess is the ithyphallic god Min, related to forces of fertility and also the protector of travelers in the eastern deserts. The presence of divinities that evoke the Syria-Palestine world can be ascribed to the mixture of nationalities and cultures found in the workers' village at Deir el-Medina.

The stele was offered by the squadron leader Ramose and by his wife Mutemuia, depicted in adoration in the lower level.

To the right of Qadesh is the oriental god Reshef, armed with a lance and sword, he too characterized by a warrior nature.

▲ Stele of the goddess Qadesh and the god Reshef, Deir el-Medina, 19th–20th dynasty, painted limestone, h 45 cm, Fondazione Museo Antichità Egizie, Turin, C. 1601.

Such rows of prisoners, sometimes ethnically typified, were symbolic of the forces of chaos that endangered the cosmic order.

This relief is part of a narration of the wars Ramses III fought against the Sea Peoples, a confederation of peoples who before invading Egypt had ravaged the coastal regions of the eastern Mediterranean.

Egypt looked upon the outside world as a possible threat to its stability; thus the pharaoh, in order to protect the harmonious order of creation, had to control whatever was foreign.

The inscriptions celebrating Ramses III's victories, in his mortuary temple at Medinet Habu, bear the names of the invaders. Among them are the Akhuau (ancient name of the Achaeans), the Peleseth (the Philistines, depicted with a tall flaring hairstyle), the Shekelesh, and the Shardana (who some identify with the Sicilian Siculi or the Sardinians).

▲ Relief with prisoners, from the mortuary temple of Ramses III at Medinet Habu, 20th dynasty.

"His majesty sent me to Elephantine to bring a false door, together with its offering-tablet, mountings, and settings and an offering-tablet belonging to the upper chamber" (The Inscription of Weni)

Court artists

The figure of the artist who makes a name for himself because of his personality did not exist in ancient Egypt, but it has been possible to identify a few of Egypt's artists. These skilled artists served the court and made works desired by the ruler himself. Since their tasks included giving a face and features to a divinity on earth, they contributed to forming the king's image. In a world populated primarily by illiterates, visual communication was crucial, and the iconographic details used in depictions of the sovereign had to make clear his greatness, power, divine nature, and magnanimity. Most of the known artists date to the New Kingdom, among them Bak and Thutmose, both active during the reign of Akhenaten. Of course, more than any other pharaoh Akhenaten exploited his image as a vehicle in a political and religious program. Artists had to serve a long apprenticeship in a workshop, often directed by a family member, where they learned techniques, uses of materials, tools, and the principal iconography. The masters whose talents were most appreciated made works of sculpture, painting, or architecture for court patrons or private persons who often permitted them greater expressive freedom.

In depth
Such semiprecious stones as granite, diorite, basalt, and porphyry involved costly mining and transportation from distant quarries; then they had to be shaped. Such material was reserved almost exclusively to royal monuments. Softer and easier to manipulate rocks like limestone, sandstone, and alabaster could be shaped with hammers and chisels.

Bibliography
Aldred 1980.

Related entries
Artisans, Akhetaten, Amarna excavations

◄Sculptors making a statue, from the tomb of Rekhmire at Sheikh Abd el-Qurna, Western Thebes, 18th dynasty.

Bak is of historical-artistic importance not only because he worked out the enigmatic artistic style of Amarna but because he was able to artistically interpret a religious message of profound intensity.

In a relief cut into rock in the area of Aswan, Bak and his father, Min, are depicted paying homage to sovereigns, Min to Amenhotep III, Bak to Amenhotep IV. Min worked under Amenhotep III, while Bak worked for his successor at Amarna, perhaps directly continuing work begun by his father, with whom he must have studied.

Bak is here depicted with his wife Taheri on a stele in the shape of a tabernacle. The couple are standing, the wife embracing her husband. Bak's protruding belly indicates his well-to-do position. In contrast to the simplified forms of the bodies, their faces are intense and are presented following the dictates of Amarnian art.

Bak claimed he had been directly "instructed" by the sovereign. This did not involve satisfying a preference or a taste or a style, for the pharaoh asked his chief sculptor to work out a completely new iconography and sensibility.

▲ Shrine of Chief Sculptor Bak and Taheri, from Amarna, 18th dynasty, quartzite, h 76 cm, Ägyptisches Museum, Berlin, 1/63.

The two portraits depict Akhenaten with two different headdresses. The details of his features are emphasized, analyzed, and perfected.

The artists working on making images of the king drew on repertories of portraits and standard iconography. Among the numerous works found at Akhetaten are examples that must have been tests or preliminary sketches made before creation of the final work of sculpture or statuary.

The workshop artists had to follow the stereotypes established by traditional propaganda while at the same time applying the style and aesthetic novelties of their time.

▲ Sculptor's model with royal portraits, from Amarna, 18th dynasty, limestone, h 23 cm, Egyptian Museum, Cairo, JE 59294.

Religion and science

◄Head of the goddess Hathor in
the form of a cow, from the tomb
of Tutankhamen, 18th dynasty,
wood and gold leaf, Museum of
Ancient Egyptian Art, Luxor.

The Heliopolitan cosmogony

Hieroglyph
Pesedjet 'at
("Great Ennead")

In depth
In addition to the
pesedjet 'at, or Great
Ennead (*ennead* from
the Greek for "the
nine"), the theologians
at Heliopolis elaborated
a *pesedjet sheryt*, or
Lesser Ennead. This
accommodated the
need to organize the
pantheon around the
central figure of Atum-
Ra and thus included
Egypt's most important
divinities: Horus, who
acted as connection to
Osiris and thus to the
Great Ennead, and his
four sons, Imsety, Hapi,
Qebehsenuf, and
Duamutef. To these
divinities were added
Thoth, Maat, Ptah,
and Anubis.

Bibliography
Baines, Lesko,
Silvermann 1991,
Chap. II.

Related entries
Maat, Ra and Apep,
The Osirian drama,
Pyramid complex

The oldest and most widespread Egyptian cosmogony was elaborated in the religious center at Heliopolis near the capital of Memphis. This related that in the beginning there was only an infinite ocean, immersed in total darkness, called Nun. Dispersed in this primordial water were the components of the god Atum, which at a certain moment assembled, permitting the god to rise from the water in the form of an enflamed spark or the sun. Thanks to his warmth Atum "dried" a small portion of Nun, creating the primordial hill on which he could rest and begin the act of creation. From his saliva or sperm, according to the version, Atum created the first divine couple, Shu and Tefnut, the first representing air, the second dew and rain. These in turn generated Geb and Nut, respectively the earth and the sky. From this pair were born Osiris and Isis, associated with the idea of germination and fertility, and Set and Nephthys, the arid desert and sterility. Together, these nine divinities formed what the Egyptians called the Great Ennead,

which, by giving the leading place in the Egyptian pantheon to Atum, the solar divinity of Heliopolis, increased the importance of that city's local clergy, in particular during the 4th and 5th dynasties of the Old Kingdom. That clergy remained an essential element in Egyptian theological thinking during later periods.

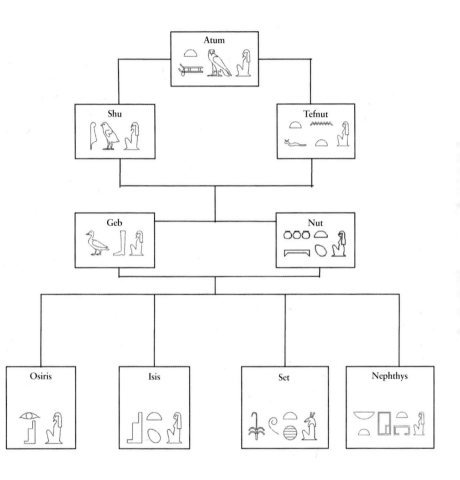

◀Statue of Horemheb offering *mu* vases to the god Atum, from the cachette of the temple of Amon-Ra at Luxor, 18th dynasty, diorite, h 171 cm, Museum of Ancient Egyptian Art, Luxor.

▲Genealogical tree of the Heliopolitan Ennead.

From the Third Intermediate Period on, sarcophagi were often embellished with numerous mythological scenes that recall the idea of regeneration. One of the most widespread and evocative images is the myth of the separation of the sky (Nut) from the earth (Geb) by the god of the air (Shu).

Egyptian myth narrates that Shu had to intervene to separate Geb and Nut, who were bound in an amorous embrace. It may well be possible that this depiction of Shu, who stands erect with his arms raised to hold up the sky, provided the original prototype for the codified iconography of the Greek Titan Atlas.

The god Geb is usually depicted in this mythological scene lying down, resting on an elbow with one knee raised. His dark color refers to the rich silt that nourished the Egyptian earth following every Nile flood.

▲ The cosmic divinities Geb, Nut, and Shu on the sarcophagus of Nespawerhefi, scribe in the temple of Amon-Ra, Western Thebes, 21st dynasty.

The body of the goddess Nut curves over the scene, representing the celestial vault. In the myth narrated in the Book of the Celestial Cow, she is said to devour her own children (the stars in the morning, the sun at sunset) only to give birth to them again each new day. For this reason her head and vulva indicate, respectively, the west and the east.

Ptah and the Ogdoad

The unification of Egypt favored the birth of a capital at Memphis, in the lower point of the Delta. The local divinity, Ptah, was considered a national divinity, making it necessary to work out a doctrine that presented this god in the role of demiurge, a role long occupied by Atum in nearby Heliopolis. The resultant myth closely followed the scheme of the Heliopolitan cosmogony, relating Ptah's emergence from primordial chaos to give life to eight divinities: Tatenen, the earth emerging from chaos, Nun and Naunet, the primordial ocean and its companion, Atum, and another four divinities whose names have been lost. A text originally composed around the 3rd dynasty, known in a late version called the *Memphite Theology of Creation*, narrates that the creation of Ptah happened by way of a thought and its enunciation. The sophisticated concept of a *logos* creator confers a strongly spiritual character on this elaboration and makes it one of the highest achievements of ancient Egyptian speculative thought. The theology of Hermopolis, instead, entrusted the creation to a group of five divinities (four dog-headed baboons, the sacred beings

of Thoth as ruler of Hermopolis, led by a hare-goddess named Unut). This group was later replaced by an Ogdoad (from a Greek word for "eight") composed of four pairs of primordial divinities: Nun and Nunet, Huh and Huhet, Keku and Keket, Amon and Amonet. Their interaction was said to have generated the sun, leading to creation.

Hieroglyph
Khemenyu
("Those of the eight")

In depth
Following the example of the Ennead of Heliopolis, other centers of worship assembled their own theological systems that grouped secondary divinities around the local divinity. The term *ennead* itself came to indicate plurality in general, regardless of the actual number. Thus the Ennead of Abydos consisted of only seven divinities, while that of Thebes put Amon-Ra at the head of a "Great Corporation" of fifteen divinities, including the Heliopolitan Ennead to which were added Mont, Horus, Hathor, Sobek, Tatenen, and Iunit.

Bibliography
Baines, Lesko, Silvermann 1991, Chap. II.

Related entries
Heliopolitan cosmogony, Ptah, Thoth

◀Portrait of the god Ptah from the tomb of Horemheb, Valley of the Kings, Western Thebes, 18th dynasty.

Ptah and the Ogdoad

In earliest times the principal worship at Hermopolis had involved a group of five divinities called the Great Five, composed of four dog-headed baboons and the ancient goddess of the province, Unut, a hare with long ears. As early as the 5th dynasty, their worship had been replaced by that of eight elementary divinities, the Ogdoad. In a later stage, Thoth assumed the role of creator, with the Ogdoad made subordinate to him.

According to the Heliopolitan cosmogony, creation occurred through the union of the divinities of the Ennead. The intellectual Memphite cosmogony puts the thought and the word of Ptah at the center of creation. Hermopolis was very different, with the affirmation of the belief that the universe resulted from a slow process that began inside a formless primordial liquid mass.

Nun is the personification of the primordial ocean. Nunet is the sky above Nun, the primordial space.

Huh and Huhet represent the concept of primordial infinity, meaning the absence of definitions in space.

Keku and Keket stand for the primordial shadows that dominated before creation of the sun, which led to the birth of the universe.

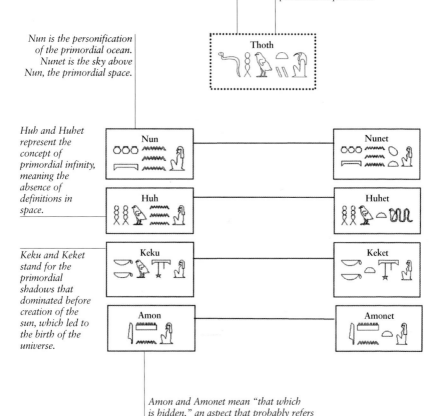

Amon and Amonet mean "that which is hidden," an aspect that probably refers to the inscrutable and indeterminate characteristics of the primordial dimension before creation.

▲ Thoth and the Ogdoad of Hermopolis.

To the sides are female figures pouring water. The circle that the water delineates represents the primordial waters preceding creation.

According to the Hermopolitan cosmogony, the birth of the sun, which led to the creation of the universe, resulted from the combined action of the members of the Ogdoad within the primordial waters of Nun. This image clearly shows the slow construction of the sun within the primordial waters and the later emergence and appearance of the sun on the horizon.

The Ogdoad is here depicted by way of eight small anthropomorphic stick figures that hold plows in their hands, symbolic of foundation, birth, and creation.

Theban theology draws on the Hermopolitan tradition, proposing a variant that locates at Thebes the origin of the events that led to the birth of the demiurge sun at Hermopolis. For this reason, images related to the myth of the Ogdoad appear on Theban mythological papyri from the 21st dynasty, such as the one shown here.

▲ Creation operated by the Hermopolis Ogdoad, from a *Book of the Dead* in the tomb of the scribe and priest of Amon-Ra Konsumes, Western Thebes, 21st dynasty, Kunsthistorisches Museum, Vienna, 3859.

Humans and gods

Hieroglyph
Netjeru
("The gods")

In depth
The most ancient and widespread hieroglyph to express the concept of god consists of a staff with a streamer at the end. Numerous interpretations have been put forward to explain the meaning of the object represented. Some scholars hold that this is a fetish wrapped in strips of material; others think the image refers to the staffs bearing streamers that decorated the pylons at the entrances to temples. Despite numerous theories, there is not yet consensus on the meaning of the hieroglyph for "god," which remains inscrutable.

Bibliography
Lurker 1994. Meeks, Faward-Meeks 1997.

Related entries
Pharaoh, Temple, Priests, The five elements of a human

Egypt's rich pantheon of divinities is a result of the unification of the country's many originally autonomous territories under a single crown. Each territorial province had its own local divinity, and instead of being eliminated upon unification, these were instead integrated within a system of divinities with the tutelary divinity of the royal house at its head. Aside from the hierarchical roles they assumed within the various theological systems, Egyptian divinities had certain characteristics in common. One of their more original features is related to the general concept of the created cosmos, understood as a sort of bubble of light perennially threatened by its possible reabsorption in the primordial water of Nun. Since the divinities were an integral part of creation, they too were exposed to this threat and thus had certain limitations that brought them closer to the human sphere. They could not travel to the territories of Nun, where they would have disintegrated; they were not immortal, but could be reinvigorated through the life-giving power of Osiris; they could suffer wounds, be mutilated, and share most human emotions, such as desire, love, and pain. A deity's zoomorphic appearance had nothing to do with the image the faithful had when worshiping the deity and was merely a means to express the deity's characteristics. In Egyptian texts, divinities reveal themselves to humans only as smells, light, voices, or even tremors of the earth, never in flesh and blood.

At dawn each morning, complex rituals were performed in each temple with the purpose of renewing the original magical power of the statue of the divinity that was venerated in the temple. The aspersion of oil on the front of the statue was a common element of such daily rituals, since with it the priest conferred upon the statue solar energy, the bearer of life, in that way preserving the presence of the divine on earth.

The solar disk contains a scarab. On the basis of this fact the divinity that bears the disk on her head can be identified as Khepri, god of the rising sun.

Over the course of time, the relationship between the divine sphere and that of Egypt's royalty changed radically, going from a situation in which the two overlapped—the king-god of the Old Kingdom—through the progressive "humanization" of the ruler, beginning in the Middle Kingdom. By the time of the New Kingdom, this process had led to a celebration of the pharaoh, who appears with far more human features than in earlier times but at the same time is invested with a personal magic, a result of the favor of the gods, who place him on a level above that of the human mass and permit him to perform superhuman deeds.

This bas-relief is part of an exceptional cycle of decorations in the mortuary temple of Seti I at Abydos. These scenes in particular present the relationship between divinities and kings in the New Kingdom. In a realm to which only the pharaoh is admitted, the relationship is expressed in the stateliness and orthodoxy of the rites, but also through a language of emotions that are more properly human.

◀ Statuary group of Tutankhamen and Amon (detail), from Thebes, 18th dynasty, limestone, h 211 cm, Fondazione Museo Antichità Egizie, Turin, C. 768.

▲ Seti I pays homage to the god Ra-Harakhty, from the mortuary temple of Seti I at Abydos, chapel of the god Ra-Harakhty, painted limestone, 19th dynasty.

Maat

Hieroglyph
Ma't
("What is right")

Iconography
Female figure with a
feather on her head.

Divine parentage
Daughter of the sun-
god Ra

**Principal centers of
worship**
The most important
known temple to
Maat was at Karnak.
Maat was the
personification of an
abstract concept, and
not many temples are
known to have been
dedicated directly to
her, but she appears on
the walls of most of the
temples in Egypt.

Bibliography
Assmann 1989.

Related entries
Ra and Apep, Death as
rebirth, Weighing the
soul

The goddess Maat is a personification of the order and harmony that the god Ra gave to the cosmos at the beginning of
creation. She is thus more a concept and a spiritual abstraction
than an individualized divine entity. Depicted with the features
of a girl with a feather on her head, Maat was thought to be a
substance that permeates all levels of creation, guaranteeing its
indispensable cohesion and preventing its disintegration and
reabsorption into the primordial waters. The movement of the
stars, the recurrence of nature's cycles, and the sequences of the
days are interconnected events whose regularity is guaranteed
by the presence of the goddess, who in this sense is often associated with Thoth, god of the exact sciences. Maat also played
a fundamental role within human society, where she becomes a
synonym for truth, rightness, justice, and concord among all
humans, thus becoming emblematic of social solidarity, all values identified with the will of the pharaoh, the sole intermediary between the gods and humans. The harmony of the
cosmos, however, is constantly threatened by the disruptive
forces of disorder (in Egyptian, Isfet), which is the reason that

in the name of Maat
both the gods and
humans strive to pro-
tect the harmony of
nature and society on
which they them-
selves depend.

▶ Statuette of the god
Thoth and goddess
Maat, 26th dynasty,
wood, bronze, gold leaf,
glass, 19.5 x 20 cm,
Kestner-Museum,
Hannover, 1957.83.

The feather she always wears on her head makes Maat, goddess of truth and justice, easy to identify. The feather alone often appears as the symbol of the goddess, as in scenes of the Hall of Double Justice in the afterlife, when the feather (or the goddess herself) is placed on a scalepan opposite the heart of the deceased to test the heart's truthfulness.

The inscription bears the following text: "Maat, daughter of Ra, who presides on earth in the kingdom of the dead."

The tomb of Seti I in the Valley of the Kings preserved this splendid base-relief portrait of the goddess Maat, goddess of justice and of the cosmic order established at the beginning of creation. The goddess is depicted as a young girl decorated in a simple way with a large bead necklace and two bracelets. Contrasted with Isfet, the earthly manifestation of evil and chaos, the goddess became extremely widespread throughout Egypt as the incarnation of a cosmic principle more than an individualized divinity.

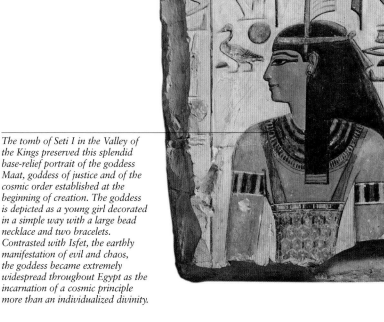

▲ Portrait of the goddess Maat, from the tomb of Seti I in the Valley of the Kings, Thebes, 19th dynasty, Museo Archeologico Nazionale, Florence, 2469.

The deceased witnesses the weighing and awaits the verdict.

According to Egyptian religious tradition, after death the heart of the deceased was judged in the tribunal of the afterlife, presided over by Osiris, to determine if the deceased could reside in the afterlife. The judgment involved *psychostasia*, the weighing of the deceased man's soul. His heart was placed on one scalepan of a balance, the feather of Maat being placed on the opposite scalepan. If the heart of the deceased proved lighter than the feather, he would be declared upright and just and would be admitted to participate in the afterlife as an excellent spirit.

Thoth, in the form of a baboon, wears the lunar crescent and solar disk on his head. He verifies the weight of the heart, writing the result on tablets and announcing it to Osiris.

The feather of Maat is sometimes replaced on the scalepan by a statuette of the crouching goddess.

The hearts of the guilty were devoured by Ammit, "the Devourer," a hybrid monster composed of a crocodile head on the upper body of a lion. Not belonging to the world of creation makes the Devourer even more dangerous. For that reason in depictions its paws are cut off to magically prevent it from doing harm to the deceased.

▲ The weighing of the heart, from a *Book of the Dead*, 19th dynasty, private collection, Leiden.

On the cosmic plane, the gods did their utmost to protect creation from the forces of chaos; on the earthly plane, these efforts were expressed in the pharaoh's constant struggle to maintain unity and peace in the kingdom, defending it against threats from foreigners or rebels and assuring the constant performance of religious rituals. During the New Kingdom, this correspondence between the efforts of the king and those of the gods was given its most coherent expression in the ritual scene of the "offering of Maat."

At the beginning of creation, Ra had provided the cosmos with Maat, who represented order and cosmic balance and came to be seen as the necessary glue holding the universe together.

This statuette, made of gold-plated silver, is an exceptional artifact because of its high artistic quality and because of the subject it represents: Seti I offering a tiny image of Maat to the gods. Beginning with the New Kingdom, this motif began to find space in the rich figurative patrimony of Egypt. The first known instances date to the reign of Thutmose III, and from the Ramessid era on, this scene of regal offering shows up in temple reliefs as well as in the decorations of royal tombs.

▶ Statuette of Seti I making the offering of Maat, 19th dynasty, gold-plated silver, h 19.5 cm, Musée du Louvre, Paris, E 27431.

Ra and Apep

Hieroglyph
R'
("the Sun")

Epithets
Ra: Lord of all.
Apep: Terrible of face,
Enemy of Ra

Divine parentage
Ra: according to
Heliopolitan theology Ra
was the creator and father
of the gods.
Apep: this divinity did not
belong to the created world
and was a personification of
chaos. According to the
theology of Isna, he had been
born from the saliva of Neith.

Principal sites of worship
Sites associated with the cult
of Ra include the sanctuary
of Heliopolis and the 5th-
dynasty solar temples in the
Memphite necropolis.

Bibliography
Quirke 2001.

Related entries
Maat, Death as rebirth,
Weighing the soul, Books
of the Dead

▶ Statuette of
Amenemope, called
Seqai, bearing a stele
with a solar hymn to Ra,
limestone, h 55 cm, 19th
dynasty, Fondazione
Museo Antichità Egizie,
Turin, C 3038.

According to the Heliopolitan cosmogony, the universe had come into being out of the primordial chaos thanks to the action of Ra. However, it was a fragile creation, forever threatened by the destructive forces of chaos, which exerted a constant action of dissolution on the world. Chaos would soon have reabsorbed the ordered cosmos had not Ra intervened every day to renew creation, rising at dawn and crossing the sky in his solar boat to then set in the west. At night, Ra dove back into obscurity, thanks to which he underwent a process of disintegration/reintegration that permitted him to be reborn the following dawn, repeating thus the creative operation of the origin of creation. From earliest times, this confrontation between Ra and the forces of chaos influenced Egyptian funerary practice, and beginning in the New Kingdom, expressed as the struggle between Ra and Apep, it was reproduced in royal tombs in the Valley of the Kings and on funerary papyri. Every night Ra crosses the kingdom of the dead during the twelve nocturnal hours. At the seventh hour, Ra confronts the serpent-god Apep, a personification of chaos who sought to prevent the renewal of creation. Having defeated Apep, the solar boat was free to move ahead toward dawn and rebirth. Since Apep represented chaos "without beginning and without end," it was the only truly immortal divinity, so that Ra would have to repeat the entire struggle the next night.

Ra: the sun at noon.

During the New Kingdom, the solar mythology of Heliopolis was assimilated into the Theban mythology, strongly influenced by the worship of Osiris, the god who dies to then arise in the afterlife. For this reason, within the canonic solar triad, the sun at sunset was often depicted in funerary texts by a ram's-headed divinity called Efu-Ra, or "flesh of Ra." In the new funerary ideology, the sun god had to "incarnate" himself to go through death in the afterlife like Osiris and then be reborn the following morning.

Khepri, the sun at dawn

Atum/Efu-Ra, the sun at sunset.

▲ The three manifestations of Ra from the tomb of Seti II in the Valley of the Kings, Western Thebes, 19th dynasty.

As early as the Old Kingdom, the theologians of Heliopolis, site of the main temple of Ra, had distinguished at least three great manifestations of solar power. These referred to the stages of the sun in its daily birth and death. The scarab Khepri represented the rising sun at dawn and could be depicted as a child crowned with the solar disk; the solar disk Ra-Harakhty represented the energy of the sun at its maximum intensity; and Atum marked the advanced age of the setting sun.

The Eye of Ra, or Eye of Horus (udjat eye), is the greatest symbol of Ra's power, and its presence in this scene is intended to ward off evil.

The sun god appears here in the form of Ra-Harakhty, or "Ra-Horus on the horizon," with the characteristic falcon face crowned with a solar disk. Behind him are Horus and Thoth tightly bound together.

A baboon-headed divinity stabs the coils of Apep with knives, striking down and destroying the monster and in that way neutralizing its danger. This condition will prove only temporary; with the passage of the solar boat the forces of chaos will reintegrate, and Apep will return to threaten the voyage of the sun the following night.

The subject of the clash between Ra and Apep has numerous mythological variations, which blend a variety of mythical and symbolic elements in ways that are not always open to easy interpretation although they are based on the same thematic nucleus composed of the two divinities.

▲ The nocturnal voyage of the sun-god Ra in the regions of the afterworld from the Heruben *Book of the Dead*, 21st dynasty, Egyptian Museum, Cairo.

Set, on the prow of the boat, defends the solar boat by spearing the head of Apep. Although representing the destructive forces of disorder, much like Apep, Set was part of the created world, which the serpent-god was trying to destroy, for which reason Set sought to protect the solar boat that daily regenerates the universe.

The scene is witnessed by the deceased Heruben, as is written in the legend in front of her face: "Heruben, just of voice, worships Ra-Harakhty, great god, lord of the sky."

Ra's boat moves forward over the blue coils of the serpent Apep, which form a design not unlike the waves of the sea, probably an allusion to the primordial waters of Nun from which the serpent, in myth, arises and into which he tries to take back the entirety of creation.

The solar boat is drawn by four jackals and four cobras, animals associated with the funerary world and necropolises.

The Osirian drama

Hieroglyph
Usir ("Osiris")

Epithets
Lord of the West, Lord of Abydos, Lord of silence, King of the living

Iconography
Anthropomorphic figure with a body swathed in mummy wrappings. On his head is the tall white crown flanked by two ostrich feathers called the *atef*.

Divine parentage
In Heliopolitan theology, he is son of Geb and Nut and brother of Set, Nephthys, and Isis; together with Isis and his posthumous son Horus, he formed the Abydos triad.

Principal centers of worship
Busiris, Abydos.

Bibliography
Griffiths 1960, 1970.

Related entries
Death as rebirth, Weighing the soul

▶ Horus and Set grab the *sema-tawy*, symbolic of the union of the Two Lands, throne of the statue of Sesostris I from Lisht, Middle Kingdom, limestone, Egyptian Museum, Cairo, CG 414.

One of the most complex and important myths elaborated by Egyptian civilization was that concerning the death and resurrection of Osiris. By way of this myth, an intricate drama was woven in which the themes of the legitimization of royal power and its succession were blended with other myths of a purely religious nature that recognize Osiris as the king arisen from the world of the dead and the catalyst for the regeneration of nature. The myth relates that before the dynasties of the pharaohs, the world was ruled by divinities and that one of the last of these was Osiris. Under his rule the world of humans went through a period of great prosperity and peace that ended when he was murdered by his brother Set. Isis, Osiris's wife and sister, managed to use her magical arts to bring him back to life long enough to generate a son, the falcon-god Horus. When he became an adult, Horus obtained his father's kingdom, but not until he had fought a bloody struggle with Set and later appeared before the tribunal of the gods. The myth thus provided a mythical justification for the procedure of succession, which served to repair the institutional rupture that occurred between the death of a ruler and the ascension of his successor; the first became Osiris, and the second guaranteed the continuity of the royal institution by identifying himself with Horus, who by defeating Set had made the throne of Egypt solid again.

Osiris wears his characteristic atef *crown composed of the tall white crown of Upper Egypt and two side feathers.*

Symbol of filial piety and conjugal love, the Abydos triad became, most of all beginning in the Middle Kingdom, the icon of a new morality based on everyday values within a human dimension.

This pendant represents one of the great masterpieces of Egyptian gold-working. It dates to the 22nd dynasty and depicts the Abydos triad, composed of Osiris, Isis, and Horus. The statuettes are made in sold gold; the pillar and the base are in lapis lazuli. The work includes both incision, for some of the details, and encrusting.

▲ Pendant with the Abydos triad, 22nd dynasty, reign of Osorkon II, gold, lapis lazuli, and red vitreous paste, h 9 cm, Musée du Louvre, Paris, E 6204.

The goddess Isis wears a tall headdress with two long horns that frame the solar disk, elements that associate her with the goddess Hathor, revealing aspects of the divine mother in Isis.

Nephthys is the sister and companion of Set. Her character is less defined than those of her relatives, and it is possible that she was created by Egyptian theologians to give Set a companion and to create a couple parallel to that of Isis and Osiris. Nephthys did not share Set's destructive nature; in the myth of the drama of Osiris, she abandoned Set and helped Isis collect the parts of the body of her brother, and she is often depicted in funerary decorations while weeping with Isis or while helping her watch over the body of her dead brother.

Set is one of the most complex and contradictory figures in the Egyptian pantheon. His iconography does not seem to be drawn, as with the other gods, from the animal world. With his elongated face and long rectangular ears, he has been variously associated with an anteater and a dog, but it seems far more likely that he was based on a fantasy animal. He can also be depicted as a ferocious hippopotamus or a turtle. As a personification of the devastating power of chaos and disorder, he constitutes a being locked in absolute opposition to Osiris and Horus, who represent the continuity of cosmic and earthly order, incarnated in pharaonic regality.

▲ Statuette of Set and Nephthys, 19th dynasty, h 17 cm, Musée du Louvre, Paris, E 3374.

Thoth

Thoth is one of the major divinities in the Egyptian pantheon, and there is no locality in ancient Egypt that does not preserve at least one monument with his carved or painted image. He was usually depicted with a human body and the head of an ibis, but his iconography extends to zoomorphic versions of the ibis, baboon-faced forms, and even a bull. Thoth was the patron of the sciences and all intellectual and rational applications of thought. Myths attributed to him the invention of hieroglyphs and saw him as the principal author of the sacred and magical texts; he was worshiped for his profound knowledge and wisdom. He was considered the patron of scribes and was himself the scribe of the gods. In relation to a religious background with an astral matrix, he was associated with the moon, and since the moon was one of the first astronomical indicators used for the measurement of time, Thoth was also seen as a great astronomer, a measurer of time and ruler of the calendar. His role as peacemaker was proverbial in the myths, as was his skill at resolving conflicts and soothing the anger of divinities using only the weapons of his intellect, his culture, and his philosophy. His worship, widespread throughout Egypt, was centered most of all at Hermopolis (in Egyptian, Khnum, "City of the Eight") in the 15th province of Upper Egypt, where the local cosmogony presented him as the only true universal demiurge, the ibis that had hatched the world egg.

Hieroglyph
Djehuti
("Thoth")

Epithets
Judicious of heart, He who fills (the *Udjat* Eye), Lord of the years, He who measures time

Iconography
Human body with head of ibis or dog-headed baboon; as an ibis or a dog-headed baboon or a bull

Divine parentage
In the Hermopolitan theology, he is a demiurge divinity and thus father of all the gods. Locally, he was worshiped at Hermopolis, together with his consort, Seshat.

Principal center of worship
Hermopolis Magna.

Bibliography
Lurker 1994.

Related entries
Ptah and the Ogdoad, Magic, Astronomy, Calendar, Writing

◄ Statuette of the god Thoth in the form of an ibis, painted terracotta, Fondazione Museo Antichità Egizie, Turin, C. 1009.

Aside from as an ibis, Thoth was frequently depicted in the shape of a baboon. This usage was probably a result of the baboon's humanlike appearance and behavior. The baboon thus seemed the ideal animal in which to discern manifestations of the knowledge and wisdom characteristic of the god.

Thoth's skill as a divine peacemaker, as in the argument between Set and Horus, had a literary expression in a very interesting story from the Greco-Roman age known as "The Myth of the Eye of the Sun; or, the Dialogue of the Baboon and the Cat." In this story, the goddess Tefnut flees Egypt in anger at her father, Ra, taking with her all moisture from the Nile. She goes to Nubia, where she takes on the guise of a cat. Thoth, disguised as a baboon, finds her and calms her anger, and she returns to Egypt, bringing great joy and happiness.

▲ Statue of Thoth in the form of a baboon, chapel of Khepri at Abu Simbel, 19th dynasty, reign of Ramses II.

Osiris sits on a throne inside a shrine. He wears the atef *crown and a white robe that covers all of his body. He holds the flail and crook, symbols of his power as ruler of the dead.*

Isis and Nephthys are recognizable by the hieroglyphic symbols that decorate their heads and that express their names. The two goddesses raise their arms toward Osiris and touch his crown and elbow in sign of protection.

Thoth holds a stylus and scribe's case, indispensable for the performance of his role.

The principal and best known role attributed to Thoth is that of scribe at Osiris's tribunal of the dead. The god of the exact sciences verified that the weighing of the heart was performed properly, wrote down the result, and announced it to the judge of the dead, Osiris.

▲ Thoth and Horus with Osiris, burial chamber of Amenhotep at Deir Durunka, long right wall, 19th dynasty, limestone, Ägyptisches Museum, Berlin, 2/63-3/63, 1/64.2/64.

According to an ancient myth, during a battle Set tore an eye from Horus and, after tearing it in pieces, cast it into the most remote regions. Thoth was charged with finding and repairing the parts, and having done so he returned it to Horus. The memory of that myth appears in certain statues that present Thoth in the form of a baboon or an ibis-headed man holding a tablet with the eye of Horus (in Egyptian, udjat) *engraved on it.*

▲ Bracelet of Sheshonk II with the Eye of Horus (*udjat*), from the tomb of Psusennes I at Tanis, chamber of Sheshonk II, 22nd dynasty, gold, lapis lazuli, carnelian, and faience, h 4.6 cm, Egyptian Museum, Cairo, JE 72184 B.

Ptah

When the sovereigns of the 3rd dynasty moved the capital of the kingdom to Memphis, Ptah, that city's local deity, rapidly assumed a central position in the Egyptian pantheon, becoming the tutelary divinity of the capital and of the ruling house. His iconography gave him an anthropomorphic shape wrapped in bandages leaving only his hands free to hold the *uas*, *ankh*, and *djed* scepter. The band on his head and his usual pedestal, together with his rigid pose, gave him the appearance of an icon. A stele in the British Museum, known as the Shabaka Stone, bears a text known to scholars as the *Memphite Theology of Creation*. This complex doctrine attributes to Ptah the role of creator of the world. In it is expressed for the first time the idea of creation by way of enunciation, a highly original doctrine with great philosophical meaning, dating at least to the end of the 3rd millennium BC. The Egyptian tradition delineated a spiritual and intellectual dimension around the figure of Ptah, a benevolent god not too far distant from humanity, a protector of artisans and guilds, defender of the cosmic order and justice.

Hieroglyph
Ptah
("Ptah")

Epithets
Fair of face, Lord of truth

Iconography
Anthropomorphic figure wrapped like a mummy with a close-fitting head band holding a scepter composed of three symbols, the *uas*, *ankh*, and *djed*.

Divine parentage
Demiurgic divinity according to the Memphite theology, thus father of all the gods. Locally, he constituted the Memphite triad together with the lioness-headed goddess Sekhmet and their son Nefertum.

Principal center of worship
Memphis.

Bibliography
Lurker 1994.

Related entries
Ptah and the Ogdoad

◀ Statue of Sekhmet, from the funerary temple of Amenhotep III, Western Thebes, 18th dynasty, Fondazione Museo Antichità Egizie, Turin, C. 252.

This statue is from the furnishings in the tomb of Tutankhamen and is an extraordinary creation of Egyptian woodworking. It is carved from wood and is entirely gilt, except for the head covering, which is made of faience. Inserts in blue vitreous paste decorate the god's eyes and eyebrows, while bronze was used for the dark parts of the sculpture, such as the flat beard and the scepter.

The scepter in the god's hands is composed of three different symbols: the uas stick (power), the djed pillar (stability), and the ankh cross (life).

Ptah is usually depicted wrapped in a white cloth that gives him the appearance of being mummified. In this case he is decorated with a feathered robe and a usekh necklace, the details of which are rendered through engraving.

Among Ptah's epithets is "Lord of truth." This relationship with cosmic harmony and justice is explicated by the pedestal on which the god stands which has the typical wedge shape of the hieroglyph ma', meaning the word "truth."

▶ Statue of Ptah, from the tomb of Tutankhamen in the Valley of the Kings, Western Thebes, wood, gold, faience, bronze, and vitreous paste, h 60.2 cm, Egyptian Museum, Cairo, JE 60739.

Aside from being the most important divinity of the city of Memphis, Ptah was considered the creator of the universe. This creator aspect of his character, united to his character as a divinity so favorably disposed toward humanity, favored his election to patron of all work that was the fruit of ingenuity as well as the work of artisan skill.

Nefertum, whose name probably means "beauty of Atum," is associated with the first lotus flower to emerge from primordial chaos, and this flower is the symbol that often appears on his head. His ties to creation made him the personification of the warmth of the rising sun.

▲ An artisan shaping a cup, from the tomb of the vizier Rekhmire, Western Thebes, Sheikh Abd el-Qurna, 18th dynasty, reign of Thutmose III and Amenhotep II.

▶ Ramses III facing the Memphis triad, from the Great Harris Papyrus, Western Thebes, Medinet Habu, 20th dynasty, reign of Ramses III, British Museum, London, EA 999/43.

Sekhmet is the "dangerous goddess" par excellence. She is a warrior divinity originally worshipped in the 11th nome of Lower Egypt. Her Egyptian name can be translated as "the Powerful," and being the manifestation of the mortal warmth of the sun she is called iret Ra ("The Eye of Ra").

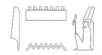

Amon

Hieroglyph
Imen
("the Hidden")

Epithets
Amon, king of the gods,
Great cackler, The
Hidden

Iconography
Anthropomorphic figure
with crown with two
feathers, ram, goose

Divine parentage
According to the
Theban theology, a
demiurgic divinity, thus
father to all the gods.
Locally, constituted the
Theban triad together
with the vulture-goddess
Mut and the ram-god
Khonsu.

**Principal centers of
worship**
Karnak, Luxor, Tanis,
Gebel Barkal.

Bibliography
Lurker 1994.

Related entries
Tutankhamen, Temple,
Thebes and Karnak

▶ The goddess Mut
nurses the pharaoh Seti I,
from the mortuary
temple of Seti I at
Abydos, second
hypostyle hall, southern
wall, 19th dynasty.

The history of religion that led to making Amon the supreme divinity in the Egyptian pantheon dates back far in time. Amon was originally a warrior divinity worshipped in the area of Thebes in Upper Egypt; he was elevated to supreme divinity when, during the First Intermediate Period, the local dynasty began to compete with the other local dynasties in which the country was then divided. When the Theban house succeeded in taking control, Amon became the tutelary god of the royal house, for which reason various 12th-dynasty pharaohs styled themselves Amenemhet ("Amon leads"), a name based on the god's name. Amon's power increased when the 18th dynasty moved the capital of the country to Thebes, site of the god's original worship. The attributes the god had already acquired were now increased, such that he became the leader of all the divinities, while his temple and clergy became the largest and most powerful religious institution in the history of Egypt. The clergy of Amon also assimilated elements of solar worship from Heliopolis, so as to give the god a cosmic and demiurgic

character in keeping with the tradition already established for the other large national divinities. Thus came into being the figure of the god Amon-Ra, king of all the gods, source of all the regality and warrior power of the pharaoh, consort of the goddess Mut, and father of the young god Khonsu, with whom he formed the Theban triad.

The crown decorated with two tall plumes constituted the typical trait of the anthropomorphic effigies of Amon. His depictions as a Theban god include such animal shapes as ram and goose; it was as a goose that he earned the epithet "Great cackler."

This splendid statute in black granite depicts the god Amon-Ra seated on a throne with his hands on the shoulders of a small statue of Tutankhamen as a sign of his protection. His face is youthful and communicates vitality and serenity. Beginning in the New Kingdom, the royal dynasty, originally from Thebes, made Amon, that city's patron god, the country's principal divinity. Later, when Amon was identified with the god Ra of Heliopolis, an identification worked by the Theban theologians, Amon became a universal god, creator of the universe and king of the gods.

The statue of Tutankhamen is missing its head, but can be identified all the same by the hieroglyphic inscriptions engraved on it, which include the pharaoh's name.

▶ Statue of Amon protecting Tutankhamen, 18th dynasty, black granite, h 220 cm, Musée du Louvre, Paris, E 11609.

The god Amon is often depicted as a ram, an animal sacred to him. The god seems to have acquired this iconography when his worship spread to Nubia. During the period of Thutmose III, a temple was dedicated to Amon at Napata, near Gebel Barkal. The local divinity worshiped there was a solar divinity with the appearance of a ram. Amon soon assimilated this iconography and his association with indigenous solar cults helped promote him to the role of creator god par excellence.

Amon is depicted in the form of a ram protecting Amenhotep III between his legs. The statue is one of a type that shows a divinity giving its favor and protection to a pharaoh. Such works range from the famous statute of Khafre and Horus in Cairo, to the statues from the period of Nectanebo II that depict Horus as a falcon protecting the pharaoh between its legs (page 91). This statue may well have been made for the temple that Amenhotep III had built in Nubia, at Soleb, and only in later times was the statue taken to Thebes.

▲ Amon in the shape of a ram with Amenhotep III, from Thebes, 18th dynasty, gray granite, Fondazione Museo Antichità Egizie, Turin, C. 836.

Beginning in the New Kingdom the worship of Amon became national, also becoming the fulcrum around which the legitimacy of the pharaohs rotated. An example of this phenomenon is the notion of the "divine birth" with which Hatshepsut, claiming to have been born through the direct intervention of Amon, sought to support the legitimacy of her assumption of power. At the queen's mortuary temple at Deir el-Bahri, an entire cycle of reliefs is dedicated to this theme, and the scenes that compose it allude to the conception, birth, and consecration of Hatshepsut by Amon.

The inscription relates the words spoken by the god to the queen: "Words spoken by Amon-Ra, lord of the sky: I give the regality of the Two Lands and the total authority to beloved daughter Maat-Ka-Ra ['Hatshepsut']. May she have health, life, and power as Ra."

This scene, depicted on the point of an obelisk, refers to the desire for legitimization by claiming the favor of Amon. In a sign of divine protection, Amon sets his hands on the shoulders of the kneeling Hatshepsut.

Hatshepsut has a very particular appearance in this depiction. Her body is explicitly masculine, and she wears the blue khopersh *war crown and the traditional* usekh *necklace.*

▲ Relief from the point of an obelisk of Hatshepsut, Karnak, 18th dynasty.

Hathor

Hieroglyph
Hut-Hor
("Hathor," meaning "house
of Horus")

Epithets
Mother of mothers, Eye of
Ra, Shining one, Beauty
that appears, Lady of the
turquoise

Iconography
A spotted calf,
anthropomorphic female
figure with long horns and a
solar disk on her head.

Divine parentage
As a cosmic divinity, she
was the mother of the astral
god Horus in archaic times.
In the New Kingdom, she
was associated with Nut as
mother of the sun Ra,
giving birth to him every
day at dawn.

Principal centers of worship
Gebelein, Cusae, Thebes,
Serabit el-Khadim.

Bibliography
Lurker 1994.

Related entries
Eroticism and seduction,
Amusements, Theban
necropolis

▶ Hathoric capitals in the
hypostyle hall of the temple
of Hathor at Dendera,
Ptolemaic Period.

Hathor is a very ancient cosmic divinity, the leading figure in an ancestral myth of the creation, in which she is presented as a young cow living in the wild marshland. Along with this zoomorphic iconography, beginning in the 4th dynasty, she began to also appear as a woman with bovine ears wearing on her head two long horns. She soon became one of the most popular divinities of the Egyptian pantheon. Her origin as a cosmic divinity explains her role as the Great Mother of both the gods and humans. This regenerative function was expressed in the funerary sphere in depictions that, most of all at Thebes, present the bovine form of Hathor emerging from the sacred mountain of the necropolis to welcome the dead. Hathor offers the spirit of the deceased the milk of the gods, which gives him rebirth as an immortal in the afterlife. Alongside this ancestral and more intellectual composite of religious values, Hathor reveals another importance within the sphere of daily worship. Her constant association with the ritual instrument known as a sistrum, with music and dance in general, and with love increased her popularity as a goddess of joy, Eros, and happiness.

The device over the head of the female figure to the left indicates that the nome depicted is the 15th of Upper Egypt, "of the hare," with its capital at Hermopolis, major center of the worship of the god Thoth.

The goddess Hathor appears at the center of the composition; the arrangement of her hair is characteristic, but most of all she is recognizable by the long horns framing the solar disk. During the Old Kingdom, she was the divine mother par excellence. Her name (in Egyptian Hut-Hor) means "house of Horus" and in all probability refers to an archaic phase in Egyptian religion during which Hathor and Horus were taken as cosmic divinities. She was then the Celestial Cow, mother of the divine falcon.

▶ Triad of Menkure, Hathor, and the nome of the hare, from the valley temple of Menkure at Giza, 4th dynasty, slate, h 83.5 cm, Museum of Fine Arts, Boston, 09.200.

In the early Pyramid Texts, Hathor is described as a primordial wild cow that, at the beginning of creation, made its way through a papyrus thicket. In myth, the Celestial Cow is the mother and nourisher of the gods and the human species, "the mother of mothers." During the New Kingdom, this ancient treatment of the goddess was expanded upon, making Hathor the protector of the Theban necropolis. Most of all it was Hathor who nourished the gods and the dead to make it possible for them to be immortal.

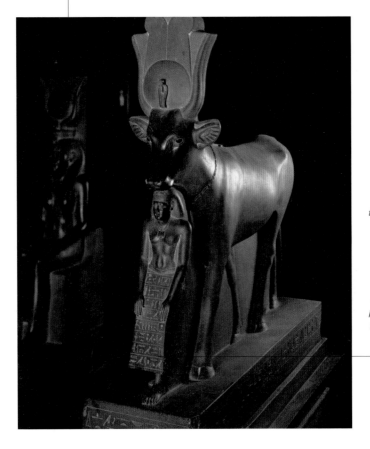

The statue depicts the protection given by Hathor, in the form of a celestial cow, to Psamtik, a high official in the 26th dynasty. The engraved writing on Psamtik's robe lists the positions he occupied, among them the important post of "supervisor of seals."

▲ Statue of Hathor with Psamtik, from the tomb of Psamtik at Saqqara, 26th dynasty, graywacke, h 96 cm, Egyptian Museum, Cairo, CG 784.

The goddess is depicted in her cosmic role as Celestial Cow while leaving the Theban mountain to offer her udders to the deceased. Her spotted hide, emblematic of the firmament, recalls the goddess's archaic celestial nature, an iconography often borrowed for images of the sky god Nut.

The image shows the typical entrance to the tomb of an artist at Deir el-Medina. Above the door is the typical pyramidion, a small pyramid in which there was often a niche to hold a stele with an invocation to the sun-god Ra.

The funerary theme of the scene justifies the presence of Anubis, here depicted as a crouching jackal. In front of him is a symbol often associated with this god, the so-called nebris, a cow's hide hung from a ritual pole. It may recall an ancient ritual in which rebirth was simulated using an animal skin as the placenta.

Beginning in the New Kingdom the decoration of sarcophagi was enriched with mythological scenes that refer to creation myths; within the funerary context, representations of the acts of creation became synonymous with the certain rebirth of the deceased. One of the many myths of creation, the one shown here is based on the myth of the Celestial Cow, a very ancient cosmic being, nourisher of both gods and humans.

▲ Funerary scene with Hathor leaving the Theban mountain, from the sarcophagus of Nespawerhefi, Western Thebes, 21st dynasty, Fitzwilliam Museum, Cambridge, E 1.1822.

The site of Serabit el-Khadim, in the Sinai Peninsula, was being exploited for its turquoise and copper mines as early as the first pharaonic dynasties. The community of workers that settled here expressed an intense religious fervor for the goddess Hathor, as indicated by the spread of the epithet for her "Lady of the turquoise." A temple was dedicated to Hathor and was enlarged over a long period of time, between the 12th and the 20th dynasty.

The pylon of the temple, which dates to the age of Thutmose I, is preceded by a long row of spaces decorated by tall votive steles, some of which are still visible in their original positions.

▲ Votive steles of the temple of Hathor at Serabit el-Khadim, Sinai Peninsula.

▶ David Roberts, The Great Hypostyle Hall in the Temple of Amon-Ra at Karnak, lithograph from Egypt and Nubia, London, 1846–49.

Temple

The Egyptian temple was conceived as a miniature representation of the universe in which a divinity was given an earthly abode. The priests cared for the god through the performance of certain daily rituals and through various purification rites performed near the statue, such as fumigations with incense, lustrations, and aspersions of oil and perfume, all intended to preserve the integrity of the god's energy and to ward off malefic forces. Unlike a modern-day church, an Egyptian temple was not a place for the faithful and was instead reserved for the personnel serving the god. The great number of sanctuaries, temples, and shrines located across Egypt composed a religious network that the pharaoh, as intermediary between the divinities and humans, made use of in order to respond on the earthly plane to the constant actions taken by the gods on the cosmic plane. In doing so, the pharaoh maintained the integrity of the universe. Beginning in the New Kingdom, the sanctuary came

to express this collection of religious values through the articulation of the elements of its architectural layout. The monumental gateway called the pylon led to an open-air court surrounded by columns; this led to a covered area supported by a large number of columns, the so-called hypostyle hall; next came the temple's *cella*, or *naos*, the inner chamber housing the tabernacle that held the statue of the god and its processional boat.

Hieroglyph
Hut-netjer
("home of god")

In depth
The temple was intended to be a miniature representation of the cosmos. The outer wall around the sacred area was constructed using courses of bricks arranged in a "wave" pattern, which some historians see as a representation of the primordial waters that surrounded the universe. The temple was symbolically located on the primordial mound, the exact top of which was occupied by the temple's *cella*. The pylons represented the horizon over which the sun rose and set, renewing creation. The floor, ceiling, and columns were, respectively, images of the surface of the earth, the celestial vault, and the pillars of the sky located at the edges of the world.

Bibliography
Arnold 1994.
Wilkinson 2000b.

Related entries
The Heliopolitan cosmogony, Humans and gods, Maat, Priests, Priesthood

The picture on this block depicts one of the steps in the ceremony called "the stretching of the cord," with which the pharaoh began the foundation of a new temple by establishing its axis. Hatshepsut is shown planting the stakes that will be used to stretch the cord and establish the temple's north–south orientation, an operation she performs together with the goddess Seshat, spouse of Thoth and like him associated with writing and measurement.

Opposite Hatshepsut is the goddess Seshat, identifiable by the symbol she wears on her head, composed of two turned-down horns above a star or seven-petal flower. Sheshat, whose name (based on the term sesh) refers to writing and scribes, was a goddess of history and record keeping and in general oversaw operations that demanded careful computation, including architecture.

Most of the rituals involved in a temple's foundation were performed at night. Dressed in ceremonial robes, the pharaoh went to the site chosen for construction of the temple and at nightfall performed a series of ritual formulas. With the help of astronomer priests, the pharaoh then observed the movement of the stars, in particular the constellation Ursa Major, which was used to determine north. The next day the pharaoh, accompanied by the court and helped by assistants, planted stakes and stretched cords between them to establish the axes to be used by the architects in construction of the new building. The ceremonies ended with the placement of the first stone.

▲ Ritual of the foundation of a temple from the Red Chapel of Hatshepsut at Karnak, 18th dynasty, pink quartzite.

Legend

1. Colossi and obelisks of Ramses II
2. Court with peristyle and pylon of Ramses II decorated with battle scenes of Kadesh
3. Chapels of Thutmose III for the boats of the Theban triad
4. Large monumental colonnade with wall reliefs depicting the procession of the sacred boats of the Theban triad during the *opet* festival
5. Court with peristyle of Amenhotep III
6. Hypostyle hall
7. Hall of the divine king
8. Rooms of the divine birth of Amenhotep III
9. Offering room
10. Sanctuary of the boat
11. Sanctuary of Imen-em-Ipet, "Amon of Luxor"

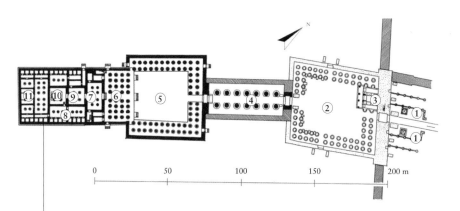

Amenhotep III had a temple built at Luxor dedicated to Amon called Amon-em-Ipet-resyt, "Amon is in the harem of the south." During the opet *festival, a procession carried a statue of the Theban triad (Amon, Mut, and Khonsu) from Karnak to the temple. This procession is the subject of the marvelous reliefs in the monumental colonnade.*

▲ Diagram of the temple of Luxor.

Legend

1. Entryway
2. Festival Hall (*Akh-menu*) of Thutmose III
3. Nucleus of Middle Kingdom temple
4. Sanctuary of the sacred boat of Amon
5. 6th pylon (Thutmose III) with reliefs of the taking of Megiddo
6. 5th pylon (Thutmose I)
7. Obelisks of Hatshepsut
8. 4th pylon (Thutmose I)
9. 3rd pylon (Amenhotep III)
10. Great Hypostyle Hall with reliefs of the military campaigns of Seti I (north wall) and Ramses II (south wall)
11. 2nd pylon (Horemheb)
12. Station of the boats of Seti II
13. Station of the boats of Ramses III
14. Colonnade of Taharqa
15. 1st pylon (30th dynasty)

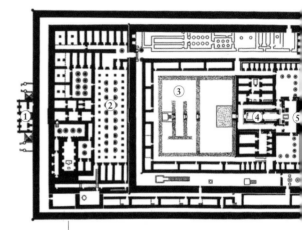

▲ Diagram of the sanctuary of Karnak.

Together with the pyramids of Giza, the most extraordinary and complex architectural creation of ancient Egypt is the Ipet-sut, the temple of Amon-Ra at Karnak, which over a short time during the New Kingdom became the true economic, cultural, and religious heart of the country. The oldest nucleus seems to date to the Middle Kingdom, but it was the New Kingdom's Thutmose I who established the original layout of the new building. After him, for about 1,500 years each sovereign made a contribution, sponsoring buildings, avenues of sphinxes, hypostyle halls, reliefs, pylons, obelisks, or sanctuaries to hold the sacred boat, each contribution symbolic of the continuity of Egypt's ruling house and thus reinforcing the legitimacy of the royal power, which was increasingly based on the benevolence accorded the ruler by the god Amon and by his powerful clergy.

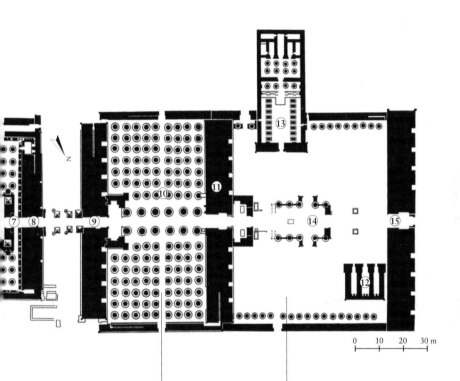

The Great Hypostyle Hall is certainly the most impressive architectural work in the sanctuary: it measures 104 m in length and 52 in width, and owes its name to the mass of 134 monostyle papyriform columns that support the roof up to a maximum height of 24 m. The hall was begun by Horemheb, continued by Seti I, who built the arrangement of 122 columns on the side aisle, and finished by Ramses II, who completed the decorative program begun by his father.

The processional boat was of fundamental importance to the religious life of Thebes. On the occasion of certain celebrations, primarily those related to the flooding of the Nile, the statue of the god Amon was taken out of its temple aboard its boat either to meet the people, who consulted it as an oracle, or to visit another temple, as was the case during the opet festival at Luxor. The statue was also taken to visit the mortuary temples of dead pharaohs, as on the occasion of the Beautiful Feast of the Valley, during which the god crossed the Nile to the West Bank of Thebes.

Priests

▶ Statuette of a praying priest, 21st dynasty, bronze, Musée du Louvre, Paris, E 3188.

Egyptian tradition held that the pharaoh was the sole intermediary between humans and the gods, and in that role he was responsible for assuring the order and prosperity of the country through the wise administration of the territory and the oversight of the religious practices in the temples of Egypt. Technically, he was in that sense the only true "priest" since he was legitimized by his pharaonic power. Since he could not be personally present in each sanctuary of the country, he delegated a special class of functionaries to carry out the necessary daily rites. The Egyptian priest was a lay functionary who, at least until the New Kingdom, served for a period limited to 30 days every five or six months. Priests were chosen from the most influential families in each region and received, in recompense for their service, a portion of the offerings collected at the temple. During the New Kingdom, some of these positions were made permanent, providing their holders with great wealth from the property owned by temples. Each temple's priests formed a hierarchy, with the so-called first prophet of god at the top. This priest administered the sanctuary and directed the various priestly tasks related to the rites and rituals of the cult.

Despite its large-scale involvement in financial and political affairs, Egypt's priesthood was the sole custodian and driving force behind the scientific and religious knowledge that has made the Egyptian civilization so famous.

The Egyptian priest was a layperson delegated by the pharaoh to perform religious functions. Not surprisingly, some of the most authoritative members of this class show up in some of the state's highest positions. Such was the case with Anen, brother of Tiy, wife of Amenhotep III. During that pharaoh's reign, Anen held the post of second prophet of Amon at Thebes.

The stars on the panther skin recall that Anen's many positions included that of priest-astronomer at the temple of Karnak. This category of priest was charged with following the movement of the stars so as to establish the hours of the night and thus begin the temple's religious rites at the correct moment. The activities of the priest-astronomer were of fundamental importance since observation of the night sky was of central importance to the ceremonies attending the foundation of temples as well as to the determination of the religious calendar.

Inscriptions running down the center of the skirt and on the pillar behind the figure list Anen's many titles, confirming the high roles he performed at court in a mixture of religious, political, and administrative positions.

A symbol of Anen's high rank hangs from his belt. On it is a cartouche bearing the Horus name of Amenhotep III, Neb-Maat-Ra.

▶ Statue of the priest-astronomer Anen, from Karnak, 18th dynasty, diorite, h 146 cm, Fondazione Museo Antichità Egizie, Turin, C. 1377.

Magic

Hieroglyph
Hekau
("Magic")

In depth
The Papyrus Harris on Magic, one of the largest papyri dealing with the magic of ancient Egypt, dates to the New Kingdom. Among its many magical formulas is the following, designed to be used to keep away or control crocodiles: "'I am Shu, image of Ra, who sits within the *udjat* of his father. If what is in the water opens its mouth, if it wags its legs, I will make it so that the earth will drop into the Ocean, so that the South will become the North, and the earth will begin to spin'—to be recited four times on a *udjat* on which there is the figure of Onouris drawn on the hand."

Bibliography
Koenig 1994.

Related entries
The Osirian drama, Thoth, Medicine, Funerary rituals, Books of the Dead

▶ Portrait of Isis from the mortuary temple of Seti I at Abydos, 19th dynasty.

The magic of ancient Egypt was based on two fundamental principles. The first was the absolute faith given the creative force of sounds: to speak the name of an object or a person meant to contact that object or person, not on the plane of reality but on a far more effective plane, one directly related to the essence of the object or person. The second fundamental principle was based on the power attributed to images. From the Old Kingdom on, the decorative cycles in Egyptian tombs, with their scenes of offerings and dances, gardens and banquets, and servants at work in the fields, were seen as magical images that would materialize in the afterlife, offering the deceased what they depicted. Egyptians believed that the gods had given magic to humans as a weapon to protect them against adversities. The substantially defensive nature of magic is made clear by the enormous quantity and variety of amulets worn by both the living and the dead. Magic was also closely associated with medicine, and doctors accompanied the administration of drugs with formulas and exorcisms evoking the power of the gods to heal the patient. Among the most recurrent themes in these formulas was the request for protection from

the bite of snakes or scorpions and from the attack of lions or crocodiles. Magic could also be employed offensively, as indicated by various undertakings of Isis, the "mistress of magic." Certainly her greatest feat was bringing back to life her husband, Osiris, torn apart by Set.

This sculpture belongs to the genre of Egypt's "healing statues," images covered with magical texts and sacred images believed to have the power to protect and heal. It was believed that water poured down the surface of the statue would come away "loaded" with the magical power of the texts. This water was collected in special bowls inserted in the pedestal of the statue.

This statue depicts a standing male, a priest or high dignitary, who after death had been elected to the ranks of the tutelary deities and thus was consulted by the common people who hoped he would intercede on their behalf among the gods.

The long-sleeved robe is rendered perceptible more by the succession of columns and rows of hieroglyphic texts that cover its surface than by the plastic rendering of its shape, which extends to the height of the ankles.

Even the head scarf is covered by hieroglyphic texts so that the only areas without inscriptions are the face, neck, hands, and a small area of the chest.

The figure bears a stele depicting the god Horus atop crocodiles. Water poured over the statue was believed to be particularly effective in the prevention of snake bites.

▶ Statue of priest covered in magical formulas, 30th dynasty, black granite, h 68 cm, Musée du Louvre, Paris 10777.

An image of the bearded face of the god Bes above the head of Horus is another good-luck element to reinforce the magical powers of the stele.

Horus on crocodiles is depicted frontally and with the characteristic iconography that presented him nude with the sidelock typical of Egyptian children.

The magical power of the image is made clear in the god's pose, grasping dangerous animals, including snakes, lions, and scorpions, while standing atop crocodiles.

▲ Stele of Horus atop crocodiles, early Ptolemaic Period, schist, h 44 cm, Egyptian Museum, Cairo, CG 9401.

The five elements of a human

Egyptian religious theories posited a highly original interpretation of human reality. On the basis of funerary texts, five elements of humans can be identified. The first of these is *ka*, which refers to the vital energy or life force that differentiates a living human from a dead one. The second highly important element was *ba*, which can be seen as the spiritual identity that makes each person unique. *Ba* was represented as a bird with a human face, and tradition held that when a person died his *ba*-bird flew into the afterlife. A *ba*-bird could return to the world of the living to collect funerary offerings. To return, the *ba*-bird needed a special place set apart to host it. The principal place for its return was the mummy itself, which for that reason had to be integral and well preserved; also a statue engraved with the name of the deceased could magically host the *ba*-bird. The third spiritual element was the person's name, which by defining with a single expression the entire identity of a person concentrated that person's essence. Speaking or thinking the name of a dead person was the same as making that person actually exist. The shadow a human cast had a particular meaning and counts as the fourth element. The fifth and last was *akh*, an illuminated spiritual state that made it possible for the deceased to join the indestructible stars.

Hieroglyph
s
("man")

In depth
According to a text preserved in a papyrus scroll of the 4th century BC, the human species came into being from tears cried by the creator god Atum. The Egyptian term for "humanity," *remetj*, sounds a great deal like another noun, *remet*, which means "tears." According to an exquisitely Egyptian point of view, the phonetic resemblance of terms indicates the existence of mythical and religious similarities in their inner meanings.

Related entries
Funerary rituals, Weighing the soul, Books of the Dead, Mastaba

◄ *Ba*-bird with Anubis, detail of funerary decoration.

The five elements of a human

The uplifted arms represent the hieroglyphic symbol for ka, *clearly identifying the nature of the statue. According to Egyptian tradition, the* ka *was the spiritual energy of each individual and together with the* ba *was what remained of an individual after death, representing a sort of "double" of the deceased.*

This statue depicts the ka *of the pharaoh Awibra Hor, a sovereign of the 13th dynasty. It was found inside its tabernacle in 1894 by J.J. De Morgan, in a tomb adjacent to the pyramid of Amenemhet III at Dahshur. The statue is probably one of the largest surviving examples in wood from ancient Egypt. The artist succeeded in creating graceful forms that would have been impossible in the stone statuary of the period, such as the open spaces between limbs and the rendering of such details as the unusually long and narrow false beard.*

The eyes were made by mounting crystal and quartz in a bronze armature, giving the face a surprising vitality and depth.

Traces of paint at the height of the waist suggest that the statue wore a painted shendyt *skirt.*

▶ Statue of the *ka* of the pharaoh Awibra Hor, from Dahshur, 13th dynasty, wood, bonze, quartz, h 170 cm, Egyptian Museum, Cairo, CG 259.

It was particularly important to the Egyptians that the spirit of the dead enjoy full freedom of movement in the afterlife, being free to leave its tomb at will and then return to it. So it is that Formula 92 of the Book of the Dead is entitled "Formula for opening the tomb for the ba and for the shadow, for going out by day and having power over legs." This vignette reproduces this desire and includes the rare simultaneous presence of both the ba-bird and the shadow (in Egyptian, shuyt).

The shadow of the deceased stands out against the entrance to the tomb, its silhouette cast by light from outside the tomb.

The ba of Irinefer is represented twice, while leaving the tomb with spread wings and while returning.

The black disk is an unusual and interesting presence, perhaps an allusion to the sun that illuminated the dark subterranean world.

▲ Illustration of Formula 92 of the Book of the Dead from the burial chamber of the tomb of Irinefer, Western Thebes, 19th dynasty.

"Do not reprove [Nut] for eating her children [the stars] since she will give them new birth" (Myth of Nut who devours her children)

Astronomy

In depth
The Egyptians attributed great ritual and astronomical importance to the stars of the firmament, most of all the so-called indestructible stars, by which the ancient astronomical priests meant the pole stars, the constellation Ursa Major, and in general the circumpolar stars, since unlike all the others these do not set below the horizon and were visible throughout the year.

Bibliography
Krupp 1983.

Related entries
Senenmut, Thoth, Priests, Calendar

Egyptian astronomy was expressed in three interconnected pursuits: the determination of the calendar and measurement of the nocturnal hours; the orientation of sacred structures; and the funerary decoration of sarcophagi and tombs. Observation of the sky had enabled astronomer-priests to perceive the "movement" of the firmament and the cyclical return of stars and constellations at certain times of the year. This made it possible for them to determine the onset of the Nile's annual floods, and they were also able to make the so-called star clocks with which they could count off the hours of the night. Doing so was made possible through reference to the so-called decans, 36 stars that, in alternation over the course of the year, rose on the horizon during the night. Observation of the sky led to recognition of the North Star and the circumpolar constellations, which were used in the orientation of temples, as well as other constellations still used in astronomy, such as Ursa Major and Orion, and the planets Mercury, Venus, Mars, Jupiter, and Saturn. Star clocks are known today because of copies made of them on sarcophagi that date to between the 9th and the 12th dynasty. Beginning with the 18th-dynasty tomb of Senenmut and continuing in the royal tombs of the 19th dynasty, the decans, constellations, and planets flowed together in the spectacular decorative programs called astronomical ceilings because they were usually located on the vaulted ceiling of the monarch's burial chamber.

▶ Clepsydra, or water clock, from the temple of Amon-Ra at Karnak, 18th dynasty, reign of Amenhotep III, alabaster, Egyptian Museum, Cairo, JE 37525.

As early as the Old Kingdom, Egyptian astronomer-priests had identified stars and constellations useful to counting off the hours of the night over the entire arc of the year. Given their great religious importance, the decans, as they were later called by the Greeks, were included on astronomical ceilings, arranged in orderly grids bearing the name of the star and its depiction as one or more stars according to whether the decan was a single star or a constellation.

Only some of the decans used by the Egyptians have been identified with certainty. The most important of them was Sopdet (Sirius), since its appearance in the morning just before the rising of the sun (once a year, at the end of July) marked the onset of the Nile flooding.

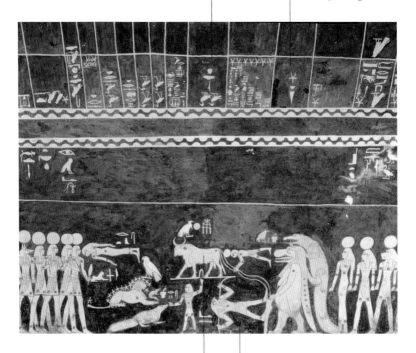

This detail illustrates the group of circumpolar constellations, presented between two groups of divinities. Among the most important of those recognizable are, to the right, the figure of a hippopotamus called Sa-mut, identified by some as the constellation Draco, while at the center the bull Meskhetyu represents Ursa Major. The crouching lion to the left may refer to the constellation Leo in the modern zodiac.

The astronomical ceiling in Seti I's tomb is one of the most fascinating and complete examples of this type of decoration. Similar images mixing the mythological and the astronomical were made in Egypt until the Ptolemaic Period, when the encounter with Greek astrology and astronomy led to the extraordinary zodiacs of Dendera, Edfu, and Isna.

▲ Northern constellations and decans from the astronomical ceiling in the burial chamber of the tomb of Seti I in the Valley of the Kings, Western Thebes, 19th dynasty.

The Egyptians divided the day into 12 diurnal hours and 12 nocturnal hours. They used sundials to measure the passage of the diurnal hours; for the nocturnal they used elaborate reference tables known today as star clocks. These are based on the rising of 12 stars or constellations, chosen by the astronomer-priests for this purpose.

The star clock is a somewhat rare type of artifact. About a dozen are known, used as funerary decorations in tombs, most of all from Asyut in Upper Egypt and dating to between the 9th and 11th dynasty.

▲ Star clock from the sarcophagus of Khu-en-sokar from Asyut, 12th dynasty, Egyptian Museum, Cairo, CG 36320.

A graphic expression of the passage of hours, the star clock was composed of a highly rational codified chart that indicated the progression of weeks on the horizontal axis and the hours of the night on the vertical axis. In this way each star moves, week by week, along a diagonal, for which reason stars clocks are also sometimes called "diagonal clocks."

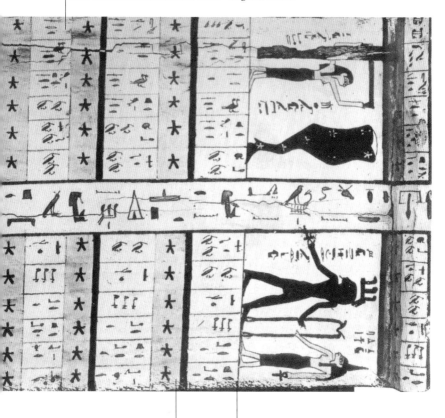

Knowing which week of the year it was, a priest could look to the east and determine which decan was rising on the horizon at that moment; looking along the column for that week on the grid of the star clock, he could then find the name of the star just observed and with it the exact hour of the night.

Along the border appear the first depictions of the principal elements of the Egyptian firmament. From top to bottom: the goddess Nut, depicted as a girl holding up the sky; the constellation Meskhetyu, corresponding to our Ursa Major; the constellation Sah (Orion); the star Sopdet (Sirius).

Legend

Decorations representing subjects drawn from Egyptian astronomical mythology began appearing on the ceilings of burial chambers in tombs in the Valley of the Kings in the 19th dynasty; such ceilings are known as astronomical ceilings. The only true prototype of this type of decoration dates to the 18th dynasty and appears in the tomb of the most powerful and learned functionary of the period of Queen Hatshepsut, Senenmut.

1. The planet Venus assumes the appearance of the sacred Benu bird (gray heron).
2. The planet Mercury appears here under its Egyptian name, Sebegu.
3. The planets Jupiter and Saturn are depicted as falcon-headed men. Mars is not cited.
4. A female figure in the dress of Isis navigates a boat and wears on her head a characteristic headdress that makes her easily recognizable as Sopdet, or Sirius.
5. Orion owes his importance to the fact that his appearance before dawn marked the arrival of the Nile flooding.
6. The list of the 36 decans.
7. The 12 months of the year are described as circles. These are divided in three groups that correspond to the three Egyptian seasons, *akhet*, *peret*, and *shemu*.
8. Divinities related to the months of the years.
9. Northern constellations.
10. The constellation Ursa Major.

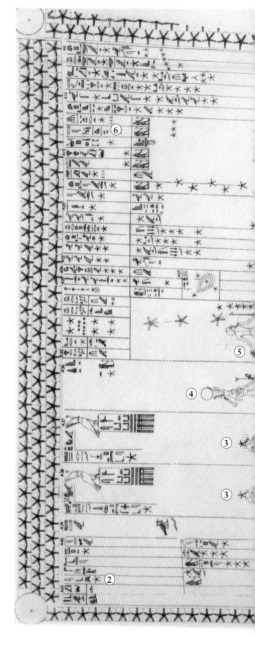

▶ Astronomical ceiling of Senenmut, tomb of Senenmut at Deir el-Bahri, Western Thebes, 18th dynasty.

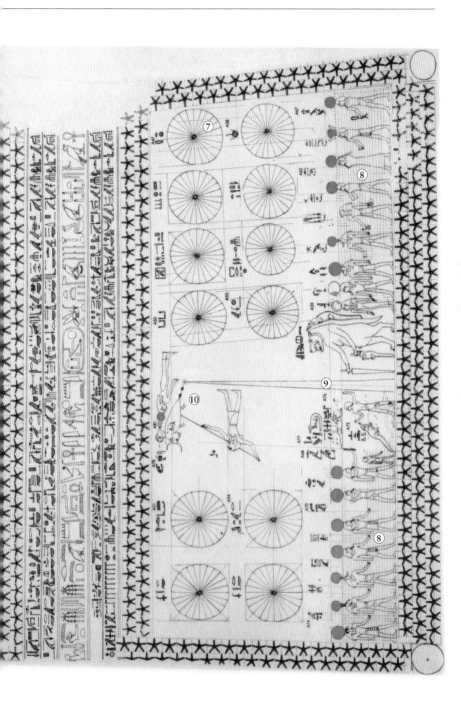

"Year 14, day 5 of the month of Pakhons, of King Psamtik [I], may he be healthy and sound eternally" (Brooklyn Papyrus)

Calendar

In depth
The Egyptian names for the 12 months are known beginning with the New Kingdom and all the way to the Roman epoch. The names were based on the agricultural festivals held in each month. In their Greek transcriptions created during the Ptolemaic administrations, they are Thoth, Phaophi, Adyr, Choiak, Tybi, Mecheit, Phamenoth, Pharmuti, Pachon, Payni, Epiphi, and Mesore.

Bibliography
Depuydt 1997.

Related entries
Thoth, Astronomy, Agriculture and peasants

▶ Fragment of a clepsydra, Late Period, red granite, h 20 cm, Fondazione Museo Antichità Egizie, Turin, S. 8.

Around the middle of the 5th millennium BC, at the beginning of the Neolithic revolution in Egypt, the need to predict and plan agricultural labors in accordance with the seasonal cycles led to the elaboration of the calendar. Egyptian agriculture was completely dependant on the flooding of the Nile, which deposited silt in the fields in the months between July and September. Since this was an annual phenomenon, offering the definition of a measurable period of time between one flood and the next, it led inevitably to the determination of the concept of a "year." This interval was first measured by lunations, then by way of a phenomenon known as the "heliacal rising of Sirius." The result was a lunar-stellar calendar composed of 12 months of 29 days each. The system proved imprecise because of a series of astronomical variables of which the Egyptians were unaware. Predynastic Egyptian society evolved more complex economic, administrative, and political necessities that required a fixed dating system, and this pressing need led to the detachment of the calendar from all natural phenomena and its expression by way of mathematical abstractions. The result was the Egyptian year divided in the three seasons of *akhet* ("flood"), *peret* ("lowering of the waters"), and *shemu* ("lowest water level") of 4 months each. The year lasted 365 days divided into 12 months of 30 days, plus 5 additional or epagomenal days at the end of the year.

"Come water, come milk, come this fresh liquid with which Horus washed his eyes for fear of blindness . . . Recite on water and milk, putting it in the eyes in the morning" (Hieratic papyrus)

Medicine

The fame of Egyptian doctors was already widespread in antiquity; it seems that such great Greek doctors as Hippocrates and Galen referred to Egyptian medical texts, which they consulted in the temple of Imhotep at Memphis. While this should not be exaggerated, there can be no doubt that the practice of embalming gave Egyptian doctors access to a wealth of anatomical knowledge and a familiarity with surgical practices that were exceptional, most of all if compared with those available to other Mediterranean cultures, where any type of contact with a dead body was taboo. An important document dating to the early New Kingdom, the Ebers Medical Papyrus, furnishes much information about the diseases known to the Egyptian medical profession and the treatments prescribed for them. A large number of prescriptions concern afflictions of the respiratory tract and problems related to digestion, such as stomach irritations, hemorrhages, and intestinal problems. Egyptian doctors knew the use of opiates as anesthetics, of suppositories, of vegetable tampons, and enemas, and made use of castor oil to loosen the bowels. The broad range of pathologies treated included headaches, such as migraines, eye infections caused by dust and sand, and dental woes, including the first instances of fillings. Egyptian doctors also treated vertebral contusions, sprains, and various fractures.

In depth
The practice of medicine was constantly accompanied and supported by prayers, exorcisms, magical formulas, and litanies drawn from the sphere of religious faith, as indicated by the text of a stele in the British Museum: "Made by the painter of Amon in the house of Maat, Nebra . . . in the name of his lord Amon, lord of Thebes . . . He made hymns in his name because of the greatness of his power . . . for the painter Nekhetamon, who lay mortally ill . . . found that the lord of the gods came on the wind of the north, sweet breeze, before him, so he could save him."

Bibliography
Manniche 1989.
Nunn 1996.

◄ Relief of lotus flowers, from the temple of Amon-Ra at Karnak, limestone, New Kingdom.

The blue lotus played an important role in Egyptian culture, being associated with a myth of the creation of the universe.

Symbol of the rising sun, regeneration, and rebirth, the lotus probably had important uses in Egyptian pharmacopoeia, and recent studies indicate that the flower has powerful relaxant properties and may well even be hallucinogenic.

▲ Princess collecting lotus, New Kingdom, 18th dynasty, painted ivory, 6.5 x 5.8 cm, Musée du Louvre, Département des Antiquités Égyptiennes, Paris.

▶ The great priest Ramessunakht with Thoth, patron god of scribes, from the cachette of Karnak, 20th dynasty, gray granite, h 7.5 cm, Egyptian Museum, Cairo, CG 42162.

"I was cast upon the island by a mighty wave and passed three days alone, with only my heart as companion" (The Shipwrecked Sailor)

Literature

Only rarely are most people reminded of the literature of ancient Egypt, yet it offers a primary key to understanding that culture. Even the briefest overview reveals that the literature of ancient Egypt was vibrant and varied, offering expression to a broad range of different voices. Setting aside the religious-funerary works, which belong to the sphere of temples and rituals, the oldest literary works are the autobiographies and moralistic teachings of the Old Kingdom, which promoted ethical values, such as loyalty to the sovereign, reserve, temperance, and respect for the hierarchy. The historical disruption and uncertainty of the First Intermediate Period was expressed in works of a pessimistic character, including the *Lamentations of Ipuwer* or the *Dialogue between a Man Tired of Life and His Ba*, a confrontation between a man determined to commit suicide and his soul, which is against the idea. With the coming of the new monarchy and the installation of a new order during the 12th dynasty, an exquisite narrative style emerged, with such masterpieces—already considered classics in the New Kingdom—as *The Eloquent Peasant, The Shipwrecked Sailor*, and *The Tale of Sinuhe*, works that exploit all the plot twists typical of modern adventure tales. The New Kingdom saw an explosion of entertainment genres, such as myths, fables, satires, hymns, love poems, and letters, coupled with a great taste for the magical and the divinatory.

In depth
A broad range of literature existed in ancient Egypt, as indicated by the following quotations, the first drawn from a book of wisdom, the second from a book of love poetry. "If you are a leader, be patient in your listening when the petitioner speaks, do not halt him until his belly is emptied of what he had planned to say. The victim loves to sate his heart even more than accomplishing what he came for" (*Teachings of Ptahhotep*, end 3rd millennium BC). "I shall lie down at home and pretend to be ill; then enter the neighbors to see me; then comes my beloved with them. She will make the physicians unnecessary, she understands my illness!" (Papyrus Harris 500, 12th century BC).

Bibliography
Lichtheim 1973, 1976, 1980.

Related entries
Scribes and functionaries, Thoth, Writing

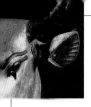

"[Scribes'] tombs are forgotten, but their names are read out on their scrolls ... making them eternal" (Papyrus Chester Beatty IV)

Writing

Bibliography
Faulkner 1972.
Grandet, Mathieu
1997. Allen 2000.

Related entries
Scribes and
functionaries, Thoth,
Literature

The Egyptian language was expressed in written form by way of three principal styles of writing: hieroglyphics, the hieratic, and the demotic. The first was monumental writing, incised or painted on the walls of tombs and temples, on steles, and on every support intended or made to last over time; it also constitutes the point of departure for the other two methods. The origin of hieroglyphs can be traced to the plant and animal depictions on Nagada pottery beginning in the second half of the 5th millennium BC. By way of a progressive stylization, the codification of an embryonic hieroglyphic system came into being around the end of the 4th millennium BC. It was used most of all for the monumental rendering of religious texts and historical or political inscriptions, while its simplified form, called cursive hieroglyphs, was used to transcribe papyrus texts of great importance, such as the *Book of the Dead*. At almost the same time the hieratic came into being, a cursive form of hieroglyphics further abbreviated and simplified, used on papyri and ostraca but most of all by state and temple administrations. Around the 7th century BC an even more stylized and abbreviated—almost stenographic—method of writing appeared. This was the demotic, used for everyday writing in place of the hieratic, which continued to be used for religious texts.

▶ Hieroglyphs in low-relief from the White Chapel, Open Air Museum, Karnak.

Hieroglyphics were used in three general ways, as phonograms (expressing simple sounds), as ideograms (direct representations for a word or thing), and as determinatives (to indicate the classification of a symbol or to avoid confusion between homophones). They are divided into monoliteral signs (representing a single consonant), biliteral (two consonants), and triliteral (three consonants).

Phonograms

1. Monoliterals

Hiero.	Trans.	Sound	Hiero.	Trans.	Sound
	ꜣ	a		ḫ	kh
	i, y	y		ẖ	kh
	ꜥ	a		z	s
	w	u		s	s
	b	b		š	s
	p	p		q	q
	f	f		k	k
	m	m		g	g
	n	n		t	t
	r	r		ṯ	tj
	h	h		d	d
	ḥ	h		ḏ	dj

2. Biliterals

Hiero.	Trans.	Sound
	bꜣ	ba
	mn	men
	nb	neb
	ḥr	her
	zꜣ	sa
	kꜣ	ka
	dd	djed

3. Triliterals

Hiero.	Trans.	Sound
	ꜥnḫ	Ankh
	nṯr	Netjer
	ḫpr	Keper
	nfr	Nefer

Ideograms

Hiero.	Trans.	Meaning
	rꜣ	mouth
	rꜥ	sun
	nṯr	god
	sꜣ	son
	kꜣ	spirit

Determinatives

Hiero.	Meaning
	man
	divinity
	foreign lands
	sun, solar light, day
	abstract concept
	city

▲ Chart of several hieroglyphs (phonograms, ideograms, and determinatives) with transliterations, sounds, and meanings.

Daily life

Village organization
Agriculture and peasants
Commerce
Livestock
Animals and plants
Hunting and fishing
Food
Servants
Home and family
Artisans
Women
Eroticism and seduction
Entertainment
Aesthetics and style
Glass and faience

◀ Group of three musicians from the tomb of Nakht at Sheikh Abd el-Qurna, Western Thebes, 18th dynasty.

"The region of Memphis totals ten thousand men consisting of free untaxed commoners; its borders are firm, its garrison is brave" (The Instruction of Merikare)

Village organization

Bibliography
David 1986.
McDowell 1999.

Related entries
Scribes and officials,
Deir el-Medina,
Akhenaten

Ancient sources hand down the names of a great number of inhabited centers, some of which were of political importance, others of economic or religious importance. Unfortunately, few important archeological traces remain of most of these. What is known of Egyptian town planning is based on what little is known of several villages created to house the workers employed on construction sites, such as Kahun and Deir el-Medina. These were designed on paper, built in a short time, and made to serve a precise social function. In both cases, the inhabited area was surrounded by a wall and traversed by one or more main roadways that divided the town into quarters; the blocks were uniform in size and juxtaposed, thus meeting the strong demand for the rational use of space. Amarna, the ancient Akhetaten, is the only city whose layout is known. It

was built from nothing by the pharaoh Amenhotep IV over the period of only a few years. It, too, displays the characteristics common to workers' villages. Its layout is orderly and schematic with places for political and religious structures and large residential areas intended for the homes of nobles as well as the homes of the ordinary population. There were also green areas, including gardens arranged around ponds integrated with the villas of the nobles.

► Statue of Shemes, from Asyut, Middle Kingdom, painted wood, h 123 cm, Fondazione Museo Antichità Egizie, Turin, S. 8653

The inside of the house is behind this columned portico, supported by eight fascicled lotus-flower columns. The well-preserved polychromy gives realism to the buds and stems.

The homes of the well-to-do had a second floor or at least a terrace. The actual rooms of the home are not reproduced in the model, which was designed to give an idea of the garden, emblematic of the abode's richness.

The model of the home of Meketra represents a luxury habitation, built around a central garden with a pond surrounded by trees. Plants and water were not merely an embellishment, for they also provided the rooms with shadows and cooler air.

What is known about domestic architecture in ancient Egypt comes not only from excavations but from scale models of homes. Many of these were made of terracotta and present homes with a court, a hearth, and sometimes a stairway leading to an upper storey.

▲ Model house from the tomb of Meketra at Deir el-Bahri, Western Thebes, 11th dynasty, painted wood, h 43 cm, Egyptian Museum, Cairo, JE 46721.

Kahun has a uniform, well-organized layout, and was built in a short time. The diagram was part of the tomb furnishings of Sesostris II, and the town was probably designed by the same architect who designed that pharaoh's pyramid and mortuary temple.

The northern area of the site of Kahun was excavated by Flinders Petrie in 1888–89 and revealed the presence of an important urban center that Sesostris II had built to house the workers and officials involved in work on the construction of his pyramid and funerary complex.

A special area (the so-called acropolis) was reserved for a single large home, separated from the rest of the area by a wall and located in a raised position; it must have been an important building, perhaps a kind of guardhouse or control center over the workers' quarters.

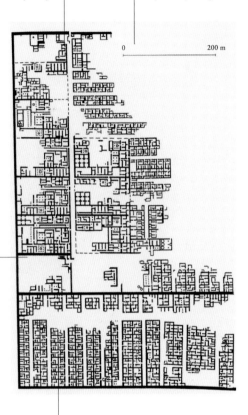

0   200 m

The town has a rectangular layout and is surrounded by walls; its interior is divided in two sections separated by a wall. The eastern part is spacious and contained important homes for officials, while the western part was inhabited by the workers, who lived in small houses built one against the other.

▲ Layout of the village of Kahun (El-Lahun), Middle Kingdom.

"Hail to thee, O Nile! You show yourself in this land, coming in peace, giving life to Egypt . . . overflowing the gardens created by Ra, giving life to all animals" (Hymn to the Nile)

Agriculture and peasants

The fertility of the soil provided by the flooding of the Nile permitted the Egyptians to practice extensive agricultural activity, supported by a vast state organization charged with the maintenance of the irrigation canals, the storage of foodstuffs, and the taxation of harvests. Egypt's agricultural economy depended on the river's annual floods, which could be scarce or could be violently devastating. Even under favorable conditions the fieldwork was difficult and along with peasants required the efforts of women, children, and animals; oxen were used in plowing and also in the phases of sowing and threshing. Cereal grains were Egypt's primary agricultural products, with surpluses being exported, along with flax, making Egypt famous as a producer of fine fabrics. Winemaking was also of great economic importance; labels found on wine amphorae indicate a production classified according to vineyard, production year, and even storage site. The vines were arranged on pergolas, and the phases of harvesting, pressing, and storing involved numerous workers. Other important agricultural products included a wide range of vegetables—squash, lettuce, onions, legumes—and fruit, including figs, grapes, and dates.

In depth
Nile flooding made the land muddy, but the peasants still had to plow and hoe to break up the fields. After the fields were seeded, flocks of sheep and pigs were driven over them to push in the seeds. The wheat was harvested with flint sickles; women gathered the sheaves and took them to the threshing floor in baskets.

Bibliography
Hartmann 1923.

Related entries
Calendar, Animals and plants, Food, Servants

◄Model of farmer from the tomb of Niankhpepi at Meir, 6th dynasty, painted wood, h 29 cm, Egyptian Museum, Cairo, CG 250.

The large landed properties produced grain in an extensive manner, satisfying the country's needs and producing surpluses that were stored for later distribution.

The computation of taxes was proportional to the size of the holding, measured every year by surveyors and by the height of the Nile during its flooding.

The operations involved a large number of workers and were constantly overseen by the owner's foremen; for the purposes of calculating taxes, state officials took careful note of the quantity of grain produced by every field.

Once the flood waters had receded, the peasants performed the phases in the cultivation of grain: plowing, where the ground was compact, sowing, reaping, and threshing.

▲ Agricultural scenes from the tomb of Menna at Sheikh Abd el-Qurna, Western Thebes, 18th dynasty.

Grapevines could be trained onto shrubs or small trees, entwined on pergolas, or planted in rows to receive more sunlight.

The most widespread grape varieties in Egypt were dark. Such grapes were also used as food and for decorative purposes. There were also pale varieties, used to make both sweet and dry wines. Dried grapes and grape seeds have been found in excavations.

Grapevines are known to have been present in Egypt even in the Predynastic Period, probably brought to Egypt from the Near East. Grape cultivation was particularly widespread in marshy areas, in the Delta, in Faiyum, and in the oases.

▲ Grape harvesting, tomb of Nakht at Sheikh Abd el-Qurna, Western Thebes, 18th century.

The stalks and skins of grapes were given a further pressing, inserted in a canvas sack, and wrung and twisted with the use of sticks.

The number of people crushing the grapes depended on the size of the vat, which was covered with a sort of canopy that the workers could hold onto to avoid slipping on the grape skins.

After the grapes were harvested by hand, they were transported to vats in which they were crushed by being trodden upon.

An outlet in the vat drew off the liquid from the pressing to smaller holding vats or directly to large terracotta amphorae that were sealed with clay stoppers wrapped tight with fabric.

▲ Wine pressing, tomb of Nakht at Sheikh Abd el-Qurna, Western Thebes, 18th dynasty.

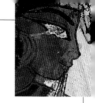

"I navigated according to the current from there to Merenra-Kanedfer, with six barges, three transport ships, and three ships eight arms long, in a single expedition" (Autobiography of Uni)

Commerce

Egyptian written sources hand down abundant information concerning the commercial contacts that Egypt, always in search of raw materials, had established with surrounding countries. From the very earliest dynasties, pharaohs were procuring wood from Lebanon, resin and spices from Ethiopia—the legendary land of Punt—semiprecious stones (turquoise, lapis lazuli, malachite) from the East, gold from Nubia, exotic animals, hides, ostrich plumes, ivory, and ebony from deeper inside Africa. This commercial traffic was directed by the royal administration and made use of the great caravan routes that crossed Nubia and ran parallel to the Nile following the route of the oases in the Western Desert, constantly crossed by teams of pack animals loaded with merchandise. The river was used for the transportation of materials from Lower Nubia, although the Nile was difficult to navigate below the Second Cataract. The produce of the Near East arrived in Egypt by land or by sea, transported on ships that sailed along the coast of the Levant. The products Egypt exported to the Mediterranean world included perfumes, articles of goldworking, wine, and grains. Very little is known about internal or local commerce; exchanges must have been regulated by a system of barter, and the value of every good was determined by its weight in pieces of copper.

In depth
The basic element of linear measurement was the cubit, about 40 to 50 cm long; this was divided into 28 fingers; 8 fingers made a hand, 12 a palm, 16 a foot, 20 an arm. The balance with two scalepans and a central lead bar was used for small weights; the basic unit of weight was the copper *deben* (about 90 grams), which was used to calculate the value of a product.

Bibliography
Partidge 1996.

Related entries
Foreigners, Nubia and Abu Simbel, Naukratis, Oasis

◀ Scene of ritual navigation toward Abydos, from the chapel of Maia at Deir el-Medina, Western Thebes, 18th century, painted plaster, Fondazione Museo Antichità Egizie, Turin, S. 7910.

Rekhmire served as vizier during the reign of Thutmose III, a pharaoh greatly involved in military campaigns and overseas operations.

Military contacts with the Near East and with Nubia were often undertaken not just to acquire territory for political or defensive reasons but also to create communication routes for trade. Egypt lacked several important raw materials, among them precious woods, metals, semiprecious stones, spices, and incense.

▲ Procession of Nubian tribute bearers, tomb of Rekhmire at Sheikh Abd el-Qurna, Western Thebes, 18th dynasty.

Egypt was in contact with the Mediterranean world from very early times, but it was during the New Kingdom that Egypt sought to greatly expand the range of its influence.

During the Minoan age, the island of Crete was famous for the high quality of its goldwork, including jewelry of minuscule size and large ceremonial vases.

The Cretans are depicted as slim and graceful, with brown skin. They wear their hair long, sometimes held back by bands or diadems. They wear simple, brightly colored skirts decorated with precious elements and wear high footwear, decorated with colored thread.

The products being presented to the Egyptians are vases of various shape made in gold and precious materials. These are mostly craters and pitchers with large handles, drinking vessels shaped like animal heads, and containers with floral applications embellished by wavy lines, spirals, and geometric motifs.

▲ Cretans with tribute, tomb of Rekhmire at Sheikh Abd el-Qurna, Western Thebes, 18th dynasty.

The principal purpose of these scenes of processions of foreigners was to call attention to the vizier's achievements and to exalt the undertakings of the pharaoh. All together, the scenes have a great deal of compositional and chromatic vivacity, with a wide variety of subjects and details.

The Egyptians were greatly drawn to the fascination of the exotic, in particular the "strangeness" of Africa's natural world, with so many interesting and unknown kinds of animals and plants.

The trade in exotic and luxury products served the well-to-do class of society, the members of which were eager to show off clothes, headdresses, and precious accessories fashioned using rare materials of distant origin.

In this part of the procession are Africans carrying elephant tusks, trunks of ebony, a leopard, a baboon, and a small monkey.

▲ African tribute bearers, tomb of Rekhmire, Sheikh Abd el-Qurna, Western Thebes, 18th dynasty.

"It is he who produces the forage that nourishes the flocks, the fruit trees for humans, he who creates that on which the fish in the stream live, and the birds beneath the sky (Hymn to Amon-Ra)

Livestock

From the Predynastic Period on, the raising of animals (cattle, goats, sheep, poultry) was one of the prevalent activities of the peoples in the Nile Valley. During the first dynasties, efforts were made to domesticate various wild species, including ibex, gazelles, antelopes, mouflon, pigs, and even hyenas. Egyptians were quite fond of wild game, the consumption of which was a privilege reserved to the nobility; various important Egyptian personages are depicted in their tombs taking part in hunts in the marshes, natural reserves of birds. Most livestock was raised for human consumption, but some species were raised for practical purposes, such as the asses used in transporation, or the dogs used in hunting. Bovines constituted one of the principal resources of the Egyptian economy. They furnished not only an important part of the diet (meat, milk products, and derivatives) but were also used to pull plows and for other difficult agricultural work. The possession of numerous head of large and small cattle was a sign of social distinction, hence the scenes of cattle counting that show up so often in tomb decorations. Even the officials involved in the activities of livestock tending enjoyed a certain social prestige.

In depth
Herodotus relates various Egyptian ritual practices, including the presence in temples of sacred animals. Bulls, he says, could not be sacrificed unless they were found to be pure, free of defect; cows, being sacred to Isis, could not be sacrificed. In the same way rams could not be sacrificed because they were sacred to Amon, as well as cats, mongooses, falcons, the ibis, and the crocodile.

Bibliography
Boessneck 1988.

Related entries
Animals and plants, Food, Servants, Mastaba

▼ Frieze of geese from the mastaba of Nefermaat at Meidum, 4th dynasty, h 27 cm, Egyptian Museum, Cairo, CG 1742.

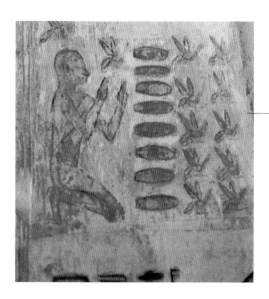

Bees were the symbol of Lower Egypt from the most ancient times, for the region was rich in pastures and flowering fields. Honey was the primary sweetener, but figs, carobs, and dates were used as sweeteners in cooking and the preparation of sweets.

This painting, made in a local workshop, makes use of unusual anatomical and perspective views; one of the men is depicted in profile and the other in a three-quarter view while twisting his body. The standing antelope partially covers the view of one of the men.

Beginning in the Old Kingdom, attempts were made to domesticate the animals from the semidesertic regions. Gazelles, antelopes, and oryxes along with various caprids were appreciated for their graceful shapes and fluid movements. Hunted for sport, they may have made up part of the diet of the most well-to-do Egyptians.

▲ Scene of apiculture, tomb of Pabasa at Assasif, Western Thebes, 26th dynasty.

▲ Antelope breeders, tomb of Khnumhotep III at Beni Hasan, Middle Kingdom.

Overseers with long staffs in their hands can be seen standing around, even leaning against walls, there to make sure the herdsmen keep control of the cattle.

Seated in the shadow of a pavilion supported on fascicled columns are the directors of the estate and its owner, Meketra, all of them there to witness the cattle census. Meketra sits on a square stool, his attendants crouching on the floor.

Some herdsmen prod the cattle, others lead them with long ropes around their horns; the cattle include a variety of types with solid, dappled, and spotted hides.

The overall composition has a sense of movement and vitality, accentuated by the perfect display of polychromy; the use of clothing made of actual fabric adds a further touch of descriptive realism.

Censuses of the cattle on an estate were taken at regular intervals, and the information was recorded and used to calculate the amount of royal tax to be paid on the livestock. The owner was present during such operations, permitting him to take stock of his wealth.

▲ Model of a cattle census, from the tomb of Meketra at Deir el-Bahri, 11th dynasty, painted wood, h 55 cm, Egyptian Museum, Cairo, JE 46724.

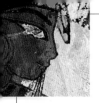

"In the river there are also otters, which the people think are sacred. They also regard as sacred the fish they call the lepidotus and the eel; these are sacred to the Nile as . . . is the fox-goose" (Herodotus)

Animals and plants

Bibliography
Manniche 1989.
Vernus, Yoyotte 2005.

Related entries
Medicine, Livestock, Hunting and fishing, Food, Servants, Faiyum and Lisht

In a natural setting in which the desert meets the fertile waters of the Nile and the sea, a great variety of animal and plant species lived together. Amid the sparse shrubs of the desert—terebinth, acacia, and tamarisk—lived snakes, lizards, hedgehogs, hyenas, wolves and jackals, antelopes and gazelles, locusts and scorpions, while among the rocky gorges there were nests of falcons and vultures. Along the border of the arid zones grew date palms, sycamores, willows; the stagnant waters of the marshes of the oases and the Delta hosted papyrus thickets, lotus, water lilies, rushes, and reeds in which found shelter crocodiles, hippopotamuses, boars, wading birds, ducks, hoopoes, colorful birds, wild cats, frogs, turtles, and various kinds of insect (flies, butterflies, bees). The fertile areas cultivated with grains and flax were used for raising bovines, sheep and goats, poultry, pigeons, pigs, dogs, and beginning in the New Kingdom horses. Grapes, olives, and pomegranates arrived in Egypt from the Near East, as did the lily and the peach. The waters of the river and the canals were populated with eel, catfish, tilapia, perch. The domestic animals found in homes included cats, dogs, and monkeys; the gardens of the well-to-do had fish and birds. The Egyptians were familiar with various exotic animals, mostly from Africa, such as lions, leopards, ostriches, elephants, giraffes, rhinoceroses. A clear manifestation of their interest in plants is the Botanical Garden Thutmose III had made in the Festival Hall at Karnak.

▶ Scene of grain being taken to a granary, from the tomb of Iti at Gebelein, First Intermediate Period, painted plaster, h circa 200 cm, Fondazione Museo Antichità Egizie, Turin, S. 14354.

Pre-Amarnian art developed themes tied to faunistic decorations, drawing inspiration from the variety of animals and plants in papyrus thickets. The flight of colorful birds amid papyrus flowers results in fanciful chromatic displays, giving the scene great vivacity and lightness.

The New Kingdom saw a highly original style of art based on the satirical depiction of reality, with the elements of normalcy overturned. In these works, animals are often given human movements, sometimes becoming emblematic of vices and virtues, much as in fables.

This papyrus depicts an antelope and a lion happily seated face to face to play a round of senet. Just visible to the right is a hyena carrying a bundle on his shoulder.

▲ Fresco with marsh scene, from the palace of Amenhotep III at Malqata, Western Thebes, 18th dynasty, painted plaster, h 80 cm, Egyptian Museum, Cairo, TR 3/5/27/6.

▲ Satiric scene, probably from Deir el-Medina, 18th dynasty, painted papyrus, 15.5 x 59.7 cm, British Museum, London, EA 10016.

The composition makes use of contrasting vertical and horizontal lines; the background is composed of a tall forest of papyrus trunks that end in bell-shaped flowers populated by birds.

The dominant color is the green of the plants, against which the lively reddish brown of the men's skin stands out.

The two men stand on a boat made of bound papyrus trunks. Each raises a harpoon in one hand while grasping with the other a cord tied around a hippopotamus.

The lower part of the picture is dominated by a horizontal motif formed by the canal and the boat; the harpoons held by the hunters form diagonal lines that follow the line of their shoulders and legs.

The mammal is located beneath the boat, crouching on the bottom of the canal along with a crocodile; these animals posed dangers to humans and domestic animals and were symbolic of all the forces of evil that constantly threaten the order of creation.

▲ Hunting hippopotamus in a papyrus thicket, from the Memphis necropolis, 5th dynasty, painted relief, h 107 cm, Ägyptisches Museum, Berlin, 2/70.

▶ Scene of fishing from the tomb of Ipuy at Deir el-Medina, Western Thebes, 19th dynasty.

"A happy day when we go down to the marsh, where we may snare birds and catch fish . . . we will give to everybody and light a brazier to Sobek" (The Pleasures of Fishing and Fowling)

Hunting and fishing

Hunting had been a fundamental element in the subsistence of the populations inhabiting the Nile Valley in prehistoric ages, but by historical time this activity was practiced only by semi-nomadic tribes and by Egyptian nobles, for whom it was a form of entertainment. On the edges of inhabited zones people hunted such wild animals as antelope and gazelles, sometimes even lions. Hunting was done on foot or from carts (beginning in the New Kingdom) using bows and arrows with the assistance of beaters and dogs to flush out the game. Marshlands were also areas for hunting, in particular birds, and nobles hunted together with their families on papyrus boats armed with bows and arrows or throwsticks; this was far more a matter of amusement than the procurement of necessary foodstuffs. The hunting of hippopotamuses did play an important role since the hippos lived in shallower waters and devastated both cultivated fields and herds. Armed with spears, rope, and harpoons, the hunters moved on lightweight papyrus boats, freeing the canals of the hefty animals. Quite similar tools were used in the practice of fishing, along with the use of nets, traps, fishing line, and bait. Fish had an important place in the diet of ancient Egyptians and were consumed fresh, dried, and salted. Hunting and fishing were looked upon as sacred and symbolic activities when practiced against animals that were seen as potentially dangerous.

In depth
Hunting was often given ritualistic and symbolic values, and many divinities were depicted in the act of hunting or harpooning dangerous beasts, personifications of the forces of chaos: Horus defeats the hippopotamus, Ra exterminates the serpent Apep. Onouris, an ancient hunter and warrior god, is depicted standing and throwing a lance or harpoon; venerated in particular at Sebennytus in the Delta, he was identified with Shu, god of the air, and wears a headdress adorned with four tall plumes.

Bibliography
Decker, Herb 1994.

Related entries
Livestock, Animals and plants, Food, Servants

The colors preserved in this painted fragment are vivid and richly shaded; the dominant color is the bright red of the flesh of the scribe Nebamun, who occupies the center of the composition. The blue and green of the water and plants mixes with the browns and reds of the animals.

Flowering plants rise from the papyrus thicket. Among the plants live several varieties of bird that rise in flight to flee the hunters and the cats that try to catch them. Many birds were seen as symbolic of the transmigration and resurrection of the human soul in the afterlife.

The canal beneath the boat is populated by various species of fish, animals often connected to rebirth, such as the Nile tilapia.

▲ Nebamun fowling in the marshes, from the tomb of Nebamun, Western Thebes, 18th dynasty, painted plaster, h 83 cm, British Museum, London, EA 37977.

Nebamun is standing, balanced atop a small boat made of papyrus trunks. In his right hand he holds three herons by the feet; with his left he is about to let fly a throwstick, a hunting weapon similar to a boomerang. He is dressed in a narrow skirt held tight at his waist and wears a wide necklace.

Depicting the deceased in the act of hunting was a means of expressing hope for a serene and carefree existence in the afterlife, but it also had a powerful regenerative and sensual value. Indeed, the scene is dominated by the massive presence of lotus flowers, symbolic of rebirth.

Behind Nebamun is the small figure of his wife, dressed in robes made of a luxurious fabric that drapes along her body, revealing her shape; she wears a long wig held by a crown of flowers and topped by a cone of perfumed ointment.

Nebamun's daughter is seated between his legs. She is nude, wears the sidelock typical of Egyptian children, and holds a lotus flower that prefigures the beatitude of the deceased in the afterlife.

Various species of fish have been caught in the net, others have already been transferred to one of the boats.

Fishing was one of the principal amusements of Egyptian nobles, who also participated in the hunting of such large and dangerous animals as hippopotamuses and crocodiles.

There are rowers at the far ends of each boat; all the other men are busy maneuvering and raising a net cast in the water.

All the elements are made of wood and are attached to a single base, including the net, also made of wood and brightly painted.

The Egyptians fished in the waters of the Nile using lightweight maneuverable boats made of tightly bound papyrus trunks; larger boats were not needed, given the small size of the fish.

▲ Model of boats with fishermen, from the tomb of Meketra at Deir el-Bahri, 11th dynasty, painted wood, h 31.5 cm, Egyptian Museum, Cairo, JE 46715.

Hunting in the desert is a subject often found in the tomb paintings of nobles and in the propagandistic literature of kings. This activity was considered suitable only for the upper classes, seen as a sport that permitted the display of physical and tactical skills.

Userhat and his chariot and horses are red and brown, while the antelope are rendered in ocher against a bare and colorless landscape background.

Userhat, scribe at the court of Amenhotep II, is standing on a light chariot, with rayed wheels, drawn by two horses. He draws his bow, about to release a long arrow, and has a quiver hanging from his back.

The animals are depicted massed in disorderly flight from the hunter. Some have already been struck by arrows and lie on the ground.

▲ Scene of antelope hunting from the tomb of Userhat at Sheikh Abd el-Qurna, Western Thebes, 18th dynasty.

> *"Some of their fish they dry in the sun and eat raw, but others they eat pickled in brine. Of birds they eat quails and ducks and small birds raw, having pickled them first"* (Herodotus)

Food

In depth
Herodotus reports that after flaying an ox for sacrifice the Egyptians removed the stomach and filled the body "with pure loaves of bread and with honey and raisins and figs and frankincense and myrrh and all the other spices." Then they cooked it, "pouring on an abundance of olive oil." What remained after the sacrifice was consumed by those who had performed the rite, as at a banquet.

Bibliography
Wilson 1988.

Related entries
Livestock, Animals and plants, Hunting and fishing

Scenes of offerings in Egyptian tombs present a great variety of foods, for the soul of the deceased would have need of sustenance in the afterlife. In the daily reality of Egypt, only a privileged few ate a well-rounded diet, most of the people getting by with the minimum needed for survival. Products derived from the working of grain formed the basis of the Egyptian diet: loaves and flat breads, biscuits, and a full-bodied beer, easily perishable because of the heat. Also consumed in large quantity were various types of vegetables, such as squash, melons, onions, garlic, lettuces, olives, and a great quantity of legumes, the high protein content of which made up for the scarcity of meat. Meat, in fact, was eaten rarely, a result of its high cost and the difficulties of preserving food. Beef, mutton, fowl, and fish were preserved by being dried, smoked, roasted, or pickled; their eventual consumption thus involved abundant spices to cover the aftertaste. There was also the widespread consumption of eggs and milk products, available at relatively low prices. The same applies to various types of fruit: figs, pomegranates, and dates. The sugar content of fruit was also used as a sweetener, alongside honey. The grapes that were the heart of Egypt's wine production were reserved almost exclusively to the wealthy.

▶ A princess dines on quail, from Amarna, 18th dynasty, limestone relief, h 23.5 cm, Egyptian Museum, Cairo.

The variety of baked goods, salted or sweet, included loaves, flat breads, and biscuits; most bread was leavened, but some was not. Bread was baked in a variety of different shapes: round, conical, triangular, braided, even in the shapes of animals or candies.

▲ Loaves of bread on a table, from the tomb of Kha at Deir el-Medina, Western Thebes, 18th dynasty, Fondazione Museo Antichità Egizie, Turin, S. 8343.

Since cereal grains were the principal product of Egyptian agriculture, products based on the working of barley, rye, and wheat composed the base of the Egyptian diet.

"I protected and freed the male and female slaves for their forbears, all gods, hoping to satisfy them by doing what their kas *wish" (Tutankhamen's Restoration Stele)*

Servants

In depth
Defining the legal status of Egypt's "slaves" remains difficult. Slavery understood in the classical sense was practically unknown in Egyptian society, if one excludes prisoners of war and the condemned. There were restrictions on personal freedom, forced labor on public works, mass conscription for service in military campaigns, and the exploitation of subject peoples. Those who refused forced labor were punished.

Bibliography
Della Monica 1980.

Related entries
Soldiers and the army, Foreigners, Home and family

▶ Model of woman grinding grain, from the necropolis of Memphis, 5th dynasty, painted limestone, h 25.5 cm, Museo Archeologico Nazionale, Florence, 3811.

The contents of Egyptian tombs included not only the furnishings and foods the deceased would require in the afterlife but also statuettes of servants and workers to carry on their labors for the deceased. In the reality of daily life, the more well-to-do families possessed skilled and specialized workers to take care of numerous tasks; these various services were perpetuated in the afterlife by way of "funerary models," statuettes reproducing activities of daily life that would magically come to life. Practically all types of daily labor are depicted: the peasant with his hoe or leading a plow drawn by oxen cultivating a field; peasants bearing baskets of grain on their heads as they move toward a granary; grain being mashed to make beer or ground to obtain the flour used by bakers busy baking conical or round loaves. Stockbreeders tend to their animals in stalls, others lead the animals before the owner so he can look them over. Butchers and cooks are busy preparing beef, game, poultry. Boats bearing men and merchandise include the necessary oarsmen; small papyrus boats carry fishermen with their nets, traps, and harpoons. Other cooks prepare fish for roasting. There are then weavers, carpenters, potters, musicians, and long rows of bearers with offerings of all types in their hands

or on their heads; the food offerings themselves are sometimes reproduced in miniature.

Servants prepared food for the members of their owner's family; much attention went to the kitchen, where it was important to maintain good hygiene and keep the foods clean and fresh.

Beef, mutton, and the meat of wild animals was roasted and eaten with abundant spices, or it was boiled or stewed to maintain its flavor and softness.

Birds were preferred roasted on charcoal or spitted; they were sometimes smoked and stored in large sealed jars.

Because of the hot weather, meat was difficult to preserve and had to be cooked before being stored. Drying was the preferred method for fish and the meat of small animals.

▲ Model of servant cooking a bird, from the tomb of Niankhpepi at Meir, 6th dynasty, painted wood, h 24 cm, Egyptian Museum, Cairo, CG 235.

The proper management of the domestic sphere was entrusted to experienced, loyal servants. The many important chores that needed to be done required the coordination of the activities of workers, stockbreeders, cooks, gardeners, peasants, and many other laborers.

Activities like fishing, hunting, and stockbreeding required numerous specialized workers, and the procurement of food supplies often meant journeys over long distances.

▲ Scene of work from the tomb of Nefer and Ka-hay at Saqqara, 5th dynasty, painted relief.

"You are young and you have taken a wife, you have founded your hearth; take interest in whom you have brought into the world, of each one that you have cradled" (Teachings of Ani)

Home and family

The great quantity of surviving documents makes it possible to delineate the salient characteristics of domestic life in ancient Egypt. Marriage was at the base of the formation of the family, although instances of premarital cohabitation are known. Marriage was seen as an agreement between the spouses and had no religious significance. In theory, husband and wife enjoyed the same rights, and all the children could inherit from both parents, although the parents could establish inheritance in wills. The birth of descendents guaranteed continuity, and the young were thus exhorted to marry and generate many heirs. Because of the high rate of infant mortality, each family brought into the world a large number of children in the hope that some would survive. A married woman was called the "Lady of the House," to indicate that she was the director of family life, in charge of the maintenance and administration of the various domestic activities. Homes were generally on a single floor, with rooms giving onto an open area. The principal areas were a reception room, private rooms, and service areas, such as the kitchen, storeroom, pantry, and washroom. The most prestigious homes also had gardens with ponds and small lakes, while farms had stalls, chicken coops, granaries, and areas for winemaking or for artisan activities, such as carpentry, weaving, and pottery.

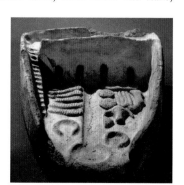

In depth
Bes was a very popular divinity during the New Kingdom, protector and guardian of family life, the home, pregnancy, and also sleep. He is a hideous dwarf with a brutish face, bushy beard, and drooping tongue. He wears a crown of ostrich feathers and carries a sword to ward off demoniac spirits.

Related entries
Village organization, Servants, Women

Bibliography
Janssen, Janssen 1990
Janssen, Janssen 1996

◄ Model in terracotta of a house, Middle Kingdom, Musée du Louvre, Paris.

The scene depicts Inherkau and his wife seated together in an attitude of great familiarity, while their two sons make offerings (only one is visible) and their grandchildren play at their feet.

Inherkau, a foreman of the necropolis workers, is shown seated with his wife dressed in long white robes, some with the long, puffy sleeves typical of the New Kingdom; the wigs are tight to the head, curly and braided, those of the males cut at an oblique angle.

The children are depicted naked, as was ordinary in Egypt, with curious hairstyles with bangs and curls; they wear bracelets and anklets.

▲ The family of Inherkau (detail) from the tomb of Inherkau at Deir el-Medina, Western Thebes, 20th dynasty.

The principal moral values of the Egyptians were those related to private life and the family. It was the duty of parents to provide the best conditions for their children's growth, while children were called on to care for their parents in old age and to provide everything necessary for their mortuary homes.

Dwarfism was a somewhat widespread phenomenon in ancient Egypt and was not a reason for social discrimination; dwarfs often held high positions at court and in harems, worked as artisans, and enjoyed the protection of the god Bes.

Seneb's wife sits beside him, dressed in white with pale skin; she tenderly embraces her husband, one arm around his shoulders.

This statuary group presents the family of Seneb, head of the royal dwarfs and funerary priest of Khufu. He is presented seated cross-legged, an expedient with which the artist manages to disguise his size.

The empty space beneath Seneb's legs is occupied by the figures of his two children. From the ideal point of view the children represent a support for their father. This positioning gives the composition symmetry while adding lively realism to the figures.

The children are naked and hold a finger to their lips. In keeping with artistic conventions, the male has dark skin, the female pale.

▲ Statuary group of the dwarf Seneb and his family, from the mastaba of Seneb at Giza, 4th dynasty, painted limestone, h 34 cm, Egyptian Museum, Cairo, JE 51280.

"The coppersmith at his toil at the mouth of his furnace, his fingers like crocodile skin, his stench worse than fish eggs"
(Satire of the Trades)

Artisans

In depth
Administrative documents reveal that workers were paid in kind: water, fish, wine, honey, oil. The workers at Deir el-Medina received about 5 kg of grain and almost 2 of barley to make bread and beer. On building worksites the overseers received 10 loaves, designers 6, foremen 5, sculptors 2, and laborers 1.

Bibliography
Lucas, Harris 1962.

Related entries
Court artists, Servants, Home and family, Ptah, Commerce

A splendid catalog of the various artisan activities performed by Egyptians can be found on the walls of the tomb of the vizier Rekhmire, who lived in Thebes during the 18th dynasty. The depictions include artists intent on woodworking and carpentry, producing furniture for the tomb. There are jewelers who make jewelry and objects of goldwork to adorn their master's house of eternity. Carpenters plane, smooth, assemble, and finish the pieces that are the framework of a boat; beside them sculptors and stone workers are busy in the creation of statues and other objects of art. Basketmakers weave plant fibers to make containers in various sizes and shapes, rope makers twist cords, potters shape containers for food and beverages, tanners work the leather with which they will produce purses and sandals, masons mix mud and straw to make bricks. Cooks produce grain, bread, and beer; butchers cut up bovines, goats, sheep, or geese, others slice roast fish and quail while perfumers create and bottle essences extracted from flowers and spices. All these products are presented to the deceased in a long procession of offering servants. The idea of providing the tomb with everything needed in the afterlife is also made explicit by the presence in tombs of funerary models, statuettes of artisans, servants, and peasants, as well as miniature replicas of their necessary tools.

► Chest for linens, from Gebelein, 4th dynasty, wood incrusted with ivory and faience, h 19 cm, Fondazione Museo Antichità Egizie, Turin, S. 15709.

The depictions are dominated by such clear descriptive realism that it is possible to recognize the typical body motions and tools for every activity. The lively composition is crowded with figures, giving the scene a sense of great busyness.

In the upper level are the leather workers: the hides, stretched for drying, were smoothed, cut, and worked for the production of various accessories, most of all sandals; footwear was also made of plant fiber.

The central part presents various stages in the work of carpenters: some cut wood with toothed saws, others plane planks, some make holes with bow drills, yet others finish a large covered chest with chisels and graving tools.

The tomb of the vizier Rekhmire, who lived during the reigns of Thutmose III and Amenhotep II, is decorated with numerous scenes of workers and artisans, probably working on objects given to the vizier.

▲ Scenes of woodworking and carpentry, from the tomb of the vizier Rekhmire, Sheikh Abd el-Qurna, Western Thebes, 18th dynasty.

Metallurgy required great experience, especially in the steps of fusion and casting. Very high temperatures were needed to make metals liquefy in melting pots. Bellows worked with the feet were used to feed the flames.

Objects produced in series, such as some architectural elements and parts for weapons, were made in molds: the liquid metal was poured into the mold and left to cool.

To make bricks, a mixture of mud and straw was poured into square molds and left in the sun to dry; once removed from the mold the brick was ready for use.

The production of building materials required a large number of workers. The mud for making bricks had to be cleaned and mixed with water and straw to achieve compactness. The mixture was made in vats, stirred, and trod upon to eliminate air bubbles.

▲ Scenes of metallurgy and building, from the tomb of the vizier Rekhmire, Sheikh Abd el-Qurna, Western Thebes, 18th dynasty.

"She is one girl, there is no one like her. She is more beautiful than any other. Look, she is like a star goddess arising at the beginning of a happy new year" (Love poem quoted in Manniche 1987)

Women

During the pharaonic period, women enjoyed the legal status of autonomous individuals. They enjoyed rights, could own goods and dispose of them at will, and were ruled by the same laws as men. Of course, belonging to a high-ranking family and having a respectable genealogy were factors of great prestige, and the ties between generations ran deep. It was considered unseemly for a child to abandon elderly parents and not recompense them for the sacrifices made to raise him. However, having reached their majority, young people could leave the paternal household, free from parental power and in possession of a personal patrimony. During the more turbulent periods of Egyptian history, when the lack of state cohesion meant individuals were not granted their full rights, women were subject to marital authority. The primary role performed by women in Egyptian society is attested to by the various important queens who often ruled as regents for children. There were also female priests invested with great financial and political power. Even so, the ideal female was still seen as the faithful wife and the loving mother, the careful administrator of the household economy. There were also different stereotypes of beauty and sensuality, as represented by dancers, musicians, and obviously prostitutes, although the wise cautioned men against their company, so as not to fall into vice.

In depth
Many divinities are associated with the world of women. Among the major gods, Hathor is the goddess of love and beauty and Isis is the loving mother and faithful wife. On a more popular level, Bes protects the home and family, while Taueret was the goddess of childbirth, often depicted as a pregnant hippopotamus with large breasts.

Bibliography
Robins 1993.

Related entries
Hathor, Home and family, Eroticism and seduction, Aesthetics and style

◄ Model of offering bearer from the tomb of Meketra at Deir el-Bahri, 11th dynasty, painted wood, h 123 cm, Egyptian Museum, Cairo, JE 46725.

During the Old Kingdom women played an important role in domestic life and in society in general, since landed properties were handed down from mother to daughter; aside from the exceptions of various queens and priestesses, women did not, however, occupy political or public positions.

Women are often depicted together with their husbands during everyday work activities, such as inspecting property, counting livestock, or overseeing the work of laborers. The presence of women at celebrations and banquets testifies to the relative social freedom enjoyed by Egyptian women compared to the women in other ancient societies.

The hierarchical differences between the sexes were very marked, especially in earlier epochs. Thus the woman was always depicted as smaller than her father or husband, sometimes kneeling before or seated to the left of her companion, emphasizing her lesser social importance.

▲ Family group from Memphis, 5th–6th dynasty, painted limestone, h 73.5 cm, Brooklyn Museum, New York, 3717E.

Beginning in the reign of Amenhotep III the "great royal wife" was depicted constantly beside the king, supporting his political decisions and personifying the gentle side of his propaganda. In the same way, the presence of Nefertiti beside Akhenaten became a constant feature of Amarnian art.

The bride of Ramses II, Nefertari Merienmut ("The most beautiful, beloved of Mut"), was the object of a particular devotion on the part of her husband, who dedicated the Small Temple of Abu Simbel to her, in which the queen assumed the form of Hathor, with these words: "Ramses II has made a temple, excavated in the mountain, of eternal workmanship, for the chief queen Nefertari, beloved of Mut, in Nubia, forever and ever, Nefertari, for whose sake the very sun does shine."

The image itself of the queen assumed a divine role, as happened for Ahmes-Nefertari, mother of Amenhotep I, for Tiy, mother of Amenhotep IV, and for the mother of Ramses II, Tuya. Temples and shrines were dedicated to their worship, and they enjoyed great popular devotion.

Just as the pharaoh was the living image of Horus, his queen represented the incarnation of the divine female essence and was identified with Isis-Hathor.

▲ Statue of Queen Tuya, mother of Ramses II, Great Temple at Abu Simbel, 19th dynasty.

With few exceptions, only the sons of wealthy families received scholastic educations; they attended the school at a temple or, in the wealthiest families, were educated by a private tutor. The children of peasants received no education whatsoever, while the sons of artisans soon enough began their apprenticeship in the workshop.

Children were nursed until the age of three; by their fourth year they could begin school. Nursing was continued a long time, providing the child with a healthy diet while postponing the mother's next pregnancy.

Women's chores were related to domestic activities: cleaning the house, preparing meals, doing the wash, collecting food. Women had the help of at least one servant in the performance of their chores, except in cases of extreme poverty.

To feed, care for, and raise a child was a chore exclusive to Egyptian women, who are often presented while holding their child in a shawl knotted behind. The mother could thus nurse the child while performing other activities.

▲ Mother with child, from the tomb of Montuemhat at Assasif, Western Thebes, 25th–26th dynasty, painted limestone, h 23.9 cm, Brooklyn Museum, New York, 4874.

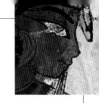

"With his hair, he throws against me his nets; with his eyes he makes me prisoner; with his ornaments, he takes over me"
(Beginning words of a spell)

Eroticism and seduction

Quite naturally, the Egyptians included good food, music, and love among the pleasures of life. The banquet scenes included in tomb decorations are populated by men and women dressed in fine, almost transparent fabrics, adorned with sumptuous jewels, wearing thick, curly wigs sometimes surmounted by perfumed cones. Dress and makeup constituted a major factor in erotic attraction, and for women wigs played an important role in the game of seduction. Many tales of mythological subjects are pervaded by sensuality, sometimes as a way of emphasizing in a ritual way the fecundating and regenerative powers of many divinities, such as Amon, Min, Hathor, and Isis. Related to this was the custom of putting in tombs dolls shaped like naked women with exaggerated sexual attributes; such "concubines of the dead" had the precise scope of reawakening virility and generative energy. Explicitly sexual or obscene images are relatively rare, limited to popular settings and perhaps used as good-luck charms. There was no lack of veiled references to the intimacy of couples, as in scenes of feasts, hunting, or music, usually accentuated by the presence of details with an erotic value, such as lotus flowers, mandrake roots, poppies, musical instruments played by women, or the jewels typical of the worship of the goddess of love, Hathor.

In depth
Aphrodisiacal formulas: to make a woman love her husband: "Grind acacia seeds with honey, rub your phallus with it, and sleep with the woman." To force a woman to enjoy intercourse: "Rub your phallus with the foam of a stallion and sleep with the woman." (Papyrus London BM 10070 and Papyrus Leiden J. 383, from Manniche 1987)

Bibliography
Manniche 1997.

Related entries
Hathor, Home and family, Women, Entertainment, Aesthetics and style

◀ Sistrum rattle with Hathoric top-piece, Late Period, bronze, Fondazione Museo Antichità Egizie, Turin.

Near the guests are always tables laden with food and drinks of every sort as well as young servants ready to be helpful.

Parties and banquets were social occasions during which upper-crust families entertained one another; naturally, they were also ideal occasions for the public display of the symbols of social status: beauty, wealth, power.

Men and women appear dressed in fine fabrics wearing wigs decorated with floral diadems or perfumed cones and show off elaborate jewelry.

Such banquet scenes are full of telling details that create an atmosphere of sensuality. The clothes are low-cut and more or less transparent, while the makeup, wigs, and jewels enhance the sense of femininity and sexual attraction.

Affectionate gestures among the guests add to the sense of intimacy; girls caress one another, adjust one another's clothes, feed one another bits of food. In such instances, eroticism is depicted by way of a fleeting gesture and is not the subject of an explicit allusion.

▲ Banquet scene from the tomb of Nebamun, Western Thebes, 18th dynasty, painted plaster, h 76 cm, British Museum, London, EA 38986.

Atop their wigs the girls wear a lotus flower, symbol of rebirth and pleasure; their clothing consists of only a belt. One of them, seen frontally to display her sex organs, looks in a mirror to apply makeup.

Objects associated with the worship of female divinities appear in the scene, including a sistrum and a vase of wine or perfume held by a man.

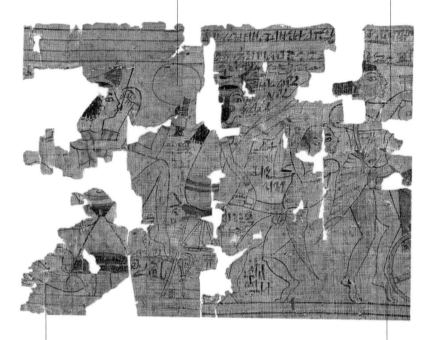

Obscene illustrations are somewhat rare in Egyptian art, but there are scenes of explicit eroticism and sexuality. Such works were usually related to the sphere of popular art and had a good-luck value in terms of promoting fecundity.

This papyrus, today preserved in Turin, has a somewhat satiric tone as a hyperbolic caricature of reality, as in the exaggerated size of the phalluses and the almost bestial faces of the men.

▲ Scene from the Erotic Papyrus, from Deir el-Medina, 19th–20th dynasty, h 21 cm, Fondazione Museo Antichità Egizie, Turin, S. 11198.

Figures of nude women with blatantly indicated sexual attributes are often found in tombs, including those of the earliest periods. They wear heavy wigs, often made of wire or foil, and jewels to enhance their feminine sexual attraction.

The girls are often supine on a bed, sometimes with the figure of a child beside them. The purpose is clear: such images were meant to serve regenerative and procreative purposes.

The statuettes were meant to reawaken the virility and fecundity of the deceased.

In a society with peasant origins, sex was understood not just as the occasion for amorous pleasure but as a fundamental aspect of procreation. Thus also in the afterlife it would be important for the deceased to come back into possession of his regenerative abilities.

▲ Statuettes known as "concubines of the dead," Middle–New Kingdom, Fondazione Museo delle Antichità Egizie, Turin, S. 1236.

"I sing to you, intoxicated by your beauty, my hands set on the harp of the singer" (Hymn to Amon, Papyrus Chester Beatty IV)

Entertainment

The social life of ancient Egyptians was often enlivened by the presence of musicians and dancers. Differing occasions called for different melodies and movements, and today it is possible to get only the most generic sense of their meaning. During sacred events, rhythmic and harmonious sounds and movements served to accompany or emphasize certain ritual gestures; sistrum rattles and crotal bells were used, along with chants and handclapping. The sounds of flutes and tambourines signaled passing time to fieldworkers, and singing served to alleviate their fatigue; far more intense were the rhythms of the trumpets and horns that drove soldiers forward into battle. Intimate social moments were accompanied by the music of harps, lutes, flutes, and tambourines, with songs that extolled the joys of earthly life and conviviality. There were also dances, often of an acrobatic nature. Funerals involved processions of musicians and dancers. Nor did the Egyptians lack games, such as the famous *senet*, played on a board with twenty or thirty squares. There was also the game of "dog and jackal." These were table games, with various types of gaming pieces whose movement was determined by throwing flat sticks or knucklebones instead of dice. As early as the Old Kingdom there was the "game of the serpent," played on a circular board in the shape of a coiled snake, its body divided in squares along which the pieces advanced.

In depth
As early as the New Kingdom, the game of *senet* (Egyptian for "plan, project") served a funerary value and was cited in Chapter 17 of the *Book of the Dead* as an indispensable tool for survival in the afterlife: victory in a game against an invisible adversary guaranteed the purity of the heart of the deceased.

Bibliography
Manniche 1991.

Related entries
Hathor, Home and family

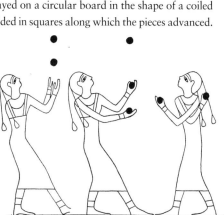

◀ Drawing of dancers playing with balls, from the tomb of Baqet III at Beni Hasan, Middle Kingdom.

The "game of the serpent" got its name from the shape of the board along which the pieces were moved. The body of a coiled serpent is divided in squares that form the route of the pieces, probably in a way similar to the classical "goose game."

The top of the box was used for playing "twenty squares," a variant of senet in which the pieces moved on the basis of points obtained by casting knucklebones.

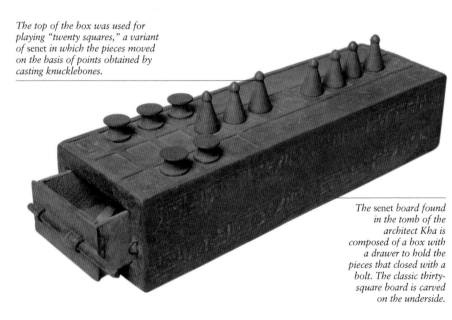

The senet board found in the tomb of the architect Kha is composed of a box with a drawer to hold the pieces that closed with a bolt. The classic thirty-square board is carved on the underside.

▲ Game of the serpent, from Qau, Predynastic Period, limestone, diameter 28.8 cm, Petrie Museum, London, UC 20453.

▲ *Senet* box and board, from the tomb of Kha at Deir el-Medina, Western Thebes, 18th dynasty, wood, h 8 cm, Fondazione Museo Antichità Egizie, Turin, S. 8451.

Dancing included purely acrobatic movements, such as that performed by this girl. She wears only a cloth at her waist and a pair of round earrings.

Men and women performed dances, but mixed groups were rare.

The girl's long, thick hair falls to the ground, giving the composition a sense of realistic movement. The pink color of the girl's skin is enlivened by darker shadings in some areas to indicate shadows.

Male or female, dancers performed in groups, as couples, or as soloists, and they created true choreography; sometimes they used objects, such as small balls, sticks, and ropes.

▲ Ostracon with figure of dancer, from Deir el-Medina, 19th–20th dynasty, painted limestone, h 10.4 cm, Fondazione Museo Antichità Egizie, Turin, C. 7052.

Dance and music were the usual accompaniments for civil and religious celebrations and for special events in social life, such as weddings and banquets.

Musical instruments were of several types: percussion (drums, tambourines, sistrums, castanets, and crotal bells), wind (panpipes, oboes, trumpets), and stringed (lutes, harps, lyres).

Certain instruments were largely used on festive occasions, and their sound accompanied occasions of pleasure and intoxication. Banquet scenes are enlivened by the presence of young female musicians wearing transparent clothes.

Harps and lutes were particularly popular for the creation of an intimate atmosphere and can be found in scenes of family life as well as amorous moments.

▲ Banquet scene with female musicians and dancers, from the tomb of Nebamun, Western Thebes, 18th dynasty, painted plaster, h 61 cm, British Museum, London, EA 37984.

► Chest for beauty products, from the tomb of Kha at Deir el-Medina, Western Thebes, 18th dynasty, painted wood, h 29 cm, Fondazione Museo Antichità Egizie, Turin, S. 8479.

"Put fine linen on your body, and for her make a bed of royal linen. Be careful in the use of bed sheets, spreading them with perfumed essence" (Ramessid lyrics: "Desires of love")

Aesthetics and style

The Egyptians devoted great attention to cosmetics not only for their ornamental value but for their ritual and therapeutic uses, especially in the prevention of eye infections and the treatment of burns. The many medical prescriptions known from papyri often relate to an aesthetic, rather than a curative, use, as with the ointments to diminish wrinkles, combat baldness, or dye hair. Perhaps staying youthful looking and pleasing was seen as a way to maintain one's health. Great attention was also devoted to personal hygiene to avoid infections and parasites; there were body deodorants and breath fresheners, and perfumes for the skin and the hair. Incense, resins, and terebinth were used to purify the air. Red ocher was used to color cheeks and lips, henna to color hair and nails, and kohl mixed with coloring powder was used to darken the outlines of the eyes. Men usually dressed in a simple skirt, women wore a top with shoulder straps. Over time, Egyptian clothing was embellished with veils and shawls, folds and draping, belts, and other precious accessories that were also a means of displaying social status. The well-to-do were distinguished most of all by their sandals, made of papyrus or leather in a wide variety of styles. Wigs were used for both hygienic and aesthetic reasons, and the styles for men and women could be braided, curled, short or long, even decorated with diadems and flowers.

In depth
"To strengthen the hair of a woman use castor beans, ground, and prepare a paste to put on the head with fat" (Ebers Papyrus, 251c). Terebinth: odorous resin, burned to purify the air. Henna: plant from the Near East, source of a strong dye for hair, skin, and nails. Kohl: colorant for the eyes and eyelashes obtained from manganese and antimony, with antibacterial properties.

Bibliography
Manniche 1999.

Related entries
Home and family, Eroticism and seduction

The eyes of the two statues are not painted but rather inlaid with quartz and transparent rock crystal; the effect is a lifelike expression still impressive today.

Rahotep is dressed in a simple skirt and wears a thin necklace with a pendant; his wig is short and tight-fitting. In keeping with the style of the period, he has a thin black mustache, typical of the portraiture of the 4th dynasty.

The two statues, although carved in blocks, represent a single group not only conceptually but artistically. The spouses are seated on a white cubic throne with a high back and stare straight ahead.

Nofret is dressed in a long white tunic with wide shoulder straps over which is a smooth cloak of the same color. She wears a wide necklace with pendants and a shoulder-length thick wig. She wears a diadem decorated with rosettes and floral motifs.

▲ Statuary group of Rahotep and Nofret, from the tomb of Rahotep at Meidum, 4th dynasty, painted limestone, h 122 cm, Egyptian Museum, Cairo, CG 3, 4.

The wig is massive, composed of groups of very thin braids held by horizontal bands and topped by a floral diadem. A two-budded lotus flower descends to decorate her forehead, covering the edge of the wig. Her face is framed by ringlets.

The eyes are large, and the line of the upper eyelid is marked; eyelashes and eyebrows are emphasized by a thick line of dark bister.

This statue was part of a group that included her husband, the general Nakhtmin; both were made in crystalline limestone, which gives them an almost glassy shininess. They originally formed a single statue that is today fragmentary.

The woman wears a gown typical of the end of the 18th dynasty, in light linen, draped on her body in a way that brings out her form. The sleeves extend to the elbow with a large pleated opening.

The jewelry the woman wears is composed of a necklace of six strands of beads and a bracelet. In her left hand she holds a menat necklace made of beads and grasped by a handle-shaped counterpoise decorated with a rosette. The jewel is associated with the worship of the goddess Hathor.

▲ Statue of the wife of Nakhtmin, from Thebes, 18th dynasty, limestone, h 85 cm, Egyptian Museum, Cairo, CG 779 B.

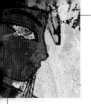

"Prestigious public collections or modest groups of personal souvenirs, every evocation of Egypt's pharaonic past inevitably includes objects in enameled paste" (F. Lavenex Vergès)

Glass and faience

In depth
"Egyptian blue" is a typical color of Egyptian glass; its imitations are opaque vitreous glass.
The term *Egyptian faience* is sometimes inaccurately applied to all the ancient Egyptian objects with a siliceous body and a glassy coating, while it is an enameling with tin oxide.

Bibliography
Verges 1992.
Nicholson 1993.

Related entries
Commerce, Artisans

The products of Egypt's artisan crafts included several special types that required the true mastery of technologies and materials. Chief among these is the art of glassmaking, known in Egypt since earliest times. The materials for the production of glass paste were abundantly present: quartz, sand, and silicates, which melt at relatively low temperature with natron or ashes. In its rough state this glass was not shiny and bright but opaque; coloration was obtained by mixing iron oxides into the base material. Beginning in the New Kingdom, probably following contact with the Near East, Egyptian glass production reached levels of excellence, as indicated by the blue containers with white and yellow rippling, sometimes made in the shape of animals, made to hold the perfumes and cosmetics exported from Egypt throughout the Mediterranean world. Egyptian faience is not earthenware but is obtained from a nucleus of quartz covered by a siliceous glaze that gives it a brilliant patina. The paste obtained in this way could imitate far more precious materials, such as turquoise, lapis lazuli, or carnelian, according to the col-

oration obtained. The chromatic range included colors like cream, red, brown, pale green, indigo, turquoise, and even black. Aside from statuettes, amulets, and jewels, the glazed paste was used to made incrustations for wood or stone statues.

▶ Statuette of seated monkey, New Kingdom, faience, h 5.4 cm, Brooklyn Museum, New York, 48181.

Small containers for cosmetics and perfumes were made by trailing molten glass over a core made of a clay mixture. Rods of colored glass were then wrapped around the body. Egyptian beauty products were renowned throughout the Mediterranean, and they were exported in containers like this.

The painted decoration of flowers and plants creates the aquatic environment in which the mammal lived.

The figure of the hippopotamus had various values in Egyptian religion. Very often the animal is identified with savage and destructive forces, but is it also the personification of the goddess Taueret, protector of childbirth and fecundity.

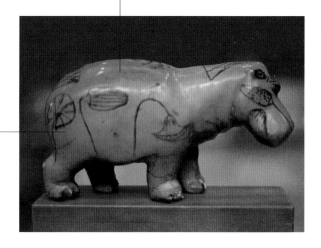

▲ Glass bottle in the form of a fish, from Amarna, 18th dynasty, blue glass with decoration in yellow and white glass, 14.5 cm long, British Museum, London, EA 55193.

▲ Figurine of hippopotamus with floral decorations, from Thebes, Middle Kingdom, faience, h 11.5 cm, Egyptian Museum, Cairo, JE 21365.

The world of the dead

◀ Funeral banquet (detail) from
the tomb of Ramose, Western
Thebes, 18th dynasty.

"He will be laid in the coffin and committed to earth; his name will not perish from the earth, for men will remember him on account of his virtues" (The Tale of the Eloquent Peasant)

Death as rebirth

In depth
With regard to death, Egyptian beliefs established a perfect continuity between the world of the living and that of the dead. The living turned to their dear departed for help, explaining their difficulties and requesting their intervention; they did this using letters, communicating with the dead exactly as they would with the living. The letter was "addressed" to the eternal resting place of the deceased, and the text was either engraved on the bowls that held the funerary offerings to the deceased or was transcribed to papyrus.

Bibliography
Assmann 2005.

Related entries
Heliopolitan cosmogony, Maat, Ra and Apep, Funerary rites, Weighing the soul, Books of the Dead

One of the most original and striking concepts elaborated by Egyptian religious thought was its concept of death. Death was perceived as an important interruption in the course of existence, but it was not looked upon as a definitive annihilation and was seen instead as an alteration that was part of a dynamic cycle of rejuvenation and regeneration. For gods as well as for humans, the transient state of the created cosmos, subject to the progressive erosion of time, could be eluded only through a constant process of death and rebirth. This implied a concept of existence characterized by continuous renewal, as was the case with nature, with its seasonal cycles, as well as with the sun, with its alternation of rising and setting. The Egyptian term *kheper*, translatable as "to become" and "transformation," indicated both the existence and the biological maturation of an individual. This dynamic aspect was the central idea in Egyptian thought concerning death: a thread that connected life and death in a single route of continuous transformation that had its ultimate completion in the assumption of the spirit of the deceased within the immutable cycles of nature, as a star in the firmament or aboard Ra's solar boat in its daily journey across the sky.

The inscription identifies the figure depicted as the draftsman (in Egyptian, sesh kedut) Inherkhau.

It seems probable that the Benu bird represents one of the principal prototypes behind the myth of the phoenix and that the image of the heron atop the primordial mound, also called the "island of the flame," furnished the mythical material later reworked into the legends surrounding the rebirth of the phoenix from its ashes.

▲ Vignette of Formula 83 from the *Book of the Dead*, from the tomb of Inherkhau at Deir el-Medina, 20th dynasty.

◄ Atum-Ra in the form of the cat of Heliopolis destroys Apep under the sacred Ished tree, from the tomb of Inherkhau at Deir el-Medina, 20th dynasty.

*The bird known to the ancient Egyptians as the "Benu bird" is the grey heron (*Ardea cinerea*), common in the Delta marshes from earliest times. The image of the bird with its legs rising from the water may have induced Egyptian mythologizers to include it in the Heliopolitan creation myth as a manifestation of the sun-god Ra rising from the primordial waters. During the New Kingdom it appeared in the* Book of the Dead, *most especially in vignettes illustrating the "formula for taking the shape of the Benu bird" (Formula 83), which the deceased followed in the hope of transforming himself into the fabulous bird so as to fly into the afterlife as a reborn spirit.*

Apep is depicted while wrapping himself to form 12 coils, the 12 nocturnal hours that Atum-Ra must overcome to rise in the morning.

The mythical encounter between Ra and Apep suggests a contrast between two different concepts of time, the dynamic and the static. Ra is born and ages every day so he can be reborn the following morning, whereas Apep is destroyed every night by Ra but returns each time in his original form because he is an expression of the immobile and immutable continuity of chaos.

This image depicts a scene from the third division of the Book of Gates, which relates one of the central myths concerning the Egyptian idea of death and the passage of time: the nightly battle between Ra and Apep. What distinguished the ordered cosmos from fearsome chaos, of which Apep is a personification, was the cyclical process of regeneration that could be found in all manifestations of creation but that was completely absent in the formless and changeless mass of chaos.

Atum-Ra slays Apep with a lance. This iconic image was to have enormous diffusion, and by way of numerous interpolations it became the prototype for the Christian iconography of St. George and the Dragon.

▲ Atum-Ra slays Apep, from the tomb of Ramses I in the Valley of the Kings, Western Thebes, north wall of Burial Chamber J, 19th dynasty.

"When they have done this [lamented the dead] they carry the corpse to the embalming. There are those who set themselves to this very trade and make it their special craft" (Herodotus)

Embalming

Egyptian funerary doctrine held that preservation of the body of the deceased was an absolute necessity, for on it depended the survival of the spirit in the afterlife. For this reason, the Egyptians became masters in the techniques of embalming corpses, a practice that led to knowledge of human anatomy and physiology and thus to notable advances in medical science. A corpse could be embalmed in a variety of ways, depending on the amount the family was willing to pay. In its most complete form, the process required about 70 days and involved at least three distinct phases: evisceration, desiccation, and wrapping, each phase accompanied by ritual recitations and funerary formulas. The body was delivered to the embalmers three or four days after death, at which point the viscera were extracted by way of an incision opened in the side, between the umbilicus and the groin. Through this opening, the lungs, intestines, and liver were removed, spread with a warm resinous glue, and deposited in canopic jars (the heart was kept in the body). The brain, to which the Egyptians attributed little importance, was removed through the nose and discarded. The body was then placed in a bath of granulated natron (sodium carbonate) for 40 days, which completely dried it. After having been repeatedly spread with oils and perfumed essences, the body of the deceased was wrapped in strips of cloth, a process that took roughly fifteen days.

In depth
The term *mummy*, commonly used to indicate the bodies preserved by the Egyptian method of embalming, is an ancient Persian word for bitumen. The term was first employed by classical authors writing about the blackish appearance of certain embalmed bodies in Egypt. This phenomenon was a result of the use of bitumen in the process of embalming, a custom that spread in Egypt only beginning in the Roman Period.

Bibliography
Ikram, Dodson 1998, chap. III.

Related entries
The Osirian drama, Death as rebirth, Funerary rites

◄ Anubis (detail), from the tomb of Horemheb I in the Valley of the Kings, Western Thebes, 18th dynasty.

These four pictures, part of the decoration of the tomb of Tjai, present stages in mummification (left) and the preparation of a sarcophagus (right). In the scene shown here, embalmers are wrapping a body.

In the upper box to the right, carpenters plane a sarcophagus.

The bandages are soaked in resin to make them bind together.

The surface of the sarcophagus is cleaned and decorated.

▲ The wrapping of the mummy and the preparation of the sarcophagus, drawing based on the decoration of the tomb of Tjai, Western Thebes, 19th dynasty.

This knife belonged to an embalmer named Min-Mesut, whose name was engraved on the blade.

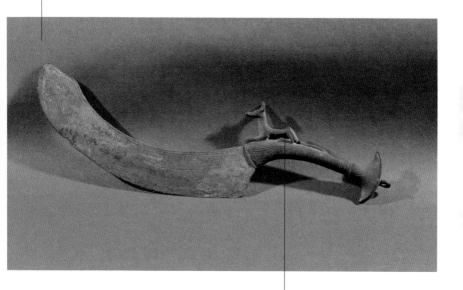

The tool is made entirely of bronze and is embellished by several details, such as the statuette of crouching Anubis and the grip ending in the shape of a papyrus flower.

▲ Knife of the embalmer Min-Mesut, New Kingdom, bronze, 24.5 cm long, Musée du Louvre, Paris, N2116.

Hapi (baboon-headed) protects the lungs together with Nephthys.

Imsety (human-headed) and Isis guard the liver.

Duamutef (jackal-headed) and Neith protect the stomach.

Qebehsenuf (falcon-headed) and Selqet are custodians of the intestines

The covers of the jars were entrusted to the sons of Horus, but the jars were protected by four goddesses: Isis, Nephthys, Neith, and Selqet. An inscription on the body of each jar bears an invocation from the goddess responsible for the jar to Osiris, asking him to protect the organs that are preserved therein. Together with the mummification of the body, the preservation of certain organs helped guarantee survival of the deceased in the afterlife.

Canopic jars get their name from a scholarly misunderstanding of the early 20th century when the jars were taken as proof of a local cult dedicated to Canopus, the pilot of Menelaus's ship, who died on the site of the ancient Egyptian city named for him. Today the usage is universally accepted.

▲ Canopic jars of the dignitary Uahibra, from Memphis (?), alabaster, h 36.5 cm. Fondazione Museo Antichità Egizie, Turin, C. 3208.

"The sky is open for you, the earth is open, the road to Duat [the underworld] lies open. You rise with Ra, you walk with broad strides" (Opening of the Mouth ceremony)

Funerary rites

Having completed the process of embalming, the deceased was ready for the funeral. Before burial, an extremely important ritual had to be performed, the Opening of the Mouth ceremony. This ceremony, first indicated in the Old Kingdom, had the precise purpose of magically getting the deceased to identify himself with his statue and then "animating" the statue so it would be able to host the spirit of the deceased each time it wanted to return to earth to receive offerings. The ceremony was usually performed in a place called the House of Gold, the workshop annexed to the temple where statues and all religious and funerary furnishings were made. The officiant magically "opened" the eyes and the mouth of the statue, touching them with a long curved instrument. This was followed by purifying fumigations, lustrations, and the recitation of formulas to animate the statute, which was then clothed and honored with offerings. During the New Kingdom, the ritual was extended to the mummy of the deceased before it was closed in its sarcophagus, and frescoes in tombs from that period indicate that the ceremony could also be performed directly in front of the entrance to the tomb.

A procession bore the deceased and his tomb furnishings to the area in the tomb where, from then on, family members would periodically go to bring food, drink, and flowers to guarantee the survival of the deceased in the afterlife.

Bibliography
Goyon 1972.
Assmann 2000.

Related entries
Priests, Magic, Embalming, Weighing the soul, Books of the Dead

▼ Funerary ceremony of Kha from the *Book of the Dead* in the tomb of Kha at Deir el-Medina, Fondazione Museo Antichità Egizie, Turin, S. 8438.

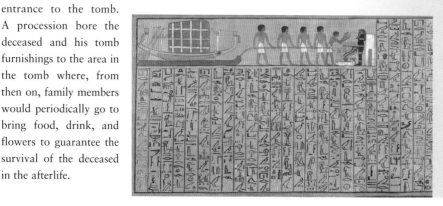

A priest wearing the characteristic panther skin offers incense, libations, and food to the deceased. Ahead of him two attendants perform the Opening of the Mouth ceremony, touching the lips of the deceased with a short curved instrument.

The god Anubis, conductor of souls, supports the mummy, preparing the deceased for the journey to the afterlife, while a group of women from his family lament his death.

Over the course of the New Kingdom, the Opening of the Mouth ceremony was added to the rituals performed at the entrance to the tomb. The version of the ritual presented here is from the tomb of the royal scribe Hunefer.

Beginning in the 19th dynasty, votive steles were no longer placed inside tombs but were set up instead outside, beside the entrance. The artist did not merely depict Hunefer's votive stele but accurately transcribed the text engraved on it.

The architecture at the far right of the composition is typical of a private tomb from the Ramessid period; the most recognizable aspect is the presence of a small pyramid atop the tomb's structure.

▲ Funerary rites performed in front of the tomb of Hunefer, from the *Book of the Dead* of Hunefer, Western Thebes, 19th dynasty, British Museum, London, EA 9901.

The central pillared chamber in the mastaba of
Mereruka is the final destination of the series of areas
leading toward the interior of the tomb. This area, used
for the presentation of offerings, was composed of a
raised surface for the offerings and the type of votive
stele known as a "false door." In the more complex
examples from the end of the Old Kingdom, this area
for offerings became the principal architectural nucleus,
around which the other rooms were arranged.

The statue of the deceased
was "brought to life"
before the funeral rituals
by the Opening of the
Mouth ceremony, which
turned the statue into a
sort of "second body," but
one that would prove
incorruptible. Thanks to
this ceremony, the soul of
the deceased could move
at will from the afterlife to
the earthly world, taking
shelter in the statue. In this
way, the deceased could
receive offerings, listen to
supplications from family
members, and intervene in
the actual world with
complete freedom.

▲ Pillared chamber from the
mastaba of Mereruka at
Saqqara, tomb of Mereruka
at Saqqara, 6th dynasty.

Below the level of the
statue, atop a short flight
of stairs, is an offering
table. Visitors to the
deceased placed offerings
of food, drink, and
flowers on this surface
for the pleasure of the
spirit of the deceased.

"I exult at the words of the Maat because I know it means salvation for whoever practices it on earth, from birth until the landing" (Stele of the mystic Baki)

Weighing the soul

Bibliography
Rachet 1996.

Related entries
Maat, Thoth,
Humans and gods,
Death as rebirth,
Books of the Dead

▼ *Book of the Dead* of
Maherpra, from the
tomb of Maherpra in
the Valley of the Kings,
Western Thebes, 18th
dynasty, Egyptian
Museum, Cairo.

The idea that at the end of earthly life the deceased had to undergo divine judgment dates to the Old Kingdom, but only during the New Kingdom did depictions of this specific moment of human existence, known to scholars by the Greek term *psychostasia* ("weighing of the soul"), become extremely popular, assuming a central part in the repertory of vignettes from the *Book of the Dead*. The scene depicts the deceased being introduced by Anubis to the presence of Osiris and forty-two judges in the hall of divine judgment, called the Hall of the Two Truths. The heart of the deceased, location of his soul and intelligence, is placed on one scalepan of a balance, and the feather of the goddess Maat, serving here as the personification of truth and justice, is placed on the other. The deceased then recites a long "negative confession" in which he declares to have committed no sins during his existence. The god Thoth makes certain that the operation of the weighing is performed correctly and announces the result. If the heart proves heavier than the feather of the goddess, the soul of the deceased is torn apart and devoured by a monster, half crocodile and half hippopotamus, called the Devourer. If not, the negative confession is declared true and the deceased is proclaimed "right of voice" and is admitted to an Edenic realm known as the Field of Rushes.

Behind Osiris, the goddess Maat raises an arm as a sign of protection. Above her the sun is depicted while rising in the east, symbolic of Nakht's coming rebirth.

Nakht, a royal scribe and overseer of the army, in the company of his wife, Tjuiu, are welcomed by Osiris to the kingdom of the afterlife.

At the center of the scene is a sort of bird's-eye view of a rectangular lake surrounded by trees and date palms. A fruit-laden branch extends toward Osiris, god of the dead and also god of the cycles of vegetation.

If the deceased passed the judgment of the tribune of Osiris, he was called "right of voice" since what he had professed in his negative confession had been confirmed by the weighing of his heart. At that point Osiris admitted the deceased to eternal life, a place of happiness and pleasure, which Egyptian tradition depicted as being conceptually similar to the biblical Eden or the Elysian Fields of Greek civilization.

▲ Nakht and Tjuiu in the garden of the blessed, from the Book of the Dead of Nakht, from Thebes, 18th dynasty, British Museum, London, EA 10471/21.

Weighing the soul

Among vignettes illustrating passages from the Book of the Dead, the most famous and widespread is that concerning Chapter 125, in which the deceased is admitted to the tribunal of Osiris and must confront psychostasia and the final judgment. Chapter 125 provided the deceased with the text for his so-called negative confession with which he claimed to have committed no impious acts during his life; he had to speak this confession facing the tribunal while his heart was weighed against the feather of Maat, goddess of truth.

The god Shaï, personification of human destiny, observes the performance of the divine judgment together with his two companions, Renenet (behind) and Meskhent (below), divinities related to nursing and childbirth.

The court of the tribunal is composed of 42 judges. More precisely, these are local demons, each one charged with punishing a certain crime. The names of the judges eloquently express their severity in the case of guilt, as indicated by the following list of judges and areas of interest: "Ghost Eater": theft; "Terror Face": murder; "The Flaming One": simony; "Bonebreaker": falsehood; "Blood Drinker": theft of ritual cattle; "Viscera Eater": illicit appropriation of goods; "The Wicked One": deceit; "The Destroyer": transgression of laws; "Backward Face": pederasty; "The Obscure One": slander.

This is the goddess Ammit, with a crocodile head, lion body, and hippopotamus rear legs. She is also known as the Devourer, for if the heart of the deceased was not found to be free of sin, she would leap on it, tear it up, and eat it.

▲ Weighing of the soul of Efankh, from Thebes, early Ptolemaic Period, Fondazione Museo Antichità Egizie, Turin, C. 1791.

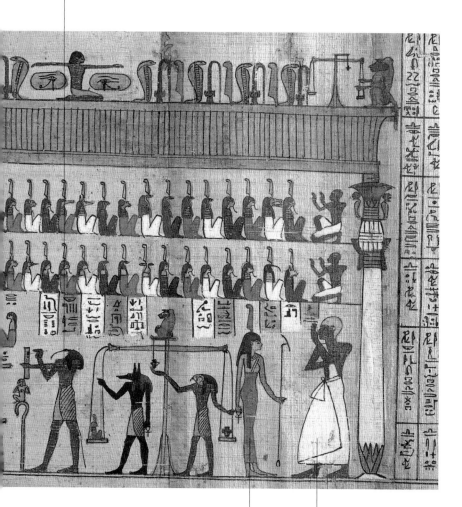

Thoth appears in the form of an ibis-headed man, taking notes on the result of the heart's weight and reporting the outcome to Osiris.

Maat, goddess of truth and justice, is identifiable thanks to the characteristic feather on her head. She welcomes the deceased to the hall of the tribunal, known as the Hall of the Two Truths.

Standing at the far end of the hall, the deceased recites the "negative confession" before Osiris seated on his throne and the 42 judges of the court arranged farther up.

"He who knows this will be among those in the boat of Ra in the sky and on earth. But he who lacks the knowledge of these images will not know how to crush the Terrible of Face [Apep]" (Book of the Dead)

Books of the Dead

In depth
Beginning in the 18th dynasty, the Egyptians began placing papyri bearing funerary formulas designed to ensure an afterlife to their possessor within reach of the deceased in tombs. This collection of formulas was known to the Egyptians as "formulas for going out in the day" (for leaving the tomb and seeing the light of day); today, they are most often referred to by the name coined around 1842 by Karl Richard Lepsius: *Totenbuch* ("Book of the Dead").

Bibliography
Hornung 1999.
Manuelian, Allen 2005.

Related entries
Ra and Apep, Death as rebirth, Weighing the soul, Pyramid complex, Valley of the Kings

▶ *Papyrus of the Dead* of Nebqed, 18th dynasty, Musée du Louvre, Paris.

The fame of Egyptian funerary culture results in part from the enormous variety of texts that were created to guide the deceased through his voyage into the mysterious world of the afterlife. These texts were designed to help the deceased protect himself from the dangers and obstacles he might encounter and also provided the information he would need to behave properly in each ritualistic situation. The most famous of these writings are the Pyramid Texts, the Coffin Texts, and the *Book of the Dead*; these represent evolutions in formulas and magic spells that belong to the same oral tradition. In the Old Kingdom, only the pharaoh could look forward to taking this afterlife journey, but it was progressively opened to nobles and then private individuals, as indicated by the various locations where the texts have been found, inside the pyramids of the Old Kingdom, on the sarcophagi of nobles and officials in the Middle Kingdom, and finally on papyri included in the funeral furnishings of ordinary individuals in the New Kingdom. At the beginning of the New Kingdom, a new generation of texts, characterized by a funerary mythology with a solar matrix, was elaborated for the

royal tombs in the Valley of the Kings. This put particular emphasis on identification of the dead king with the sun that is reborn at dawn after its nocturnal voyage through the world of the dead. These texts are the *Litany of Ra*, the *Amduat* ("What is in the netherworld"), the *Book of Gates*, *Book of Caverns*, *Book of the Day*, and *Book of the Night*.

Funerary texts could also be placed on amulets that accompanied the deceased. Among these, the most characteristic is the so-called heart scarab, which was placed over the heart of the deceased. A text was engraved on it, most often Chapter 30 of the Book of the Dead, which contains formulas to prevent the heart from testifying against the deceased during the weighing of the soul.

Chapter 30 of the Book of the Dead: *"O my heart, which I received from my mother, my heart of the different ages of my life, do not stand up against me as a witness! Do not create opposition to me among the judges! Do not tip the scales against me in the presence of the keeper of the balance! You are my soul, which is in my body, the god Khnum who makes my limbs sound. When you go forth to the hereafter my name shall not stink to the courtiers who assign people to their fate. Do not tell lies about me in the presence of the great lord of the West [Osiris]—Speak these words above a scarab of nephrite mounted in yellow amber with a ring of silver. Place on the neck of the spirit [the deceased]."*

▲ Funerary scarab belonging to the prince Isek, 22nd dynasty, green steatite, Fondazione Museo Antichità Egizie, Turin, C. 5982.

The Pyramid Texts are so called because they were first found in the burial chamber of the pyramid of Unas; they were then found in the pyramids of the pharaohs and in those of some of the queens of the 6th dynasty. They constitute the first written compilation of a ritual and religious patrimony that until then had been transmitted orally. They are referred to as texts because they present an enormously varied and heterogeneous collection, including spells, prayers, and hymns from different epochs.

▲ Antechamber with Pyramid Texts from the pyramid of Unas at Saqqara, 5th dynasty.

The Pyramid Texts offer a great deal of information about the more archaic religious practices of ancient Egypt. The overall background is a sort of astral mythology in which the sun-god Ra represents the principal divinity. He is the creator of the universe and crosses the sky in his celestial boat every day, being reborn at dawn and thus renewing the first day of creation every morning. Against this mythical context, the pharaoh goes through his elevation to divine status as the earthly incarnation of Ra. Relating this complex tradition on the walls of royal tombs, the Pyramid Texts magically supported the soul of the sovereign in its ascent to the sky, in its later assimilation among the gods, and finally in its transformation into a star of the firmament.

The 4th hour of the Amduat *describes the passage of the solar boat from the rich and fertile landscape of the Nile waters to the desert of Ra-Setu, also called "the land of Sokar who is on his sand." The boat continues its journey across the sand, for which reason it must be dragged by helpers. An innumerable host of infernal spirits populate this region, as shown by the many serpents that have wings and legs and can therefore move more easily, endangering the sun god.*

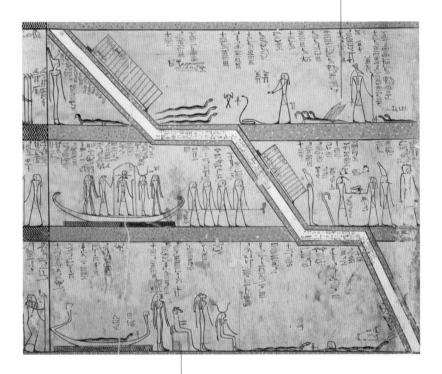

▲ 4th hour of the book of *Amduat* ("What is in the netherworld"), from the tomb of Thutmose III in the Valley of the Kings, Western Thebes, left wall of Hall J.

Amduat, *Egyptian for "what is in the netherworld," is the title given one of the most famous funerary texts of the New Kingdom. As indicated by its title, the purpose of the text was to provide the deceased with the knowledge necessary to undertake the journey to the afterlife, at the conclusion of which he would be reborn at dawn together with the sun as an immortal spirit. For the Egyptians the voyage through the afterlife involved navigating the great celestial river that the sun followed in its daily course. This river flowed over the horizon to enter what was considered the most obscure and dangerous region, the night.*

"Your [earthly] mother carried you ten months and nursed you three years. I will carry you for an indeterminate amount of time and never give birth to you" (Louvre Papyrus 3148)

Sarcophagus

In depth
Beginning in the 1st
millennium BC, the use
of the sarcophagus was
progressively replaced by
a more economic system
known as cartonnage. In
place of a coffin made of
shaped and painted
sycamore or cedar, a
mixture of papyrus
fragments held together
with glue was directly
applied to the
mummified body as a
covering. This was then
covered with white
stucco, resulting in a
surface well suited for
painted decoration, the
application of gold leaf,
or even the creation of a
mask with the painted
portrait of the deceased.

Bibliography
Ikram, Dodson 1998,
chap. VII-VIII.

Related entries
Embalming, Funerary
rites, Tomb furnishings

► Sarcophagus of the
prince Duaenra, son
of Khafre, from Giza,
pink granite h 112 cm,
Fondazione Museo
Antichià Egizie, Turin,
S. 1838.

The coffin made to hold the body of the deceased is the result of an evolution that began in the Predynastic Period with the use of mats made of woven plant fiber. The deceased was wrapped in the mat before being deposited in a circular ditch in a fetal position. During Egypt's earliest historical periods, the dead were buried, still bent inward, in short, wide wooden boxes. Even at that early period, however, members of royal families were being buried in elongated rectangular stone sarcophagi made to hold mummies. During the Old Kingdom various high-ranking nobles used stone sarcophagi, decorated with the classic "palace-façade" motif. The Middle Kingdom continued the traditional use of an elongated sarcophagus but embellished it with painted and carved decoration of a religious or superstitious character; the funerary inscriptions found inside many of these are the basis of the Coffin Texts. Beginning in the Second Intermediate Period, and especially from the New Kingdom on, sarcophagi began to have an increasingly anthropoid shape, to emphasize the integrity of the body contained. The decoration, most often painted, came to cover all the available space, both inside and outside. There was then the custom of fitting several coffins one inside the other to form enormous stone or wooden sarcophagi to better protect the mummy and at the same time to display the wealth of the deceased.

The interior of the coffin and its cover could be covered in magical and auspicious depictions, most often including the goddess Nut, symbol of the sky across which the solar boat travels, and the djed pillar, the backbone of Osiris, symbolic of stability.

Anthropoid shapes began appearing at the end of the Second Intermediate Period. These often presented highly detailed renderings of some aspect of the deceased: the face, hair dressing, jewelry, hands.

The end of the New Kingdom saw the unusual phenomenon of the reuse of funerary equipment. All that was needed to reuse a sarcophagus was to remove or add elements that indicated the sex of the occupant.

The body, wrapped in linen strips after embalming, is reproduced in its mummy form on the sarcophagus itself; this part of the coffin was soon decorated with prayers and funerary texts. In many cases there are depictions of canopic jars or funerary amulets.

▲ Series of sarcophagi in stuccoed and painted wood.

The oldest stone sarcophagi were decorated very simply with palace-façade motifs or funerary inscriptions; sometimes they were only smoothed and polished. The habit of engraving texts and funerary formulas on sarcophagi began in the Middle Kingdom.

Large stone coffins were usually square, sometimes with rounded sides, making it easier to work the hard materials.

Anthropomorphic-shaped stone coffins appeared in the New Kingdom. There were also those shaped like a cartouche with the form of the deceased carved in high relief. In the Late Period there was a return to more classical models with austere shapes, but with the outer surfaces richly engraved with inscriptions and processions of divinities, as with this example.

Inside the large stone sarcophagi were usually others, made of wood, inserted one inside another like Russian dolls; this style came into widespread use in the New Kingdom, when Egypt had a middle class of state officials with the right to a dignified burial.

▲ Sarcophagus of Ankh-Hor, Late Period, granite, Ägyptisches Museum, Berlin, inv. 41.

"I have prepared myself an excellent tomb . . . I have exquisitely furnished the place of my burial in the rock of the desert of eternity" (Tomb of the vizier User-Amon)

Tomb furnishings

Proper embalming and the magical spells of rituals could not alone provide for a happy afterlife. Also needed were the many furnishings that would accompany the deceased in the tomb. These included funerary objects and articles of daily use. Tombs of a certain prestige were sure to contain one or more sarcophagi, containing the mummy, along with the canopic jars with the viscera extracted during mummification. During the earliest periods, the deceased was provided with objects needed for survival: weapons, containers with food and drink, clothes, and various personal ornaments. The "middle class" of officials and professionals that came into being during the New Kingdom brought about a great multiplication of funerary objects. Aside from models of servants busy performing the most varied duties, there were also crowds of mummiform figurines of the deceased bearing agricultural tools. At the call from Osiris to begin work in the fields, these would magically take the place of the deceased and do his work, responding in his name. They are thus called *shabti* (from the verb *usheb*, "to answer"). There was also the custom of furnishing the tomb like a normal house with furniture, tableware, clothing, foodstuffs, work tools, cosmetics, objects for beauty and hygiene, for hunting and sport, for traveling and for show. Naturally, the less well-to-do Egyptians did not enjoy such privileges, and their tombs were ditches dug in the ground.

In depth
Chapter 6 of the *Book of the Dead* gives instructions for magically activating the *shabti*, or "answerer," statuettes, which would perform chores for the deceased in the afterlife. "Chapter for making the *shabti*s do work in the necropolis. Speak these words: Oh, you *shabti*s, if Osiris justifies [name of the deceased] and he is called upon to do any of the work required there in the necropolis at any time, put yourself in his place to cultivate the fields, to irrigate the riverbank fields, to ferry sand from west to east. You must say: 'I will do it! Here I am!'"

Bibliography
James 2000.

◀ *Shabti* of the lady Sati, Saqqara, New Kingdom, 18th dynasty, reign of Amenhotep III (?), faience, h 25 cm, Brooklyn Museum of Art, New York, Charles Edwin Wilbour Fund, n. 37.123E.

The collection of objects found in the tomb of Tutankhamen is without doubt the most astonishing both in terms of their enormous quantity and for the quality of their workmanship and the value of their materials. Other important tombs, such as those of Yuya and Tuya and Kha and Merit, contained furnishings that were less impressive but equally informative.

The abode of the soul had to be supplied with everything necessary for the new existence in the afterlife; the most grandiose and complete furnishings were composed of vast collections of goods to make the next life comfortable.

Many objects included among the tomb furnishings had probably been used by the pharaoh during his earthly life, while others had a purely funereal use. Some articles had been made at the time of his ascent to the throne, as indicated by the presence of his original name, Tutankhaton.

A parade cart in gilt wood, complete with wheels, finishings, and harness had been disassembled, with all its parts deposited inside the tomb. Today it is preserved, completely reassembled, in the Egyptian Museum in Cairo.

The entrance to the first room in the tomb of Tutankhamen was protected by two guardian statues; inside were many pieces of furniture: beds with leonine and bovine top-pieces, stools, trunks of linen, boxes for food, and containers for drinks.

▲ Reconstruction of the interior of the first chamber of Tutankhamen's tomb.

▶ Bas-relief with scene of fording the Nile, from the mastaba of the vizier Kagemni at Saqqara, north side of Hall 2, 6th dynasty.

"Make your house in the necropolis excellent, and make your seat in the west splendid . . . the house of death belongs to the living" (Teachings of Hordjedef)

Mastaba

The term *mastaba* refers to the Egyptian tomb of the Old Kingdom, made for the kings of the 1st and 2nd dynasties and for the functionaries of later dynasties. A mastaba is composed of an underground tomb with a visible superstructure in stone or brick. It has the shape of a box with inclined walls, enlivened by architectural decoration composed of projections and indentations called "pilasters." The basic concept of the tomb was that of providing the deceased with a home that would be resistant to time, for which reason tombs are like apartments, decorated with exceptional painted reliefs. At first, such tombs were dug into the ground along with other mortuary spaces to hold the sarcophagus and necessary furnishings; later they were arranged inside the superstructure. The place of worship was always located to the east, where the sun rose, and initially was indicated on the exterior by the simple presence of a votive stele that could also take the form of a so-called false door, a false entrance to the tomb that symbolically connected the inside of the tomb with the outside world of the living. The site of worship was also furnished with an offering table which evolved from a simple slab to forms with highly varied decorations.

In depth
The necropolis of Saqqara preserves the most interesting and splendid private mastabas of antiquity. The walls of the rooms into which the mastabas are divided are decorated with magnificent reliefs that present a tapestry of all the administrative activities performed by the deceased when alive. These activities are described in great detail but also with a surprising awareness of and attention to the more delicate and poetic aspects of existence. The most important mastabas are those of Ti (5th dynasty), Kagemni (6th dynasty), Mereruka (6th dynasty), and Mehu (5th dynasty).

Bibliography
Lauer 1977.

Related entries
Pyramid complex, Ancient centers, Memphite necropolis

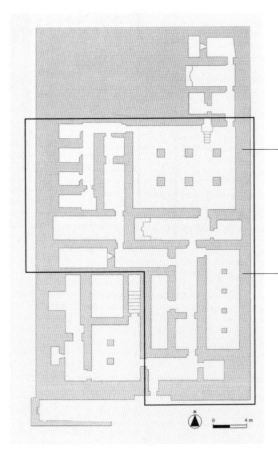

Mereruka served as judge and vizier during the reign of Teti, at the beginning of the 6th dynasty. His mastaba was built immediately to the north of the pyramid built for his sovereign at Saqqara and must have represented one of the most spectacular achievements of private funerary architecture of the Old Kingdom.

The layout of the mastaba reflects its use as eternal dwelling place. The building is divided into 32 rooms in three sections: 21 rooms dedicated to Mereruka alone, 6 to his wife, Uatet-khethor, and 5 to their son Meriteti. These areas were designed as true personal apartments with pillared chambers, long halls, shrines, storerooms, and sealed-off rooms. The internal walls of the structure are covered with a rich decoration of painted bas-reliefs that present the world seen through the eyes of the deceased.

▲ Layout of the mastaba of Mereruka at Saqqara.

Mehu served as vizier and administrator of justice during the reign of Teti in the 6th dynasty. His mastaba, discovered at Saqqara by Auguste Mariette, is very large and has preserved two famous false doors. They are decorated over their entire surfaces with a delicate polychrome relief that reproduces both images and texts. The vizier is depicted in the upper central area while sitting in front of an offering table covered by tall loaves. The inscription above lists Mehu's titles as well as the offerings given him.

Worship in the tomb usually consisted of the presentation of an offering to the deceased. From the earliest times, the offering was brought to the exterior of the tomb and set upon an offering table. In the most archaic times, the offering table was a simple mat placed on the ground, probably with the hieroglyphic ideogram hetep, *meaning "offering," represented by a loaf set on a mat.*

▲ False door of Mehu from the offering chamber in the mastaba of the vizier Mehu at Saqqara, 6th dynasty, limestone.

▶ Offering table of Nakht, 12th dynasty, limestone, Musée du Louvre, Paris, AE 10226.

Seated on a zoomorphic chair, the princess is depicted in the stylized gesture of holding one hand to her chest while extending the other toward the loaves of bread arranged on the offering table.

This votive stele, made for Princess Neferetiabet, a daughter of Khufu, is an exceptional artifact; thanks to the extraordinary state of preservation of its painted decoration, it reveals the magnificent levels reached by the artisans of the Old Kingdom.

The panther skin Neferetiabet wears emphasizes her noble birth but is also a powerful symbol, making reference to the celestial firmament. The splendidly rendered spots were compared to the stars, for which reason such skins were used in the ceremonial and funerary spheres, considered bearers of celestial energy.

▲ Votive stele of Neferetiabet, 4th dynasty, painted limestone, h 38 cm, Musée du Louvre, Paris, E 15591.

▶ Panorama of the plain at Giza, 1880.

"Who will raise a finger against this pyramid and this temple of Pepi and his ka . . . will be cursed and will be one whose body is devoured" (Pyramid Texts)

Pyramid complex

At the beginning of the 3rd dynasty, the architect Imhotep was charged with designing a monumental funerary complex around the mastaba of his king, Djoser. The result was grand, but the great number of buildings and, most of all, the powerful outer wall around the entire area put in shadow what was supposed to be the heart of the celebratory complex, the ruler's mastaba. Through a series of later reworkings, Imhotep arrived at the so-called Step Pyramid, which became the point of departure for the later architectural evolution of the royal tomb, the pyramid complex. The founder of the 4th dynasty, Snefru, carried ahead the idea of his predecessor and began construction of three pyramids. The stages in their construction, from attempt to attempt, reveal the highly experimental character of the design and make it possible to follow the maturation, over the course of the work, of technical knowledge and building experience. The funerary complex that began taking shape in the 4th dynasty had evolved into a canonical style by the 5th and called for four basic architectural elements: the pyramid, a temple built against the face of the pyramid, a valley temple that served as the monumental entrance to the entire complex, and a causeway connecting the valley temple to the pyramid. The know-how acquired during the reign of Snefru was immediately put to use by his son Khufu, with whom the great period of the pyramids at Giza began, true apogee of pyramidal architecture.

In depth
How did the Egyptians manage to raise such heavy blocks so high? Here are the opinions of Herodotus and Diodorus Siculus, two of the leading historians of antiquity. "When they had first made this base, they then lifted the remaining stones with levers made of short timbers, lifting them from the ground to the first tier of steps . . . As many as were the tiers, so many were the levers." (Herodotus, *The History*, II:125). "The stones, they say . . . were raised by making mounds of earth; cranes and other engines not being known at the time." (Diodorus Siculus, *Historical Library*, I:63).

Bibliography
Lehner 1997.
Verner 1999.

Related entries
4th dynasty, Heliopolitan cosmogony, Books of the Dead, Memphite necropolis, Faiyum and Lisht

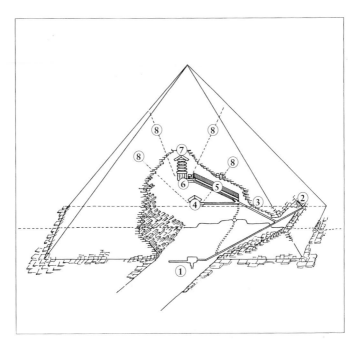

Legend:

1. The function of the subterranean chamber in granite is still unclear. Some scholars think it was an emergency tomb, built in case the ruler died prematurely. Others think it represents the symbolic cavern of the death god, Sokar.
2. The original entrance to the pyramid was located on the north side and led to a descending passage leading more than 30 m under the level of the base of the pyramid.
3. Ascending passage.
4. The so-called Queen's Chamber. In reality, the function of this space has not been established. Presumably it must represent the original burial chamber of the ruler, later replaced by the King's Chamber.
5. Grand Gallery.
6. The King's Chamber is made entirely of pink granite from Aswan and has a low ceiling composed of nine large blocks weighing 400 tons. Khufu's sarcophagus, located against the rear wall of the chamber, is also made of pink Aswan granite. Diodorus Siculus repeated the legend according to which Khufu was never buried in the pyramid, an opinion shared by many even today.
7. Relief chambers. The enormous weight of the King's Chamber was absorbed by the arrangement of five hollow rooms set one upon the other (called relieving compartments) and separated by flat blocks of granite for an overall height of 15 m. At the top are two slabs arranged to form a slope to distribute the force of pressure.
8. Ventilation shafts.

▲ Diagram of the Great Pyramid of Giza.

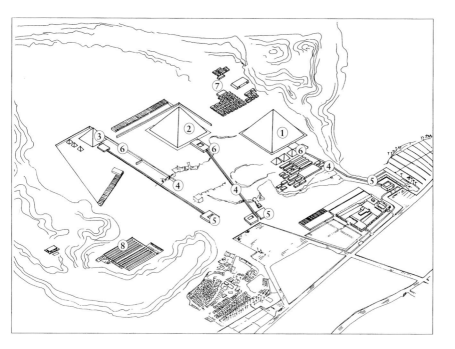

Legend:

1. Great Pyramid of Khufu
2. Pyramid of Khafre
3. Pyramid of Menkure
4. Processional ramp used in the transfer of the ruler's body from the valley temple to the mortuary temple. It was usually covered and decorated, as indicated by examples from the 5th dynasty.
5. During the funerary ritual, the valley temple served as landing spot for the boat bearing the body of the deceased ruler. The temple was also used to store the simulacra of divinities visiting the sepulcher, most of all during religious festivals.
6. The funerary rituals were performed in the mortuary temple, which was the point of interconnection between the earthly world and the otherworldly residence of the ruler represented by the pyramid.
7. Western necropolis of dignitaries.
8. Workers' village.

▲ Schematic diagram of the pyramids and funeral temples at Giza.

Within the sphere of the internal design of pyramids, the so-called Grand Gallery in the Great Pyramid of Khufu is a completely unique architectural feature. The gallery is about 46 m long, 2 m wide, and 9 m high. It constitutes the only access route to the King's Chamber, and it is believed that its entrance was originally sealed with blocks of granite that were rolled down it.

The walls are composed of seven rows of granite blocks that narrow upwards a constant distance of 7.5 cm. The astonishing use of the technique of the "false vault" to close off the gallery had a single precedent in the inner chambers of the pyramid of Snefru. Although on a decidedly smaller scale, the technical experience matured in the age of Snefru was a precious point of reference for the architects who had to confront the continuous challenges and unknown dangers of this impressive undertaking.

▲ View of the Grand Gallery in the pyramid of Khufu at Giza, 4th dynasty, granite.

"I am Ra who is in the sky, I enter the shadows at sunset, I open the door of the sky in the West. Take me" (Book of the Caverns)

Valley of the Kings

Pyramids like those of the Old Kingdom were still being built in the Middle Kingdom, during the 12th dynasty, but the style had been abandoned by the start of the New Kingdom, when, beginning with Amenhotep I, the pharaohs decided for logistical and security reasons to separate the tomb and the mortuary temple, placing them in two different locations on the bank of the Nile at Thebes. Later the tombs were located in the Valley of the Kings with the mortuary temples on the plain opposite it on the West Bank at Thebes. The tombs followed a relatively simple layout based on the repetition of certain architectural elements: an entrance corridor, a pit, a columned antechamber, and a pillared burial chamber that held the sarcophagus of the king. These elements were recurrent but were not locked into a set arrangement, such that each pharaoh made slight modifications that made his tomb differ from the others. With time, the sizes of the tombs increased, and the general layout changed, moving toward a "deviated axis" at the beginning of the 18th dynasty, a "bayonet" arrangement at the end of the 18th, and a "rectilinear" form at the end of the 19th dynasty.

The walls of the tombs were completely covered with impressive funerary texts elaborated during the New Kingdom to accompany and guide the deceased king on his journey to the afterlife. These are excellent works of pictorial art that still astonish observers today with their artistic and intellectual richness.

Bibliography
Reeves, Wilkinson 1996.
www.thebanmappingproject.com

Related entries
Amenhotep I, Amon, Hathor, Books of the Dead, Theban necropolis, Deir el-Medina

▼ Ramses I among the souls of Pe and Nekhen, from the tomb of Ramses I in the Valley of the Kings, Western Thebes, 19th dynasty.

The tomb of Thutmose III is 21 m deep, and the sequence of its rooms follows an "elbow" layout to cover a total length of 54 m. It is thought to be the first New Kingdom tomb to clearly show the two principal changes in funerary architecture inaugurated in the Valley of the Kings by the pharaohs of the 18th dynasty: the separation of the mortuary temple from the tomb itself and the use of an underground tomb opened in the heart of the Theban mountain.

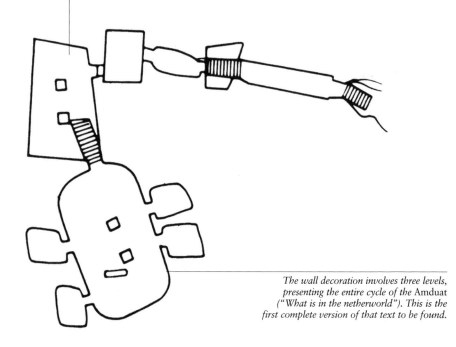

The wall decoration involves three levels, presenting the entire cycle of the Amduat *("What is in the netherworld"). This is the first complete version of that text to be found.*

▲ Layout of the tomb of Thutmose III.

The pillars are decorated with the first known version of the Litany of Ra, a funerary text that describes the divine mystery of the regeneration of the sun. In order to unite with Ra and take part in his continuous rebirth, the pharaoh had to know the names of the sun god's 75 manifestations and to invoke them one by one in front of their respective images. The ceiling is decorated with a motif of the night sky, while the walls bear an impressive list of the 741 divinities that inhabit the regions of the hereafter.

The burial chamber of the tomb of Thutmose III has an antechamber with two square pillars that support the ceiling, 3.31 m high, decorated with a blue background completely covered with yellow stars in imitation of the firmament.

▲ View of the burial chamber with the *Litany of Ra*, from the tomb of Thutmose III in the Valley of the Kings, Western Thebes, 18th dynasty.

The wall decoration in the burial chamber of Thutmose III is concise and stately, with an expressive power that is absolutely unique of its kind. The artists serving the pharaoh managed to transfer to the walls the contents of the text of the Amduat, *until then preserved only on papyrus. Standing out against the yellow-beige background are the stylized silhouettes of hundreds of divinities and fantastic animals, all accompanied by explanatory captions.*

The Amduat *("What is in the netherworld") is a composition created at the beginning of the New Kingdom that has as its main subject the nocturnal voyage of the sun through the world of the dead, which lasts the 12 hours of the night. The purpose of the text is to furnish the deceased with a guide to protect him from the perils of the journey.*

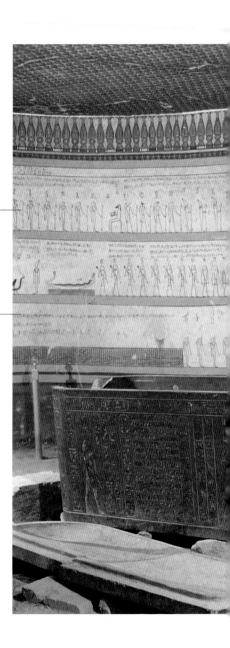

▶ View of the burial chamber with sarcophagus and *Amduat* from the tomb of Thutmose III in the Valley of the Kings, Western Thebes, 18th dynasty.

The sarcophagus is shaped like a cartouche, as is the burial chamber. It is made of pink quartzite and measures 2.35 x 0.85 m with a height of 0.96 m. At its head appears the figure of Isis, at its foot the figure of Nephthys, thus depicting the moment in the Osirian drama when the two goddesses protected the body of Osiris. The decoration also includes the four sons of Horus.

Sites and monuments

◀ Colossal head of Ramses II,
from the second court of the
Ramesseum, Western Thebes,
19th dynasty, black granite.

Ancient centers

Hieroglyph
Tjeny ("Thinis")

Location
Upper Egypt, between
20 km (Naqada) and
150 km (Thinis) north
of Thebes

Chronology
Naqada has cemeteries
from the Predynastic
Period and from the
first two dynasties;
Abydos has monuments
from all periods.

**Principal archaeological
excavations**
Flinders Petrie (Naqada-
Tukh and Abydos),
J. De Morgan (Naqada).

Bibliography
Midant-Reynes 1992.

Related entries
Menes and Narmer,
Historical sources,
Sir Flinders Petrie.

The last phase in Egyptian prehistory, which during the 4th millennium BC laid the basis for the future pharaonic civilization, is named for a site in Upper Egypt, Naqada. It is the location of important cemeteries dating to the Predynastic Period that are the source of numerous ceramic finds that made possible the establishment of a chronology for the Predynastic Period. Among the most important monuments is a large mastaba (54 x 27 m) in mud bricks with a "palace-façade" decoration on all its exterior walls. This style was to be characteristic of the tombs of the first dynastic period, which began around 3150 BC and is named for the city of Thinis (Thinite Period), about 130 km north of Naqada, source of the pharaohs of the 1st and 2nd dynasties. Their tombs have been found in the necropolis of Abydos, site of the ancient worship of the god Khenti-amentiu ("Lord of the Westerners," meaning the dead, who dwell in the west), identified with Osiris during the 5th and 6th dynasties. The city was visited by pilgrims, especially for celebration of the "mysteries of Osiris," the sacred representation of that god's death and resurrection. During all the pharaonic age, many Egyptians sought to share this destiny by building cenotaphs near the temple where his tomb was believed to be located. Outstanding examples are the mortuary temples of Seti I and Ramses II, dedicated to the cult of the king of the dead identified with Osiris.

▶ "Black-topped" pottery
from Upper Egypt,
Predynastic Period,
terracotta, Fondazione
Museo Antichità Egizie,
Turin.

Stone palettes decorated with battle scenes and fantastic animals are the only direct sources from the Predynastic Period, an age before writing. Such palettes often have a roundish cavity in the center, a sort of small cup, in which to grind powders to make ritual makeup.

The cities destroyed are depicted as diagrams seen from above, square shaped and surrounded by turreted walls. Inside are the blocks knocked down. Enclosed in the walls are symbols of the cities, probably totemic images. Such images may have been the origins of the hieroglyphic signs used to indicate the cities' names.

The back of the slab bears two levels of depictions of wild asses; such faunistic scenes, with real and imaginary animals, are a recurrent motif in predynastic art.

The scene depicts the destruction of cities by a royal power: the destroyers are a falcon, a lion, a scorpion, and another two falcons on standards; these symbolic images of royalty are also found in the historical period. The animals hold a plow between their feet, that being the tool the ruler used to knock down the enemy cities.

▲ "Cities Palette," from Hierakonpolis, Predynastic Period, graywacke, 64 x 42 cm, Egyptian Museum, Cairo, CG 14716.

Above the king's name is an impressive image of the falcon-god Horus, a divinity originally from Hierakonpolis, an ancient religious center about 200 km south of Abydos. Horus soon became the protector of Upper Egypt and, following Egypt's unification, of the ruler himself.

The king's name is expressed in a single hieroglyph, which is read dj, the meaning of which is the idea depicted by the sign itself, "serpent." The symbol is framed by a richly decorated rectangle, which is the sign called serekh, which during the first dynasties enclosed the name of the pharaoh and represented a stylization of the façade of the royal palace.

The top of the elongated mortuary slab is rounded. The center of the stele is framed by a raised border, while the lower part is smooth since it had to be set in the ground.

▲ Funerary stele of Djet, from Abydos, 1st dynasty, limestone, h 143 cm, Musée du Louvre, Paris, E 11007.

The tombs of the rulers of the first dynasties were put in subterranean chambers closed by a super-structure shaped like a tumulus, the mastaba, built of sand and mud bricks; the outer walls were shaped with projections and niches in which steles bearing the names of the owner were located.

Memphis and Saqqara

Memphis, Egypt's first capital city, was in the north, on the border between Upper and Lower Egypt; the city was a highly important administrative and religious center until the Roman Period. The foundation of Memphis dates to the earliest phases of the history of unified Egypt, and its original name was Inebhedj, "White Wall" (the walls of the city were probably made of limestone); the name *Memphis* is from the Greek pronunciation of the expression *Menefer-Pepi*, "the perfection of Pepi is stable," that being the name of the pyramid of King Pepi I, which was later applied to the entire inhabited area. Although the settlement was probably quite large in antiquity, few traces of it remain today. It may be possible to see certain of its characteristics in the funerary complex of King Djoser at Saqqara. The structures around the Step Pyramid, about 60 m high, probably reproduce the urban reality of the capital. Here too temples and buildings were surrounded by a high all in white limestone, and all the rooms are built in stone. Djoser had celebrated the *sed* festival in the sanctuary, thus reconfirming his power in the presence of the gods of Upper and Lower Egypt. Since Memphis was the first large city a foreigner reached on entering Egypt, it became the symbol par excellence of the entire country; the name *Aigyptos* (Greek for "Egypt") is derived from the name of the sanctuary of the Memphite god Ptah, called *hut-ka-Ptah*.

Hieroglyph
Ineb-hedj
("White Wall")

Location
Lower Egypt, about 30
km south of Cairo

Chronology
From the 2nd dynasty
until the Greco-Roman
age

**Principal archaeological
excavations**
Flinders Petrie
(Memphis), J. P. Lauer
(Saqqara), Quibell
(Saqqara), Z. Gonheim
(Saqqara).

Bibliography
Lauer 1977.

Related entries
Djoser and Imhotep,
Mastaba, Pyramid
complex, Memphite
necropolis

◀ Wall around the
complex of Djoser at
Saqqara, 3rd dynasty.

For the first time in the history of Egyptian art, the mortuary monument of King Djoser was built entirely in stone; this is a tangible demonstration of the solidity of his power as well as a promise of perpetuity. The complex very probably repeats the buildings of the capital, Memphis.

On the western side of the court are constructions symbolizing the principal sanctuaries of Upper and Lower Egypt, two buildings with barrel vaults; in reality these are false structures without entrances built to serve a purely religious function. The archaic sanctuaries were made of wood, reeds, and mats.

The great court was used for celebrations of the sed festival, the jubilee of the pharaoh held in the thirtieth year of his reign. The rite confirms the physical vigor of the king, who was called on to guarantee the ordered cosmos and the social harmony of the country.

The outer walls of the funerary complex were surrounded by a ditch that made access to the tomb even more difficult while also serving a symbolic value: from the primordial waters of chaos emerged the mound on which creation took place.

▲ The funerary complex of Djoser at Saqqara, 3rd dynasty.

King Djoser's tomb was originally a simple mastaba *(Arabic for "bench")* that covered the mortuary pit; the mastaba was then enlarged to cover collateral pits and came to be transformed into a pyramid, first with four and later six steps; the structure reached the height of 60 m.

The court around Djoser's pyramid is surrounded by a wall in blocks of white limestone 11 m high. The exterior facade of the outer wall has a molded surface, created by the alternation of projections and indentations. This decoration was derived from the façades of ancient royal residences, supported by pillars and closed off by mats.

Very probably the façades of the pyramid were filled with blocks of limestone that gave the construction a more homogenous and smooth appearance.

To the north of the complex is a small room called a serdab *(Arabic for "cellar")* that held a life-size statue of the ruler dressed in his jubilee robes. From that room he could magically observe the court through two slits in the wall.

▲ Funerary complex of Djoser at Saqqara, 3rd dynasty.

The museum that today holds the colossal statue of Ramses II stands near the walls of the temple of the god Ptah, the city's patron deity.

The Memphite necropolis also holds tombs from the New Kingdom and an immense cemetery for the Apis bulls, the cult of which was tied to that of Ptah. The chapels and religious areas near the tombs of the bulls composed the famous Serapeum, cited by classical authors.

Ramses II built numerous monuments in the ancient Egyptian capital and restored the temple of Ptah. He had some statues that portrayed him in colossal size erected beside the monumental doors to the religious complex.

The importance that the city of Memphis had for Ramses II is reflected in the role assumed by his son Khaemweset. As great priest, he promoted the creation of important works, but he is recalled primarily as the "archaeologist prince" because he undertook a vast program of restoring antique mortuary monuments.

▲ Head of the colossus of Ramses II, from the temple of Ptah at Memphis, 19th dynasty, alabaster, circa 10 m long, Museum of Mit Rahina, Memphis.

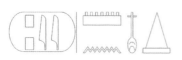

Memphite necropolis

The cemeteries located near the capital extended into the area between the Nile and the Western Desert and occupied a territory about 30 kilometers long. These necropolises hosted tombs of kings and nobles, with about fifty impressive pyramids surrounded by a myriad of lesser monuments. The farthest from Memphis is the site of Abu Rawaysh, which hosts some of the oldest tombs and which is the site of the unfinished pyramid of Djedefre. To the west of the city is Giza, dominated by the massive pyramids of Khufu, Khafre, and Menkure, all connected by causeways to temple structures. In addition to the funerary complex, the remains of a workers' village have been found. Aside from several pyramids, Abu Ghorab and Abusir are home to two important temples for the worship of the sun god erected during the 5th dynasty by Userkaf and Nyuserra; the sun was worshiped in large open-air courts, and the god's simulacrum was a low obelisk, the *ben-ben*. Saqqara, the largest cemetery and also the one nearest the capital, was used even after the pharaonic period; aside from the Djoser complex, it is the site of numerous tombs of high officials from all periods, together with catacombs and the burials of the Apis bulls, living images of the god of the Nile. The southernmost Memphite cemetery is Dahshur, which has the pyramid of Snefru, who experimented with various construction techniques there, as well as those of several Middle Kingdom kings.

Hieroglyphic
Menefer-Pepi
("The perfection of
Pepi is stable")

Location
Lower Egypt, area
of Cairo

Chronology
Giza preserves
monuments from the
Old and New Kingdoms.
Abusir has Old Kingdom
pyramids and tombs
from various periods.
Meidum has tombs from
the Old Kingdom.

**Principal archaeological
excavations**
R. Lepsius, F.A. Mariette,
Flinders Petrie,
G. Reisner, H. Junker,
S. Hassan, Z. Hawass.

Bibliography
Verner 1999.

Related entries
4th dynasty, Heliopolitan
cosmogony, Pyramid
complex, Memphis
and Saqqara

◀ The pyramid of Huni
at Meidum, completed
by his son Snefru,
4th dynasty.

The pyramid of Menkure is the smallest, being 66 m high. Aligned along its southern side are three satellite pyramids made for royal wives, each of which had its own mortuary temple.

▲ The pyramids of Menkure, Khafre, and Khufu on the plain at Giza, 4th dynasty.

The pyramid of Khafre is slightly smaller than that of Khufu and is the only one of those at Giza to preserve intact part of its external limestone dressing. When G.B. Belzoni entered it in 1818, he found only the empty granite sarcophagus, its cover lying broken at its side.

The pyramid of Khufu is one of the most impressive and best preserved monuments in the world, with a base of 230 m on each side and a height of 146 m. The entrance is located to the east, and a gallery covered by projecting blocks of granite leads to two rooms opened in the heart of the pyramid, fitted with air conduits and connections to the exterior.

The pyramid had a religious complex composed of a valley temple, connected to the Nile, and another upriver, reachable by an ascending causeway. Alongside the causeway is the monumental Great Sphinx, 57 m long, carved out of the natural rock, which reproduces Khafre in the form of a lion with a human head.

Ditches have been found at the base of the pyramid containing pieces of wooden boats. One of these, with an overall length of 43 m, has been assembled and is displayed in a special museum beside the pyramid.

The passage from the Step Pyramid to the smooth-sided pyramid involved an adaptation of building techniques and structural calculations. The sudden change in the sloping sides of the first pyramid of Snefru at Dahshur was probably the result of a structural flaw. Unlike all other examples, this so-called Rhomboidal (or Bent) pyramid has two entrances.

The Faraun Mastaba is the mortuary monument of Shepseskaf, last king of the 4th dynasty; the decision to construct a mastaba instead of a pyramid was probably the result of the premature death of the king, who was then buried in the subterranean structures.

Two kilometers to the north of the Rhomboidal (or Bent) pyramid, Snefru made another pyramid, this with a broad base (220 x 220 m) and a very low slope, such to give the monument a somewhat "blunt" appearance. It is known as the Red pyramid because of the color of the limestone blocks used for its core.

▲ The necropolis of Dashur.

The group of buildings stands out for the high quality of the materials used (Tura limestone, basalt, and pink granite) and for the refinement of its relief decorations.

The rulers of the 5th dynasty preferred the site of Abusir for their burials. The funerary complex of Sahura is composed of a valley temple connected by an ascending causeway to a temple in the shadow of the pyramid.

The necropolis has the pyramids of six 5th-dynasty kings: Userkaf, Sahura, Neferirkara, Raneferef, Nyuserra, and Menkauhor. It was also the site of the discovery, early in the 20th century, of administrative papyri from the reign of Neferirkara, documents concerning the direction of the mortuary cult of the dead kings.

In the northern area of the archaeological site of Abusir is the oldest Egyptian sun temple, built by Userkaf, first pharaoh of the 5th dynasty, who left the monument unfinished; the idea was repeated by Nyuserra, who built a solar temple at Abu Ghorab.

▲ The pyramid of Sahura at Abusir, 5th dynasty.

The decorations in the entrance rooms present themes related to the earthly life of the deceased destined to be repeated in the world of the afterlife. Thus Ti appears while inspecting his holdings, overseeing agricultural work, stockbreeding, fishing, hunting, and various activities being performed in artisan workshops.

The nobles were buried in mastabas with complex layouts composed of a great number of richly decorated rooms. One of the most complete examples is the tomb of Ti, inspector of the pyramids and temple of Sahura.

The decorations in the mortuary rooms are of a more strictly ritual type: long processions of servants bring the produce of his properties to the deceased: fruits of the land, animals, artisan works, and tomb furnishings. Farther in are scenes relating to the funeral, with the presence of family members and administrators.

▲ View of the interior of the mastaba of Ti.

Beside the tombs of the pharaohs and their families were the tombs of the most important officials and priests; the rigid hierarchy of the Old Kingdom is reflected in how close each of these tombs is to that of the ruler, thus carrying into death the ranks they held in life.

Faiyum and Lisht

During the 12th dynasty, the capital of Egypt was moved to Itjtawy, a newly founded city about 40 kilometers south of Memphis, probably the place of birth of the new rulers. The location of this city has still not been determined with any certainty, but it must not have been far from Lisht, its necropolis. The cemetery holds the two pyramids of Amenemhet I and Sesostris I, today in ruin, and the tombs of members of the royal family and officials. Standing out among the objects found that belonged to various queens and princesses are jewels and valuables that exalt the glory of the pharaoh. Not far off is the fertile region of Faiyum, an oasis connected to the Nile by canal. Its palm groves and marshes were home to large numbers of birds and wild animals. The crocodile-god Sobek was made the principal divinity of the oasis, given the high presence of this reptile in the region. The marshy areas of Faiyum were drained during the Middle Kingdom, for the exploitation of its important agricultural and hunting resources. Unfortunately, the archaeological remains of this period have almost all been lost, except for the

Hieroglyphic
Itjet-Tauy
("Conqueror of the
Two Lands")

Location
Lower Egypt, oasis
of Faiyum

Chronology
From the Middle
Kingdom to the
Greco-Roman age

Bibliography
Baines, Malek 1982.

Related entries
Amenemhet I,
Pyramid complex

necropolis of Hawara; the site was visited by the Greek historian Herodotus, who nicknamed the mortuary temple attached to the pyramid of Amenemhet III the Labyrinth because of its complex layout. There are important urban and religious sites from the Greco-Roman age, among them Karanis, Soknopaiou Nesos, Arsinoe, Narmouthis, and Tebtynis.

◀ Statue of Sesotris I, from the mortuary temple of the pyramid of Sesostris I at Lisht, 12th dynasty, limestone, h 200 cm, Egyptian Museum, Cairo, CG 414.

Access to the pyramid was through a stairway leading to the subterranean structures, dug into the rock. The burial chamber was probably sealed by large blocks of quartzite, but they failed to keep tomb robbers out.

Amenemhet III had a pyramid built at Dahshur but was buried in the monument in Hawara. The pyramid is built in mud bricks and dressed in thin layers of limestone.

The relocation of the capital to near Lisht, during the 12th dynasty, resulted in the hydrological reclamation of the oasis of Faiyum. The local divinities are strongly related to the marshy setting: the crocodile-god Sobek and the serpent-goddess Renenutet.

To the south of the pyramid are a few remains of one of the most famous buildings of antiquity, visited and described by many classical writers, including Pliny and Herodotus, who named it the Labyrinth. This was the mortuary temple for the cult of the spirit of Amenemhet. The size of the complex and its complicated maze of rooms and hallways leads to the conclusion that its function was not exclusively funerary but that it also served an administrative role.

▲ The pyramid of Amenemhet III at Hawara, 12th dynasty.

Their hair is divided in three parts, with long ringlets tied behind the head in a thick braid. The rounded beards are rendered with concentric semicircles.

The two figures have powerful musculature, as was typical of portraiture during the reign of Amenemhet III, the period to which the work belongs. The eyes project slightly, covered by heavy lids; the nose is large and important, the mouths firmly set and severe.

The figures wear skirts depicted with dense vertical lines, and heavy bracelets on their arms.

The two offerers have been variously interpreted as fishermen or inhabitants of the marsh, as the king, or as personifications of the Two Lands made fertile by the Nile, producing and offering abundant economic resources.

Hanging from the trays are cascades of aquatic plants and lotus-flower garlands in which fish and birds are visible.

▲ Statuary group depicting two Nilotic spirits, from Tanis, 12th dynasty, gray granite, h 160 cm, Egyptian Museum, Cairo, CG 392.

The rectangular plaque hangs from a necklace of elongated drop-shaped beads of carnelian and lapis lazuli alternating with gold. The scene on the pectoral is enclosed in an architectural frame.

The vulture-goddess Nekhbet, with her wings spread wide, holds the symbols of life (ankh) and stability (djed) in her legs, offering them to the ruler.

This is an openwork jewel, the front parts composed of intaglios in carnelian, lapis lazuli, turquoise, and faience, set in a light cloisonné.

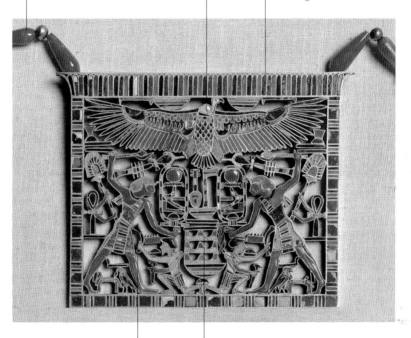

In one hand the king grasps the hair of an enemy kneeling in front of him, while in the other he holds a white mace.

The axis of symmetry of the entire composition is the name of the king, Amenemhet III Nimaatra, "perfect god, lord of the Two Lands and of all foreign lands."

▲ Pectoral of Amenemhet III, from the tomb of the princess Mereret at Dahshur, 12th dynasty, gold, turquoise, carnelian, lapis lazuli, vitreous paste, h 7.9 cm, Egyptian Museum, Cairo, GC 52002.

Provincial centers

The end of the Old Kingdom led to a weakening in the central power of Memphis, releasing control of the territory to the nomarchs (heads of Egyptian provinces). Of particular importance were the families of warrior princes of the center and the south of Egypt, at Heracleopolis, Asyut, Hermopolis, and Thebes. The decorations of the tombs of the provincial leaders reveal a great cultural and artistic agitation, as in the tombs at Asyut, Beni Hasan, and Gebelein in central-southern Egypt. A similar political situation took place at the end of the Middle Kingdom, but in that case the power vacuum was filled by the families of the southern nomarchs and by the settlement of a Semitic population—the Hyksos—in the north. While little remains of the Hyksos except a few artifacts (ruins dating to this period are at Tell ed-Daba and Tell el-Yahudiya in the eastern Delta), the sites of Upper Egypt reveal great artistic vivacity. Among these, Thebes emerges as the most important political center since it was home to the dynasty that drove the Hyksos beyond the eastern border and took power over a reunified country. The tombs of these Theban princes are located in the zone of Sheikh Abd el-Qurna, in Western Thebes; all the later rulers of the New Kingdom chose the valleys in the Theban mountains for their tombs, thus affirming their ties to the rulers who had defeated Egypt's enemies.

Hieroglyph
Sepaut-Kemet
("The provinces of Egypt")

Location
The territory of Egypt was divided into 42 administrative provinces, 22 in Upper Egypt and 20 in Lower Egypt.

Chronology
The provinces of Middle and Upper Egypt were made independent during the first two Intermediate Periods. "Asyut was content under my direction, Heracleopolis thanked me. Upper and Lower Egypt said, 'He is like those who are instructed by the king'" (*Autobiography of Khety*).

Bibliography
Aufrere, Golvin, Goyon 1991

Related entries
Mentuhotep II, Scribes and officials

◄ Wall painting (detail) from the tomb of Khnumhotep III at Beni Hasan, Middle Kingdom.

The rock tombs of Middle Egypt are usually composed of a porticoed entrance, with a pair of columns recessed in the façade, from which one enters a single room supported by pillars.

The paintings in the burial chamber of the tomb of Khety, who lived at Asyut during the First Intermediate Period, present scenes of pairs of men training for battle and sports. Numerous physical exercises are presented and many positions of hand-to-hand fighting.

In provincial necropolises, the construction of tombs dug directly into rock dates back to as early as the Old Kingdom. Behind the custom are reasons of security and also the physical nature of the territory, dominated by the mountain chain of the Western Desert.

The pictures are related to the military sphere and reflect the large-scale militaristic activities of the nomarchs of Asyut, supporters of the kings of Heracleopolis.

The necropolis of Asyut, capital of the nome of Lycopolis, presents an elevated level of artistic execution and has been found to contain furnishings of great prestige.

▲ Interior of the tomb of Khety at Asyut, First Intermediate Period.

The international range of influence of some Egyptian nomarchs shows up not only in their wealth but in the interesting pictorial cycles in their tombs, as in this tomb of Khnumhotep III, which includes a procession of Syrians bearing gifts, weapons, and musical instruments.

The Syrian men are depicted with their characteristic large hairstyles, which fall to their shoulders, and their typical pointed beards. They are dressed in long short-sleeved tunics and wear footwear laced at their ankles.

The Syrian women wear clothes that cover one shoulder, leaving the other bare, and wear their hair long, held by a band across the forehead. The colors of the clothes are lively, in tones of blue, purple, and brown; the fabrics are decorated with squares, stripes, or geometric motifs.

The necropolis of Beni Hasan has the rock tombs of the governors of the nome of Oryx who lived during the 11th and 12th dynasties. Their autonomy was severely altered by the centralization of power operated by the 12th-dynasty pharaohs, but nothing ever interrupted their control over the major caravan routes across Middle Egypt.

▲ Wall painting from the tomb of Khnumhotep III at Beni Hasan, Middle Kingdom.

Thebes and Karnak

Hieroglyph
Uaset
("The powerful," Thebes)

Location
Upper Egypt

Chronology
The city rose in
importance during the
Middle Kingdom; it lost
its political importance
during the Late Period,
but was still of religious
importance in the Roman
Period.

Bibliography
Portman 1989.
El-Saghir, Hegazy,
Goyon, Golvin 1989.

Related entries
Amon, Temple, Priests,
Valley of the Kings,
Theban necropolis

The dynasty of princes that unified Egypt after the domination of the Hyksos moved the capital of the state to Thebes, the dynasty's city of origin, as had already happened five centuries earlier, when the Theban king Mentuhotep II had put an end to the anarchy of the First Intermediate Period. Amon, the patron of the city, became the national divinity, and the largest religious complex in Egypt was erected in his honor. The great sanctuary of Karnak was a true divine city, with temples and shrines dedicated also to other gods, including Ptah, Sekhmet, and Maat; the buildings were embellished with further contributions up until the Ptolemaic Period, and the entire area must have seemed like a construction site in continuous operation. A large outer wall (circa 1500 x 800 m) was built around enclosed areas dedicated to the city's triad—Amon, Mut, and Khonsu—and to Montu, an ancient local divinity. Most of all it was the temple of Amon that was worked on and enlarged over all the periods, coming to have a T-shaped layout. The original main structure had an east–west alignment, but as early as the New Kingdom a body oriented north–south had been added. The principal sanctuary of Amon had a sort of appendix in the temple of Luxor, the "harem of the south," to which it was connected by an avenue flanked by sphinxes; during the *opet* festival the statue of the god was taken in procession.

▶ Avenue of leonine sphinxes
that connects the temples of
Karnak and Luxor.

The temple entrance was decorated with the great pylon built by Ramses II and decorated with scenes narrating the battle of Kadesh. In front of it still stand colossal statues of Ramses II and an obelisk; it was once matched by an obelisk on the other side, which is today in the Place de la Concorde in Paris.

The body of the temple, built by Amenhotep III, is composed of a colonnaded hall and a large court surrounded on three sides by a double row of columns. The sanctuary itself is entered by way of four antechambers surrounded by service areas.

Beyond the pylon is a court surrounded by a double peristyle on four sides in which are located colossal statues of Ramses II and a small temple with three shrines, each one dedicated to a god of the Theban triad, Amon, Mut, and Khonsu.

The sanctuary of Ipet-resut ("harem of the south" of Thebes) was dedicated to Amon of Ipet, who here took the form of an ithyphallic god.

▲ Entry pylon, temple of Luxor.

Reused stone blocks indicate Intef II (First Intermediate Period) had work performed here, later continued and enlarged under Sesostris I, during whose reign the famous White Chapel was built, today reconstructed in the Open Air Museum of the sanctuary.

The last constructions date to the Libyan dynasties (the "Bubastite Portal") and to the Ethiopian, to which is owed a central shrine marked off by ten 21-m-high columns, of which only one remains. During the 30th dynasty, Nectanebo II had the court closed of with the 1st pylon and worked a radical rearrangement of the entire sacred precinct.

▲ Sanctuary of Karnak.

The sanctuary is closed by an elongated building, supported on pillars, built by Thutmose III and called the Akh-menu ("Festival Hall"), designed to perpetuate celebrations of that king's jubilee by presenting the temporary structures used in the actual celebrations made instead of stone.

The large sacred lake was symbolic of the primordial waters of Nun out of which creation began. It was used for ceremonies with the sacred boat that carried the simulacrum of the god. An adjacent building was used to house the geese sacred to Amon, and nearby were the residences of the priests.

Past the large hypostyle hall of Ramses II, between the 3rd and 4th pylon, stands a new wing of the temple oriented in a north–south direction, and thus perpendicular to the main east–west axis. This structure, which dates back to the period of Thutmose III and was further worked on by Horemheb, was probably made so as to more easily reach the temple of the goddess Mut.

The center of the sanctuary is the large hypostyle hall of Ramses II, supported by 140 columns 13 m high; the twelve central papyriform columns are taller than the others, creating openings through which illumination enters. This "forest of columns" is probably meant as a monumental rendering in stone of the primordial papyrus thicket through which the sacred cow made its way with its horns.

Theban necropolis

Hieroglyph
Kheret-netjer
("The necropolis")

Location
Upper Egypt, Western
Thebes

Chronology
From the Middle
Kingdom to the
Greco-Roman age

Bibliography
Leblanc 1989.
Weeks 2001.

Related entries
Valley of the Kings, Deir
el-Bahri, Deir el-Medina,
Tomb of Tutankhamen

▼ Burial chamber in the
tomb of Thutmose III in the
Valley of the Kings, Western
Thebes, 18th dynasty.

Opposite the Thebes "of the living" arose, on the opposite bank of the Nile, a city reserved entirely for the dead. According to tradition, the West was the kingdom of the dead; the human soul was tied to the route of the sun and was thus destined to set in the west and then rise again in the east. An area facing the capital, with an extension of about 10 kilometers, was used for the tombs of the pharaohs, for members of the royal family, and for high-ranking nobles and priests. There were also mortuary temples used for celebrations of the worship of the dead. The valleys and gorges that cut into the side of the Theban mountain bear the names of their illustrious guests: from north to south there are the Valley of the Kings, Deir el-Bahri and Assasif, the Valley of the Queens, and Medinet Habu. The Theban tombs of the New Kingdom are underground and extend for tens of meters, sometimes introduced by superstructures housing mortuary shrines. On the plain between the slopes of the mountain chain and the Nile are the "Temples of Millions of Years" dedicated to the souls of Seti I, Ramses II, Amenhotep III—of which remain only the colossi of the façade, called "of Memnon"—and of Ramses III, to cite the most famous. The religious structures were furnished with palaces, service rooms, and storerooms. In the southern area of Western Thebes, Amenhotep III had his residence built, the palace of Malqata, of which there are but few remains.

The narrow valley located immediately to the north of the plain of Deir el-Bahri is today known as the Valley of the Kings (Biban el-Mulk, in Arabic) and hosts 62 royal tombs, to which can now be added a 63rd, recently discovered.

All the pharaohs of the New Kingdom were buried in the Valley of the Kings, the only probable exceptions being Amenhotep IV/Akhenaten and his direct successor, Smenkhkare.

The tombs of the New Kingdom are hypogeums, with a long corridor, sometimes fitted with stairs or ramps. The entrances to the tombs were probably disguised to prevent theft, and the tombs in the necropolis were periodically inspected to verify their integrity.

The members of the royal family were buried in the Valley of the Queens or in other adjacent sites. The few exceptions to this rule include the tomb of Yuya and Tuya, the parents of Queen Tiy, consort of the pharaoh Amenhotep III.

▲ Aerial view of the Valley of the Kings, Western Thebes.

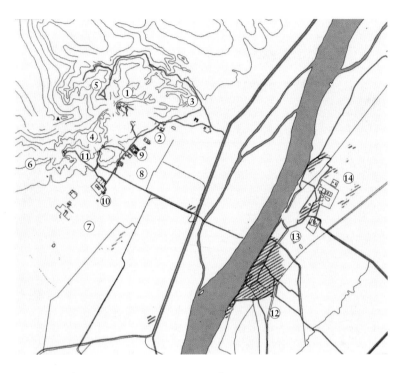

West Bank
1. Deir el-Bahri
2. Assasif
3. Dra Abu el-Naga
4. Sheikh Abd el-Qurna
5. Valley of the Kings
6. Valley of the Queens
7. Malqata
8. Colossi of Memnon
9. Ramesseum
10. Medinet Habu
11. Deir el-Medina

East Bank
12. Temple of Luxor
13. Avenue of sphinxes
14. Temple of Karnak

▲ Map of the Theban area.

In a gorge located to the south of the Valley of the
Kings are the burial sites of royal wives and royal
princes, most of all from the Ramessid period. In
ancient times this was called the "place of beauty,"
perhaps because it was used for the burial of queens.

The tomb of Nefertari is
composed of a descending
stepped access way, with an
antechamber with two side areas
halfway along its route. The
burial chamber is supported by
four quadrangular pillars and
has secondary annexes.

The tomb was discovered
in 1904 by an Italian
archaeological mission
from Turin's Museo Egizio
led by Ernesto Schiaparelli,
who found it had already
been violated by thieves.

▲ Interior of the tomb of Nefertari
in the Valley of the Queens,
Western Thebes, 19th dynasty.

The wall paintings in the tomb are based on
scenes from the Book of the Dead; in them,
the queen appears before numerous divinities.
The quality and state of preservation of the
decoration make this one of the outstanding
examples of ancient Egyptian funerary painting.

Deir el-Bahri

Hieroglyphic
Inet-Nebhepet-Ra
("Valley of Nebhepet-Ra,"
the temple of Mentuhotep II)

Location
Upper Egypt, Western
Thebes

Chronology
From the Middle Kingdom
to the Greco-Roman age.
In 1881, G. Maspero and
E. Brugsch discovered the
hiding place of fifty-odd
mummies of pharaohs,
queens, and priests.

Bibliography
Arnold 1979.

Related entries
Mentuhotep II, Hatshepsut,
Senenmut, Valley of the
Kings, Theban necropolis

The oldest graves in Western Thebes are located on the site of Deir el-Bahri, where the Theban mountain forms a sort of natural amphitheater, dominated by the sharp peak of the Qurna ("the horn"). Since the Middle Kingdom, many hypogeum tombs have been dug into the cliff, a site well protected by its relative inaccessibility. During the same period, the pharaoh Mentuhotep II (circa 2060 BC) had his mortuary temple erected, arranged on two overlapping terraces illuminated by the presence of colonnades and tamarisk and sycamore trees. The king's tomb was probably dug into the rock and topped by a pyramidal tumulus. Six centuries later, this architectural model was adopted by Queen Hatshepsut of the 18th dynasty; once again the three terraces were joined by access ramps, and every level was introduced by a porticoed colonnade. The relief decoration on the internal walls depicted the queen's undertakings—the

▶ Hathoric capital,
shrine of Hathor,
mortuary temple of
Hatshepsut, Deir el-
Bahri, Western Thebes,
18th dynasty.

dedication of obelisks to Amon and the expedition to the Eritrean land of Punt—her divine birth, and her coronation. The funerary complex also includes shrines dedicated to Anubis (the god of embalming) and Hathor (guardian diety of the Deir el-Bahri area). Thutmose III, the queen's stepson and successor, built a third and smaller mortuary temple in the limited space remaining between those of his predecessors.

The painted decoration in the temple of Hatshepsut at Deir el-Bahri includes religious and narrative themes. The queen affirms her legitimacy to the throne by narrating the episode of her divine birth: the god Amon assumes the appearance of Thutmose I and generates the future queen, who is fashioned by the pottery god Khnum ("the molder").

Also famous are the painted reliefs showing the Egyptian expedition to the land of Punt, today's Eritrea. The trip south was undertaken by ship, moving along exotic landscapes past unknown animals; the boats and sailors are depicted with lively realism and with an effective descriptive flair.

The famous painted block presenting the royal spouses of Punt has great realism. The king has short hair and a pointed beard, while his wife is depicted as obese and almost deformed, dressed in a long tunic and a showy necklace. The servants are based on standard typologies and have dark skin.

▲ Block depicting the queen of Punt and her cortege, from the mortuary temple of Hatshepsut at Deir el-Bahri, Western Thebes, 18th dynasty, painted limestone, h circa 100 cm, Egyptian Museum, Cairo, JE 14276,89661.

The shape of the mortuary temple of Mentuhotep II, founder of the Middle Kingdom, was probably suggested by structures of the Old Kingdom; its pyramidal form is a result of the overall shape of the overlapping terraces, while the idea of putting a colonnaded portico on each level was based on the prostyle tombs of the preceding period.

A processional route flanked by statues of Mentuhotep II led to the court in front of the temple, decorated with plants. The court was closed off by the portico of the first terrace, connected to the second by a ramp. The construction was completed by a tumulus, the shape of which cannot be established with precision. Beneath it was a tomb of only symbolic value.

▲ Aerial view of the mortuary temples of Deir el-Bahri.

In an open area between the mortuary temples of Mentuhotep II and Hatshepsut is a third temple, made for the funerary cult of Thutmose III, the queen's stepson and successor.

On the second terrace are two side areas with shrines, one to Hathor, the other to Anubis, the two divinities considered the tutelary gods of the Theban necropolis.

The architectural scheme of the Middle Kingdom temple was adopted by Senenmut, the architect of Queen Hatshepsut, for her mortuary temple. A paved causeway leads from a valley temple to a garden with ponds around the monument. The temple is composed of three overlapping terraces opening onto courts with colonnaded porticoes connected by two ramps.

Akhetaten

Hieroglyphic
Akhetaten
("Horizon of the Aten")

Location
Middle Egypt

Chronology
New Kingdom, 18th
dynasty, reign of
Amenhotep IV/Akhenaten
(1352–1338 BC)

**Principal archaeological
excavations**
Flinders Petrie,
L. Borchardt

Bibliography
Aldred 1988.

Related entries
Amenhotep
IV/Akhenaten, Amarna
excavations

The supremacy of Thebes was challenged, if only for about twenty years, by King Amenhotep IV/Akhenaten. His religious reform in favor of the single god Aten included the foundation of another capital, called "Horizon of the Aten," meaning the site where Aten appears; the city was planned in detail to glorify the ruler and his god. The city (today's Amarna) stood in Middle Egypt on virgin soil on the east bank of the Nile. Although archaeological excavations have involved a very large area (roughly 10 kilometers), only traces of the ancient settlement have been found. In fact, the city was taken apart immediately after Akhenaten's death, and its building materials were reused in other places. In the central area have been identified the royal quarters, while in the southern area must have been private residences. Among the city's main monuments was the great temple of Aten, composed of a series of open-air courts. A road ran through the center of the city from north to south, with the offi-

cial palaces and court residences arranged along its sides and connected by an elevated bridge. The private homes included the workshop of the court sculptor Thutmose, creator of the famous bust of Queen Nefertiti in painted limestone. Tombs for nobles and dignitaries were dug into the walls of the mountains surrounding the site, but most of them were never used because of the abandonment of the city.

▶ Boundary stele of
Akhenaten at Tuna
el-Gebel, 18th dynasty.

The sudden end to the occupation of the site of Akhetaten has made it possible for archaeologists to carry out large-scale excavations of the ruins, which are preserved unchanged from the moment the site was abandoned.

It has been determined that the city was built on virgin soil; the landscape was dominated by hills and may have resembled the hieroglyphic akhet ("horizon"), a sun rising between two mountains, from which the city derived its name.

The sacred area of the terrain of Akhetaten was marked off by boundary steles that defined a territory about 20 km long.

The heart of the capital was its central zone, location of both the great temple of Aten and the royal palace. This palace occupied land on both banks of the Nile, to the east the private residences with space for public appearances, to the west the reception areas.

▲ Excavations at Amarna (Akhetaten).

The sudden and tragic death of Akhenaten was followed by the destruction of his capital; the buildings were torn down, the site razed, and the materials were taken away and reused. The small sandstone talatat blocks (the size of three hand-breadths; talata is Arabic for 3) could be easily removed and transported, being manageable and relatively light.

Visible above are workers storing grain and other food supplies in the storerooms of a temple. Below are several scenes of stockbreeding, the care and feeding of cattle. Temples usually had enormous reserves of food and lived as autonomous entities.

Scenes of work and food storage are depicted on the walls on different levels.

In the lower level are depicted several stages in the activities of an artisan workshop and in the shops belonging to the temple. Rows of servants move furniture, vases, and goods of various kinds, while geese eat grain from a jar; below, other servants carry birds and other foods to a storeroom.

▲ Blocks from Amarna found as filling material in the 9th pylon of the temple of Karnak, 18th dynasty, painted limestone, circa 18 m long (reconstructed wall), Luxor Museum, Luxor J223.

Deir el-Medina

To guarantee a worthy burial to the rulers of the New Kingdom, teams of artisans and workers were kept busy digging and constructing tombs; the work was supervised by foremen, superintendents, and scribes. The life of the "servants in the place of truth" took place entirely on the West Bank at Thebes, where the workers also had their homes. In fact, the village of Deir el-Medina was built by Amenhotep I to optimize the work and movements of these workers. This small village consisted of about seventy houses, all facing the road that ran through the inhabited area, surrounded by a perimeter wall. In this area the artisans lived with their families. The survival of the population was guaranteed by the state administration, which paid the workers salaries composed of food, cereal, meat, fish, vegetables, wine, and other foods, as well as clothing. When this payment failed to arrive during the 20th dynasty it set off a wave of strikes among the workers, as recorded on several papyri. The burial sites of the workers were located not far from the village; these tombs were small-scale imitations of the great pharaonic tombs. Excavations at Deir el-Medina have brought to light a great abundance of details, revealing many aspects of the daily life of the town's inhabitants.

Hieroglyph
Pa-Demi ("The village,"
Deir el Medina)

Location
Upper Egypt, Western
Thebes

Chronology
From the New
Kingdom to the
Greco-Roman age

**Principal archaeological
excavations**
E. Schiaparelli,
B. Bruyère

Bibliography
Janssen 1997.

Related entries
Amenhotep I, Village
organization, Artisans,
Valley of the Kings

◄Satirical ostracon
depicting a cat leading
geese, from Deir el-
Medina, 19th–20th
dynasty, painted
limestone, h 11 cm,
Egyptian Museum,
Cairo, JE 63801.

The western hill is the site of a necropolis in which the artisans and leading people of the village of Deir el-Medina were buried. Their tombs have a mortuary chapel topped by a small brick pyramid, with the burial itself relegated to subterranean rooms.

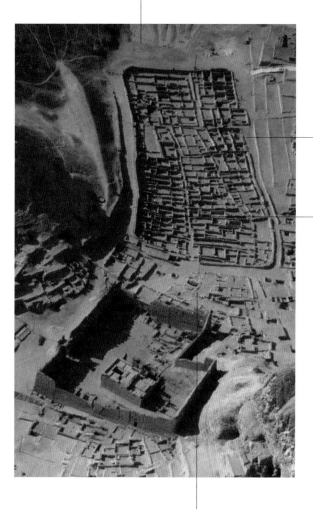

The village was built in successive phases, the first of which dates to Amenhotep I. Later enlargements of the area of the village made it possible for it to host from 60 to 120 workers with their families.

The houses were composed of at least four rooms arranged in sequence with the entrance directly off the street. There was an entry area with a reception space adjacent to a kitchen and storeroom and a bedroom. Many houses had a cellar, and the roof could be used as a terrace.

The layout of the village follows an elongated quadrangle, enclosed by a wall. A north–south road runs the entire length of the village, with the houses arranged to face onto it. There was one portal in the exterior wall, and it was closed at night.

▲ Aerial view of the excavations of the village of Deir el-Medina.

The size and elaborateness of a tomb's interior decoration depended on the financial state of the individual, and naturally the most attractive tombs from the necropolis of Deir el-Medina belonged to the village's administrators.

Accompanied by his wife, Lyneferti, the deceased appears before numerous divinities in the netherworld. In the paradise of the Fields of Iaru, the couple lives in eternal bliss.

The pictorial decoration reveals that the construction of the tomb dates to the 19th dynasty, and its owners are depicted in the style of the epoch: Sennedjem wears pleated skirts, finely pleated wigs, and a short beard under his chin; his wife wears large pleated robes and long three-piece wigs.

▲ Interior of the tomb of Sennedjem at Deir el-Medina, Western Thebes, 19th dynasty.

Tanis

Hieroglyph
Djanet (meaning uncertain;
it is the Zoan of the Bible,
Tanis of the Greeks, today
San el-Hagar)

Location
Lower Egypt, eastern Delta

Chronology
Third Intermediate Period,
21st–22nd dynasty

**Principal archaeological
excavations**
F. A. Mariette, Flinders
Petrie, P. Montet

Bibliography
Montet 1952.

Related entries
Sheshonk I, Royal tombs
of Tanis

This city of the northeastern Delta represents one of the most densely occupied sites in the area, and its overlapping structures make archaeological excavations and understanding difficult. The city was the capital of the 21st and 22nd dynasties in the Third Intermediate Period, after which the high priest of Amon dominated in the south of Egypt, while the north was ruled by kings from the Delta. Although building materials and statues from other areas and dating to earlier periods, in particular to that of Ramses II, have been found at Tanis, the building of the city must have taken place under Psusennes I toward the end of the 11th century BC, as is demonstrated by seals stamped in bricks. This king probably also created the temple of Amon, the heart of the city, surrounded by two circles of walls, the outermost of which measured 430 x 370 meters, with a thickness of about fifteen meters and a height of ten. Today, Tanis is nothing but rubble, but it was in that rubble that an extraordinary discovery was made in 1939: the Egyptologist Pierre Montet found

▶ Bust of a statue of
Ramses II, from Tanis, 19th
dynasty, gray granite, h 80
cm, Egyptian Museum,
Cairo, CG 616.

a practically intact group of royal burials containing the tomb furnishings of the pharaohs Psusennes I, Amenemope, Sheshonk II, Osorkon III, Takelot II, and Sheshonk III. Standing out among the many objects brought to light were the silver sarcophagi and gold masks that protected the mummies, along with numerous masterpieces of goldworking.

The human elements of the composition are limited to the sovereign's face, framed by a thick mane and leonine ears. The entire arrangement of the figure has a sense of great vigor, the masses compact and muscular; the pharaoh wanted to communicate the idea of regality based on power and solidity.

This statue was found at Tanis, together with other sphinxes of this type, and was long thought to be a product of Hyksos art. The portrait instead reveals the features of Amenemhet III, whose name does not appear on the inscriptions: this statue is tangible proof of the usurpation of monuments that occurred at Tanis.

The inscription on the base refers to Ramses II, builder of the capital Per-Ramesse, also located in the eastern Delta.

An inscription on the right side of the lion contains the double cartouche of Merenptah, king of the 19th dynasty and son of Ramses II.

On the chest of the sphinx is the cartouche of Psusennes I, king of the 21st dynasty, who had Tanis as his capital.

▲ Sphinx of Amenemhet III, from Tanis, 12th dynasty, gray granite, h 150 cm, Egyptian Museum, Cairo, CG 394.

During the building of the city of Per-Ramesse, during the reign of Ramses II, many monuments from Heliopolis and Bubastis were reused. Later, the kings of the 21st dynasty enriched their capital, Tanis, with building materials from various places in the Delta.

The blocks on the top are covered with inscriptions bearing the royal titulary of Ramses II, whose materials were largely reused in the building of Tanis.

Another cartouche, positioned vertically, bears what may be the name of a Ramessid king.

This block bears the cartouches of a local king, Sheshonk I, the Shishak of the Bible. Founder of the 22nd dynasty, he invaded Palestine and won victories over the kingdoms of Judah and Israel.

This block reveals the overwriting of the titulary of a Ramses (most probably Ramses II) over an earlier text, of which can be seen to the right a letter (the quail) canceled only halfway.

▲ Ruins of Tanis.

Nubia and Abu Simbel

The region to the south of the First Cataract (located at Aswan), on the border between Egypt and Sudan, is called Nubia. This name was probably derived from the mines of gold (*nub*, in ancient Egyptian) from which the Egyptians took the raw materials for their goldworking. From the earliest epochs, these territories carried on commercial exchanges with the interior of Africa. To maintain their political and economic domination of the region, the pharaohs built fortresses and temples along the route of the Nile. Many of these monuments, threatened by creation of Lake Nasser following construction of the Aswan High Dam in 1960, were dismantled and moved from their ancient sites. The outstanding symbol of this effort was the relocation of the two rock temples of Ramses II at Abu Simbel, moved almost 300 kilometers to the south of Aswan. The site bears two sanctuaries that Ramses II had cut into the rock, one dedicated to him, the other to his royal wife Nefertari, together with the goddess Hathor. The Great Temple gives onto a court, accessible by a pylon, with a façade decorated by colossi about 21 meters high depicting the king. Inside is a first hypostyle hall supported by Osirian pillars and then a second, leading to the sanctuary, site of the niche with the cult statues. On the façade of the Small Temple are six colossi representing members of the royal family; the temple is composed of a hypostyle hall and the sanctuary.

Hieroglyph
Per-Ramessu-Mer-Imen
("Temple of Ramses,
beloved of Amon,"
the Great Temple of
Abu Simbel)

Location
Lower Nubia

Chronology
New Kingdom, 19th
dynasty, reign of
Ramses II
(1279–1213 BC)

Bibliography
Friedman 2002.

Related entries
Ramses II, Foreigners,
Commerce, Nubian
temples

◀ Façade of the Small
Temple of Abu Simbel,
19th dynasty.

The structures were cut directly into the wall of rock, a technique somewhat common in the sanctuaries of the Upper Delta and Nubia, perhaps because of the configuration of the land. Such rock temples may also be an evolution of the caves in which the earliest cult worship was performed.

The entrance to the monumental complex is through a portal that gave access to a large flat space; the façade of the Great Temple has four colossal images of the king seated on a throne accompanied by his wife and princes.

▲ Great Temple of Abu Simbel, 19th dynasty.

The temples of Abu Simbel were built around year 25 of the reign of Ramses II under the supervision of the viceroy of Kush, Iuny. A few years later an earthquake collapsed one of the colossi on the façade, and it was never repaired.

Above the entrance is a niche with an image of the standing god Ra, flanked by depictions of the goddess Maat and a scepter with an animal head. Like a three-dimensional rebus, these three elements compose the prenomen of the king (User-Maat-Ra): User *(the scepter)*—Maat *(the goddess)*—Ra *(the god)*.

A vestibule with four pillars leads to the cult niche; carved into the rear wall of the sanctuary are images of the divinities of the temple: Ptah, Amon-Ra, the pharaoh himself, and Ra-Harakhty

Around October 20 the rising sun comes into line with the temple, its first morning rays illuminating the statues; that date may have been Ramses' birthday, or perhaps it was the date of the temple's inauguration.

The floor slants slightly downward moving inward, and the ceiling tends to lower as one approaches the inner sanctum, giving the area an increased sense of depth.

The walls of the vestibule bear scenes of worship; the king, accompanied by Queen Nefertari, watches the procession of the boat of Amon-Ra, decorated with emblems of the ram-headed god. Such ceremonies probably took place near the sanctuary itself, and pieces of the sacred boat have been found there.

▲ Inner sanctum in the Great Temple at Abu Simbel, 19th dynasty.

Naukratis

Egypt's contacts with the Mediterranean world date to ancient times, as indicated by the presence in Egypt of imported trade goods and evidence of Minoan and Mycenaean (circa 15th–12th centuries BC) art. The number of Greeks on Egyptian territory increased enormously during the 26th dynasty, which had Sais, in the western Delta, as its capital. Around the middle of the 7th century BC, Psamtik I began hiring large numbers of Carian and Ionian mercenaries, and as veterans with certain rights and privileges they acquired land in the Delta. A century later, Ahmose II made Naukratis the center of trade with the Mediterranean, a sort of emporium. The city thus came to host a large number of foreigners, most of all Greeks, involved in commercial activities. Naukratis was located near Sais on the Canopic branch of the Nile. Today the canal is dried up, but in antiquity it was the only canal navigable the entire year and suitable for cargo ships along its entire length; this branch of the Nile Delta connected the Mediterranean with Memphis, which even in the later pharaonic period was a city of great administrative importance. A decree dating to Nectanebo I, at the beginning of the 4th century BC, established that all the cargo ships that passed Naukratis had to pay one-tenth of the value of their goods to the Egyptian treasury, which had a tax-collection office in the city.

Hieroglyph
Niut-Karetj ("The city of Karetj")

Location
Lower Egypt, western Delta

Chronology
From the 26th dynasty to the Greco-Roman age

Principal archaeological excavations
Flinders Petrie, W. Coulson–A. Leonard

Bibliography
Möller 2000.

Related entries
Psamtik I, Foreigners, Commerce

◄ Portrait of Siamon, priest and dignitary of Greek origin (as indicated by the beard), tomb of Siamon at Gebel Mawta, Siwa, 26th dynasty.

Nectanebo I, founder of the 30th dynasty, erected the so-called Naukratis Stele in his first year of reign (380 BC). It contains a fiscal decree in favor of the temple of the goddess Neith at Sais.

The text ends with the king's instructions that the stele be "placed in Naukratis on the bank of the Anu. Then shall my goodness be remembered for all eternity."

The existence of the stele had long been hypothesized, but a copy of it was found only a few years ago in the waters of the bay of Abukir (site of the ancient port of Canopus). It is today displayed in the National Museum in Alexandria. Its text includes instructions that the stele be located at the arrival port for merchandise (Honé, or Canopus): "At the mouth of the Sea of the Greeks, in the city of Honé after the province of Sais."

The text of the decree begins in the eighth column: "Let be given one-tenth of the gold, of the silver, of the timber, of manufactured goods, of everything coming from the Sea of the Greeks, of all the tolls paid into my treasury in the town called Honé, as well as one-tenth of the gold, of the silver, of everything which is in Naukratis, on the bank of the canal Anu, and that be registered with the royal administration to preserve and protect the divine offering to my mother Neith forever."

▲ Naukratis Stele, from Naukratis, 30th dynasty, black granite, h 200 cm, Egyptian Museum, Cairo, JE 34002.

Oasis

Historically, the western oases were a borderland between the agricultural civilization of the Nile Valley and the nomadic populations of the desert. They were located along a line of depressions in the rocky plateau from which groundwater occasionally rose to form springs. This position made them strategic points in the commercial routes between inner Africa and Egypt. Numerous caravan routes made possible the transportation of exotic products along the Mediterranean coast as well as toward the Sahara. Since the Old Kingdom, Egypt's pharaohs had sought to rule these territories, installing governors and undertaking construction works first in the oases of Kharga, Dakhla, Farafra, and Bahariya; later on, these state interventions went as far as Siwa on the Libyan border. Among the most important monuments of the western oases are two important sites from the late pharaonic age: the temple of Amon of Hibis at Kharga and that of Amon at Siwa. The first was erected by the Persian king Darius at the time of the Persian conquest of Egypt, around the middle of the 6th century BC; constructed in the most traditional Egyptian style, the sanctuary was dedicated to Amon and was enlarged by Nectanebo II and by the Ptolemaic kings. The second temple is located at Aghurmi, in the Siwa Oasis; according to legend, after conquering Egypt, Alexander the Great went there to consult the oracle, which legitimized him as pharaoh.

Hieroglyph
Uhat ("oasis")

Location
Western Desert

Chronology
From prehistoric times to today

Principal archaeological excavations
After the work of A. Fakhri at Siwa, Bahariya, and Farafra in the 1950s, there was the activity of the missions of the Germanic Institute (Siwa) and of the IFAO (Kharga, Dakhla).

Bibliography
Aufrere, Golvin, Goyon 1994.

Related entries
Foreigners, Commerce

◀ View of the Siwa Oasis with the temple of Amon on the hill of Aghurmi.

Kharga represented a stopover point for the caravans between the Western Desert and Nubia. It was drained and its hydraulic network was improved during the period of the Persian domination of Egypt.

Today the temple stands in the center of a luxurious palm grove and is one of the two buildings of worship built by the Persians in the oasis. The main temple was begun by Apries and Ahmose II in the 26th dynasty and was completed by Darius I, king of the Persians.

The temple is dedicated to the Theban triad of Amon, Mut, and Khonsu, but some of the reliefs, in a good state of preservation, are dedicated to the god Set, protector of deserts and oases. He is depicted here with a falcon head.

The building follows the classical layout of an Egyptian temple; the large entry portal was added during the Roman age.

▲ Entrance portal of the temple of Hibis in the Kharga Oasis, 27th dynasty.

Built beginning in the 26th dynasty, the temple of Amon was the site of an oracle famously visited by Alexander the Great to legitimize his power in Egypt.

The northern structure of the temple overlooks a cliff; various parts of it have been shored up to keep them from collapsing.

According to a legend handed on by Pliny the Elder, the impious Persian king Cambyses, having invaded Egypt, planned to destroy the temple of Siwa but his army was buried in a sand storm while marching toward the oasis.

The temple is entered by way of the main door of the ghost town of Aghurmi. The settlement has a well and subterranean passages that may have been used for the storage of provisions; one of these passages leads to the temple of Umm Ebeida, farther downriver.

▲ Temple of Amon at Siwa, 26th dynasty.

The history of Egyptology

◀David Roberts, *View from below of the great door of the temple at Philae*, watercolor, 1846–49.

"I am going to be much longer in my history of Egypt. And this because it has more wonders in it than any other country in the world and more works that are beyond description" (Herodotus)

Greeks and Romans

In depth
In Italy, the principal temples of Isis were in Rome (at the Quirinal, the Caelian Hill, in the Campus Martius, in the Capitol), in Porto, Ostia, Lake Nemi, Palestrina, Benevento, Pompeii, Cumae, Pozzuoli, Florence, Fiesole, Bologna, Industria (Monteu da Po, near Turin), Aquileia, and Verona.

Bibliography
Lollio Barberi, Parola, Toti 1995. Gallo 1997, p. 290-296.

Related entries
Naukratis, Historical sources

For a long time, the Western world's vision of Egypt was based on the description of that land given by the Greek historian Herodotus in the second book of his *History*, written around the middle of the 5th century BC. During that period, Egypt was dominated by Persia and for several centuries had been inhabited by Greek peoples, but Herodotus, without making great distinctions, relates official reports, legends, myths, and prejudices, blending information on pharaonic Egypt with ideas from the Egypt of his day. Herodotus presents the image of an ancient civilization based on sensible laws and ancient religious beliefs with a wealthy and wise population; in the eyes of a Greek, of course, even the Egyptians were "barbarians" with bizarre customs, monstrous divinities, and inexplicable traditions. This mixture of reverence and wonder shows up in many later authors, from Plutarch to Diodorus Siculus to Apuleius. After its conquest by Octavian, Egypt clamorously entered the Roman world, fascinating most of all for the religious doctrines related to the myths of Isis and Osiris, with their promise of a serene afterlife; the

worship of these gods spread across the Roman Empire. Images and objects from Egypt became part of the empire's daily life, from the obelisks that decorated city squares to the statues of gods and pharaohs or locally made imitations of those statues. There were also the grandiose architectural reproductions by Hadrian in his villa at Tivoli, including a reproduction of the Canopus canal.

This mosaic, probably from the sanctuary of Fortuna Primigenia, was moved to various sites and restored; today, it is in a local museum. Its dating is disputed, but the Alexandrian taste of its subject and style suggest a period between the 1st century BC and the 1st century AD.

In the collective imagination of Rome, the Egyptian landscape was composed of the desert with its ferocious beasts, the Nile with its many boats as well as fish and animals, and a landscape of ancient and mysterious monuments.

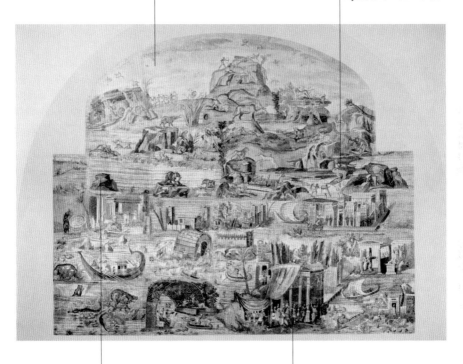

The upper area presents the course of the Upper Nile, along which move Africans armed with bows and arrows to hunt game; the arid landscape is populated by wild animals, including lions, hyenas, gazelles, giraffes, chimpanzees, and snakes.

Lower Egypt, depicted in the lower area, is a land of cultivated fields and inhabited towns; the territory is occupied by religious structures, palaces, boats, garrisons, and villages.

◄ The pyramid of Caius Cestius Epulone at Rome, 12 BC.

▲ Nilotic mosaic, Museo Archeologico Prenestino, Palestrina.

The monumental complex testifies not only to the artistic eclecticism of imperial Rome but also to the spread of Egyptian cults to Rome. The emperor Hadrian, dedicated to the study of ancient cultures, was a great admirer of Egypt.

The emperor's favorite, the young Bithynian Antinoüs, drowned in the Nile; the worship of his soul was assimilated to that of Osiris and included the celebration of mysteries and initiation rites, some of which took place in the "Canopus" in the Tiburtine villa. Hadrian founded the city of Antinoöpolis in Egypt in memory of Antinoüs.

Hadrian visited Egypt in AD 130 and spent much time there; as proof of his passage he had his name carved into one of the colossi of Memnon. Hadrian reproduced some of the images he saw during this trip in the stone creations of his complex at Tivoli.

▲ Maritime Theater, Hadrian's Villa, Tivoli, mid-2nd century AD.

"But the way of writing the Egyptians used in these things . . . can be easily interpreted . . . by the entire world of learned men"
(Leon Battista Alberti)

Renaissance

During the Middle Ages, the image of Egypt was filtered through reading of the Old and New Testaments. Egypt became the background to the stories of Joseph and Moses, the Flight of the Holy Family, and the martyrdom of saints Mark and Catherine of Alexandria, among others. Only with humanism and the birth of philological studies did ancient Egypt become the subject of serious study. In 1422, a pamphlet arrived in Italy entitled *The Hieroglyphics of Horapollon of Nilopolis*, which attempted an interpretation of the mysterious Egyptian images. The end of the 15th century saw publication of the *Hypnerotomachia Poliphili*, which narrates a dreamlike voyage among architecture covered with hieroglyphics, illustrated in woodcuts accompanying the text. With the Renaissance, Egyptian culture was looked upon as the oldest civilization, the cradle of knowledge and also of mysteries. To add status to their names, important families traced their lineage back to the pharaohs. At the same time, the style of things ancient became popular, especially at Rome, resulting in a search for historical objects: obelisks and statues became a key to reading the past, no longer merely urban decorations. An Egyptianized artistic style came into being that reinterpreted ancient images on the basis of the propaganda of Italian courts. Examples are the frescoes in Palazzo Massimo alle Terme in Rome and Palazzo Te in Mantua.

In depth
During the Renaissance, texts in Greek, such as the *Hieroglyphika* of Horapollon and the *Corpus Hermeticum*, began to circulate in the West, influencing philosophical thinking. The classics of historiography and geography were rediscovered, such as Herodotus, Strabo, Polybius, and Diodorus Siculus.

Bibliography
Ciampini 2004

◄ Lion of Nectanebo I, 30th dynasty, discovered in Rome's Campus Martius in the 15th century, Museo Gregoriano Egizio, Vatican.

329

One of the woodcut illustrations from the Hypnerotomachia Poliphili, *attributed to Giovanni Colonna, includes the depiction of an elephant bearing an obelisk located near a mausoleum; it may have served as the inspiration for Bernini's monument.*

The obelisk was found in 1665 in the Campus Martius in Rome and was erected in the Piazza della Minerva. The statue's popular name, "the Piggy" (later changed to "the Chick") may reflect the animal's shape, which looks more like a pig than an elephant; according to tradition, Bernini aimed the animal's rear end at the palace of the Jesuits as a deliberate insult.

The Latin inscription on the base of the obelisk reads: "Whoever sees here that the symbols of the Egyptian sage, inscribed on the obelisk, are carried by the elephant, the strongest of the beasts, understand that it is proof that a strong mind is needed to support solid knowledge."

▲ Egyptian obelisk from the 26th dynasty, end 7th century BC, atop an elephant, by Giovanni Lorenzo Bernini, known as the "Pulcino della Minerva," Piazza della Minerva, Rome, 1667.

The head in Turin was the subject of studies and debates during the 17th century because of the marks engraved on the face. Many interpreted the signs as hieroglyphs and attributed meanings to them related to the mysteries of the cult of Isis.

In 1761, these symbols were compared to Chinese ideograms, and an attempt was made to compare the two languages. Studies have established that the marks are, in fact, astrological symbols.

Among the many to weigh in on this question was the German Jesuit and scholar Athanasius Kircher, who arrived in Rome in 1635 and taught mathematics and Hebrew at the College of Rome. His was the first methodical attempt to interpret hieroglyphic inscriptions, but his reasoning was still based on concepts related to esoteric concepts and mysteries.

▲ Head "of Isis," black stone, Fondazione Museo Antichità Egizie, Turin.

The walls are decorated with large landscapes in which pyramids rise from desert sands, surrounded by palms; between the paintings are the figures of telamons in Egyptian-style dress that stand out against the lapis-lazuli-blue background. Sphinxes are set on wall brackets.

Egypt-inspired decorative themes appeared as early as the Middle Ages, most often as illustrations for passages from the Old and New Testaments, such as the story of Joseph, Exodus, and the Flight into Egypt.

Other examples of this Egyptian style can be found in the Loggia del Museo of Palazzo Te in Mantua, the Casino of Villa Borghese in Rome, and the Borgia Apartments in the Vatican; it was 17th-century popes who carried out the first archaeological excavations at Rome, leading to the discovery and reuse of ancient monuments.

▲ Interior of the Egyptian room in Palazzo Massimo alle Terme, Rome.

"Soldiers, from the heights of these pyramids forty centuries are watching you!" (Napoleon)

Napoleon Bonaparte

Egypt finally emerged from the myths during the 18th century. Travelers and missionaries wrote reports, illustrated by woodcuts, that awakened Europe to a still unexplored country. Egyptian symbolism and iconography were adopted by the Freemasons and various other secret societies, contributing to their diffusion. The extraordinary tidal wave of information that swept over the West resulted from a military expedition, Napoleon's 1798 invasion of Egypt, which was then part of the crumbling Turkish Empire. Along with an army of soldiers Napoleon took scholars, led by Vivant Denon; these scholars were charged with classifying, describing, and drawing what they saw. Despite an epic battle fought on the plain of the pyramids at Giza, the French conquest of the north of the country proved ephemeral and was canceled by the major defeat inflicted on the French fleet at Abu Qir by the British admiral Nelson. Even so, the work of the savants did not cease until the final surrender to the English in 1801. By 1803, publication had begun

of the monumental *Description de l'Égypte*, which was completed only thirty years later and contained roughly 4,000 pages and 600 illustrations. Napoleon's campaign had an immediate effect on contemporary figurative arts, which were further enriched by decorative elements that were at the same time both exotic and ancient.

In depth
Among the principal travelers to visit Egypt in the 17th and 18th centuries were J. Vansleb, F.I. Norden, C. Sicard, R. Pococke, and V. Donati.

Bibliography
Herold 1962.

Related entries
Jean-François Champollion

▼ F. L. Watteau, *Battle of the Pyramids*, Musée des Beaux-Arts, Valenciennes.

In 1797, *following his great victories in Europe, Napoleon prepared to invade Egypt, then part of the crumbling Turkish Empire. The French fleet set off from the port of Toulon in May 1798, en route to Alexandria with a large team of scholars as well as an army of soldiers.*

After various ups and downs and the solid defeat of the fleet at Abu Qir, the French troops were forced to leave Egypt in September 1801.

On July 21, 1798, Napoleon's forces battled the Mameluke troops serving the Turks and supported by the English on the plain of Giza, opposite the pyramids. Following this victory, Napoleon made a triumphant entry into Cairo, but the success proved short-lived: on August 1, the British navy under Admiral Horatio Nelson badly defeated the French fleet off Abu Qir near Alexandria.

▲ F. J. Couche, *The Battle of the Pyramids,* 19th century.

The work of the French savants *was the first scholarly investigation of Egypt, and it laid the basis for later works of Egyptology; its importance is a result of not only the enormous pile of information collected but the homogeneity, a result of the excellent coordination among the team of scholars.*

The goal of the scholars was to collect as much information as possible concerning the nature, geography, history both ancient and recent, and customs of Egypt.

Among the savants *who took part in Napoleon's expedition were the mathematician Gaspard Monge, the chemist Claude-Louis Berthollet, the geologist Dieudonné Dolomieu, and the artist and archaeologist Vivant Denon.*

▲ Frontispiece to the *Description de l'Égypte*, 1829.

"Je tiens l'affaire!" ("I have the key!")
(Jean-François Champollion)

Jean-François Champollion

Without question, the outstanding moment in the history of Egyptology came in 1822 when the French linguist Jean-François Champollion succeeded in deciphering hieroglyphic writing. Born at Figeac in the Dauphiné, he studied at Grenoble; from the time of his youth he was determined to find the key to the reading of the ancient language of the Egyptians, which had fallen into oblivion nearly fifteen centuries earlier. He thus set about learning all the ancient languages then known and reviewed all the preceding attempts at the interpretation of hieroglyphs. He was convinced that the symbols were not merely ideograms but that they also had a phonetic meaning. He was unable to demonstrate his hypothesis with the texts at his disposal; then in 1810 he obtained a copy of the stone found in 1799 at Rosetta. This was a bilingual document in which the same text was inscribed three ways, in hieroglyphic, in demotic (for the Egyptian version), and in Greek. Knowing the Greek letters for the names of kings and queens enabled him to isolate the phonetic elements that in the Egyptian version gave the transcription of those names, and he created a grid of signs, later enriched with biliterals, triliterals, and

determinatives. His studies led him to visit many museums, including the one in Turin, Italy. He undertook an expedition to Egypt on behalf of the Louvre and obtained the first chair in Egyptian archaeology at the Collège de France. Death prevented him from seeing publication of his research in Egypt, published by his collaborator Ippolito Rosellini between 1832 and 1844.

▶ Leon Cogniet, *Jean-François Champollion*, Musée du Louvre, Paris.

The stone was found in 1799 at Rosetta (el-Rashid in the northern Delta) during work near Fort Julien. The discoverer, a captain Bouchard, immediately realized it was an inscription and decided to ship it to Cairo.

Champollion received a copy of the texts on the stone in 1810; the availability of a bilingual translation made it possible for him to confirm many of his theories. In particular, it was the transcription of the names of Ptolemy and Queen Cleopatra that made possible the isolation of the monoliteral signs, used in this case for their phonetic value.

The text is a decree from Ptolemy V inscribed in two languages and three writing styles; the Egyptian is written in hieroglyphs in the upper level and in demotic in the central, while the Greek translation is on the bottom.

After the defeat of Napoleon's army, the stone fell into the hands of the British, for which reason it is today in the British Museum, London.

▲ Rosetta Stone, from El-Rashid, Ptolemaic Period, basalt, h 114 cm, British Museum, London, EA24.

"I had the pleasure of discovering . . . one of the two famous
pyramids of Giza, and some tombs of the kings at Thebes . . . the
famous bust of the young Memnon . . . I opened the temple of
Abu Simbel" (G.D. Belzoni)

Giovanni Battista Belzoni

Chronology
Giovanni Battista
Belzoni (Padua,
1778–Gwato, Benin,
1823)

Bibliography
Christophe 1979.
Belzoni 1988.

Related entries
Valley of the Kings,
Nubia and Abu Simbel,
The consuls

The extraordinary figure of the Italian Belzoni is emblematic of
the climate of Egyptian fervor awakened by publication of the
Description de l'Égypte and by the rush to find Egyptian antiquities. After a life wandering Europe when not performing in
music halls, Belzoni was in Malta when he came in contact with
an agent of Muhammad Ali who convinced him to go to Egypt
and present a waterwheel he had perfected. The waterwheel
failed to attract interest but put Belzoni in contact with the
French consul Bernardino Drovetti, the Swiss traveler Ludwig
Burckhardt, and the English consul Henry Salt. Belzoni began a
long journey along the Nile, intending not only to procure
objects for Salt—which included a colossal bust of Ramses II—
but also to visit ancient sites until then never reached by a West-
erner. His goal was the legendary Abu Simbel. Arriving there in
July 1817, he freed the front of the Great Temple of sand. Later,
at Luxor, he discovered several tombs in the Valley of the Kings,
including that of Seti I, still considered among the largest and

Giovanni Belzoni

best decorated in Egypt. He
removed the heavy alabaster sarcophagus of the pharaoh, which
is today in London. At Giza he
managed to find an entrance to
the pyramid of Khafre and documented his exploits with exciting
descriptions and watercolors
that were the inspiration for a
large-scale exhibition held at Pic-
cadilly between 1820 and 1822,
to great public acclaim. He died
of dysentery in West Africa, traveling to Timbuktu.

▶ Portrait of G. B. Belzoni

In order to find the entrance to the pyramid of Khafre, Belzoni dedicated himself to the study of the internal structure of the pyramid of Khufu.

Having identified the entrance, he had the halls dug out, and after about a month reached the burial chamber; the tomb was empty, broken into in the ancient era. All that remained was the pink granite sarcophagus.

The sarcophagus of Khafre, carved out of a monolithic piece of Aswan granite, is still on the site and an inscription recalls its discovery: on a wall of the burial chamber is written "G. B. Belzoni, 1818."

▲ R. Bowyer, *Visitors to the Interior of the Great Pyramid of Giza*, in Luigi Mayer, *Views in Egypt*, 1801.

Belzoni came in contact with the Swiss explorer Ludwig Burckhardt, one of the first Europeans to adventure into Nubia, famous for having discovered the site of Abu Simbel in 1812. Burckhardt had not been able to remove the sand from the entrance and visit the interior.

Belzoni wanted to find the entrance to the Great Temple at Abu Simbel and went there with a group of workers in July 1817. After a month of work, the façade of the temple of Ramses II was freed of sand. Belzoni explored the interior of the temple, finding only a few remains, and wrote a detailed description of his visit, illustrated with watercolors.

Although he produced a rich documentation of his exploits, Belzoni was never considered an archaeologist, but rather an explorer. The methods of excavation typical of the period were rough and hardly respectful of the monuments themselves, directed more at the search for precious objects than historical documentation.

▲ David. Roberts, *Façade of the Great Temple of Abu Simbel*, watercolor, Victoria and Albert Museum, London.

Belzoni's primary discovery at Thebes was the tomb of Seti I, father of Ramses II. It is one of the largest tombs in the Valley of the Kings, more than 100 m long, and it is decorated with splendid painted reliefs.

On his return from the expedition to Abu Simbel, Belzoni concentrated his efforts in the Valley of the Kings at Thebes. In 1817, he discovered the tombs of Ramses I and Prince Amonhekhepeshef, son of Ramses II.

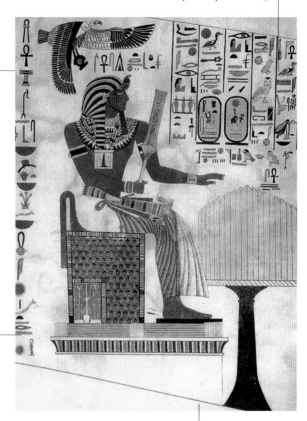

The tomb of Seti I is still being restored in an effort to stabilize the structure and to document its decoration.

Belzoni made important contributions in his reproduction of the layout of the tomb and his record of its wall decorations, collected in his book about Egypt and Nubia; the plates reproduce some of the most beautiful funerary painting of the New Kingdom.

▲ G.B. Belzoni, *Painting from the Tomb of Seti I*, lithograph, in G.B. Belzoni, *Narrative of the Operations and Recent Discoveries in Egypt and Nubia*, 1825.

"The imagination . . . stops and falls impotent at the feet of the one hundred forty columns in the hypostyle hall of Karnak"
(Letter from J. F. Champollion to his brother, 1824)

The consuls

▼ Interior of an Egyptian tomb, illustration from 1804.

Napoleon's expedition had an enormous impact on Europe, and the rulers and nobles of the period plunged into a race to acquire antiquities with which to embellish their private collections. Such objects could be bought on the antiquities market, and the many agents acting on behalf of governments or wealthy individuals stooped to every sort of subterfuge and deceit in their competition for these objects. An early case was the acquisition by Charles Albert of Savoy of the important collection amassed by the French consul in Egypt, Bernardino Drovetti. Originally from Italy, Drovetti had served in Napoleon's army before becoming a French diplomat; around 1830 the French commissioned him to find objects for the Louvre; the British consul Henry Salt provided other pieces. Britain too made use of Salt, who was assisted by the Italian-British G. B. Belzoni, and in a short time the section of Egyptian art in the British Museum became one of the most important in Europe. Nor did Germany remain without an important collection, thanks to the efforts of Baron Johann von Minutoli and the Italian antiquarian Giuseppe Passalacqua; soon the Staatliches Museum in Berlin had become a point of reference for scholars of Egyptology. Over the period of a few decades, numerous other museums came into being in Europe and the United States, and these then sponsored important archaeological campaigns, bringing to light works of fundamental importance to the growing discipline of Egyptology.

Born in 1769 in a village in Macedonia, Muhammad Ali undertook a military career in the Ottoman army. He settled at Cairo and in 1806 obtained the title khedive *("governor"); he used the great power he acquired to modernize the economy and the administration of Egypt. He died in 1849, and his remains are today in the mosque he had built on the hill of Muqattam at Cairo.*

With the defeat of the French troops and their withdrawal from Egypt, the country once again became part of the Ottoman Empire; Muhammad Ali, commander of the Turkish troops, soon established power in Egypt and installed himself at Cairo.

In Bernardino Drovetti, Muhammad Ali found an ally and a trustworthy collaborator. The French consul helped him defeat cholera, making available doctors and medical facilities, and oversaw the activities of technicians and engineers in the rearrangement of Egypt's water supply and the Nile canals.

Because of his friendship with Muhammad Ali, Drovetti was able to provide assistance to the French-Tuscan expedition of Champollion and Rosellini and personally took part in the mission to explore and document sites in the oases of the Western Desert.

▲ Portrait of Muhammad Ali, engraving, circa 1875.

As early as the beginning of the 19th century, the explorer Burckhardt had tried to remove the granite bust of Ramses II from the mortuary temple in the Ramesseum on the West Bank of Thebes. The undertaking proved too difficult, until in 1816 the English consul Henry Salt asked G.B. Belzoni to transport the statue to London.

Known as the "young Memnon," the statue was moved by about eighty men, using rollers and sledges. The statue, which weighs more than 7 tons, is today preserved in the British Museum, London.

Britain's Consul Salt managed to assemble an important collection of antiquities to enrich the London museum; disappointed by his earnings from the sale, he put together a second collection that he sold instead to France, by way of Champollion as intermediary.

▲ G.B. Belzoni, *The Bust of the Young Memnon Being Transported from the Ramesseum*, colored lithograph, from G.B. Belzoni, *Six New Plates*, 1822.

Both official and clandestine acquisitions were behind the formation of Europe's principal museum holdings in Egyptian art, including the Louvre in Paris, the British Museum in London, the Staatlisches in Berlin, the Museo Egizio in Turin, and the collections in Bologna, Florence, Rome, Brussels, Copenhagen, Moscow, Vienna, Leiden, and Geneva.

The discovery of Herculaneum and Pompeii during the second half of the 18th century and the studies by Winckelmann awakened renewed interest in antiquity, making the rulers of Europe even more eager to procure relics from the past. There were also the exciting reports from European travelers, which only increased the fascination of Egypt's civilization.

Many museums and "antiquities cabinets" came into being during the 19th century to meet the demands of Europe's crowned heads, to which must be added an infinity of private collections. The result was a flourishing antiquities market, fed by the increasingly numerous expeditions to carry out excavations on Egyptian territory. Given the great demand from European buyers, there were also plenty of fake objects on the market.

▲ Carl Goebel, *View of the Egyptian Collection in the Vienna Museum*, watercolor, 1889, Kunsthistorisches Museum, Vienna.

"After the demigods came the first royal house, which had eight kings, the first of whom was Menes of Thinis . . . he reigned 62 years and died torn apart by a hippopotamus" (Manetho)

Historical sources

In depth
Classical authors:
Herodotus, *The History*
Manetho, *Aegyptiaca*
Ptolemy, *Tetrabiblos*
Polybius, *Histories*
Plutarch, *Isis and Osiris*
Horapollon, *Hieroglyphica*
Jambicus, *The Mysteries of Egypt*
Diodorus Siculus, *Geography*
Strabo, *Geography*

Bibliography
James 1972.

Related entries
Greeks and Romans, Jean-François Champollion

Until the 19th century, reconstructions of the historical events of Egyptian civilization were based on the information in the *History* by Herodotus and in the *Aegyptiaca* by Manetho. The latter work, compiled during the Greek Period by an Egyptian priest, provides a report of the main events in the years of the reigns of each ruler; Manetho is responsible for the division of Egyptian history into dynasties, a division still used today in most Egyptological studies. Once hieroglyphics had been deciphered, scholars had access to Egyptian historical sources, which permitted a direct reconstruction of events. One of the earliest important historical documents is the Palermo Stone, which gives the history of each king's reign from the mythological rulers to the rulers of the 5th dynasty. There are then the king lists of the New Kingdom at Karnak, Abydos, and Saqqara. These relate the lineages of the pharaohs beginning with the legendary Menes. The Turin Canon, while similar to these lists and fragmentary, is of particular importance because it includes the Hyksos kings. The compilation of a precise chronology is still difficult, one of the primary reasons being the dating system the Egyptians used, which was based on counting the years of each sovereign's reign, beginning again at zero with each new pharaoh.

► King list of Abydos (detail), from the mortuary temple of Seti I, Abydos, 19th dynasty.

The Palermo Stone bears an engraved list of the kings of Egypt from Aha (1st dynasty) to at least Neferirkara (third king of the 5th dynasty). It is thus an important historical document, and it presents its information in an analytical manner. The years of each king's reign are indicated on the basis of memorable events (foundation of a palace, construction of royal boats, livestock censuses), and the stone includes records of the level of water in the Nile for the years cited.

"Year in which was built the Praise of the Two Lands ship, 100 cubits long in meru wood, and 60 [boats of 160 cubits] for the king. The land of the Nubians was raided, and 7,000 prisoners (men) were taken and 200,000 head of cattle, large and small. The fortress of Upper and Lower Egypt was built [in the reign of Snefru]. Forty boats full of [trunks of] pine were brought. Level of the Nile: 2 cubits and two fingers."

▶ Palermo Stone, 5th dynasty, black basalt, h 43 cm, Museo Archeologico Regionale, Palermo, 5416.

The relief shows Seti and his son honoring a king list with pharaohs from the origins to his time. The list does not include Hatshepsut, Akhenaten, and Tutankhamen, eliminated for various political reasons. Ramessid propaganda claimed they had not been legitimate rulers.

Ramses II was still a child, as indicated by the sidelock reaching to his neck. The overall composition drives home the idea of pharaonic succession and makes clear its intention of presenting Ramses as the legitimate heir to Seti.

▲ View of the corridor with the royal list of Abydos, mortuary temple of Seti I, Abydos, 19th dynasty.

*"At that moment, a passage from Strabo flashed through my mind:
'There is also a Serapeum at Memphis, in a place so very sandy that
dunes of sand are heaped up by the winds'"* (A. Mariette)

Auguste Mariette

Auguste Mariette made a fundamental contribution to the preservation and documentation of Egypt's archaeological patrimony.
Born in 1821, he worked as a designer, draftsman, and teacher.
He became interested in antiquities because of a cousin who had
taken part in Napoleon's Egyptian campaign. He worked as a
conservator in the Louvre and went to Cairo to acquire objects
for the museum's collection. There he used the funds he had been
given to undertake several highly successful archaeological campaigns that led to the discovery of the Serapeum at Memphis and
other monuments at Luxor. Thanks to his friendship with Said
Pasha, the successor to Muhammad Ali, Mariette was able to create the Egyptian Antiquities Service, still in operation today, for
the control and direction of Egypt's antiquities; he also laid the
basis for the future Egyptian Museum in Cairo in Midan Tahrir,
which came into being only in 1904. Until then the antiquities
were stored in a museum in a suburb of Cairo along the Nile that
was periodically damaged by the river's flooding; during one of
these events Mariette's unpublished notes were destroyed. He
died in 1881 without witnessing the construction of the
museum he had planned. He
was also a friend of Ferdinand de Lesseps, constructor
of the Suez Canal, and
assisted in writing the libretto
for Giuseppe Verdi's opera
Aida, which was first performed, at the Cairo Opera,
in 1871 in honor of the inauguration of the Suez Canal.

Chronology
François-Auguste
Ferdinand Mariette
(Boulogne-sur-Mer,
1821–Bulaq,
Cairo, 1881).
In 1879, because
of the merit he had
earned from the
Egyptian government,
he was named *pasha*
("prince"); at his death
he was buried in a
sarcophagus later
moved to the garden
outside the Egyptian
Museum in Cairo.

Principal works
1857: *Le Sérapéum
de Memphis*
1875: *Dendéreh* (5 vols.)
1875: *Karnak: Étude
topographique et
archéologique*
post-1883: *Les Mastabas
de l'Ancien Empire*

Bibliography
Dawson, Uphill 1995.

Related entries
Memphis and Saqqara,
Memphite necropolis

◀Portrait of
A. Mariette, 1861.

Gaston Maspero succeeded Mariette in the direction of the Cairo Museum and carried ahead Mariette's plans, reinforcing the bureaucratic and administrative structure of the Antiquities Service, instructing officials, and setting them in place to control archaeological activities in Egypt.

Mariette's activities, most of all the creation of the Antiquities Service and the Egyptian Museum in Cairo, brought an end to the indiscriminate plunder of Egyptian art objects. As promoter of these reforms, Mariette was buried in the garden of the museum he had hoped to build; in the 20th century his mausoleum was decorated with busts of the most important Egyptologists.

▲ Excavations by A. Mariette at Saqqara, 1878, Collection B. Garrett, Paris.

▶ Garden and entrance to the Egyptian Museum, Cairo.

"A tomb was being cleared which had been plundered anciently; the sarcophagus was empty, and nothing was anticipated. In a clearing . . . were a few rings of thin gold" (Sir Flinders Petrie)

Sir Flinders Petrie

The first example of modern methodological archaeology, applied to one type of artifact, is the immense work performed by Sir Flinders Petrie, an English scholar who arrived in Egypt initially to study the structure of the pyramids. Beginning in 1883, he dedicated himself to the study of the material remains of Egyptian culture, collecting and cataloging all the artifacts during excavations performed at Faiyum and in the Delta. After ten years he decided to concentrate his attention on sites that preserved traces of the transitional epoch between the Predynastic Period and the unification of the country by the legendary King Menes; he intended to confute the theory according to which the origins of the Egyptian civilization were to be found in the Near East. Excavations in the localities of Koptos, Naqada, and Ballas in central-southern Egypt led to the discovery of more than three thousand tombs, to which must be added several hundred more later found at Hu, between Abydos and Dendera. The type of artifact most heavily present was terracotta vases, of which Petrie unearthed thousands and of which he compiled a detailed classi-

Chronology
Sir William Matthew
Flinders Petrie
(Charlton, 1853–
Jerusalem, 1942).
Totally dedicated to
archaeology, Flinders
Petrie led an austere
life, permitting himself
no luxuries during
excavations.

Principal works
1883: *The Pyramids
and Temples of Gizeh*
1894–1905: *A History
of Egypt*
1896: *Naqada and
Ballas* 1895 (et al.)
1901: *The Royal
Tombs of the
Earliest Dynasties*
(with F.L.I. Griffith)
1920: *Prehistoric
Egypt*
1937: *Funeral
Furniture of Egypt*

Bibliography
Petrie 1931.
Drower 1985.

Related entries
Ancient centers

fication. The characteristics of each kind were written on strips of paper and later grouped, following principles of typological and decorative evolution. The result was the method of "sequence dating," a chronology of the roughly 700 types of ceramic identified, further divided in 50 sections and nine main groups corresponding to the span of the 4th millennium BC.

◀ Sir Flinders Petrie.

The bicolor pottery known as "black topped" gets its characteristic coloring from the technique of its manufacture: the color was not added later, for the pieces were fired upside down with the mouth stuck in ashes. The lack of oxygen prevented the oxidation of the iron content of the clay.

The typological study of predynastic pottery is also based on stylistic variables; the handles of the containers were made in various forms, including those with wavy lines. Most of all, however, it was the forms and themes of the painted decoration that made possible distinctions; from geometric motifs they passed gradually to the stylized depiction of humans and animals.

▲ "Black-topped" and "white-on-red" pottery, Predynastic Period, Fondazione Museo Antichità Egizie, Turin.

▶ Vases with painted decoration, Predynastic Period, Fondazione Museo Antichità Egizie, Turin.

"Beginning in 1894, Ernesto Schiaparelli . . . sought to fill in the most obvious documentary lacunae in the Turin collections"
(A. Bongioanni, R. Grazzi)

Ernesto Schiaparelli

By the early 20th century, the Egyptian collection in Turin had come to include numerous precious objects, but all of them dated to late periods in Egyptian history, from the New Kingdom on. In 1894, direction of the museum was given to Ernesto Schiaparelli, born in nearby Biella but educated in France; he had already served as director of the Egyptian section of the Florence museum. To complete the museum's documentation he commissioned several specific acquisitions, then in 1903 he began taking part in archaeological excavations in Egypt through the creation of the Italian Archaeological Mission, sponsored by the Academy of the Lincei with financial support from the Italian state. The first site explored was Heliopolis, from which came a relief of the pharaoh Djoser and a tabernacle of Seti I. At the same time he excavated the mastaba of Iteti and the tomb of Prince Duanera at Giza. The same years also saw the beginning of exploration in the Valley of the Queens in the Theban necropolis, where he dug up the tomb of Princess Ahmose, those of the sons of Ramses III,

Sethherkhepeshef, Khaemwaset, and Amonkerkhepsehef, and that of Queen Nefertari, Ramses II's consort; in the nearby workers' village of Deir el-Medina he found the tomb of the painter Maia and the intact tomb of the architect Kha. Other excavations were opened in Middle Egypt, at Asyut and at Qau el-Kebir, as well as at Gebelein near Thebes; these sites gave up artifacts dating to the Predynastic Period, the Old and Middle Kingdoms, and the First Intermediate Period.

Chronology
Ernesto Schiaparelli
(Occhieppo Inferiore,
Biella, 1856–
Turin, 1928).
He was senator in
the Kingdom of Italy
and a promoter
of philanthropic
works, including the
construction of Italian
schools and hospitals
in Asia Minor.

Principal works
1881–90: *Il libro
dei funerali degli
antichi Egiziani*
1924: *Esplorazione
delle "Valle delle
Regine" nella
necropoli di Tebe*
1927: *La tomba
intatta dell'architetto
Cha nella necropoli
di Tebe*

Bibliography
Reeves 2000.

Related entries
Provincial centers,
Theban necropolis,
Deir el-Medina

◄ Portrait photo of
Ernesto Schiaparelli.

In his explorations of the Valley of the Queens
between 1903 and 1906, Schiaparelli found the burial
sites of Princess Ahmose, the prefect Imhotep, and the
noble Nebiri, aside from those of Queen Nefertari and
the sons of Ramses III.

Nefertari was the "great royal
wife" of Ramses II. Her name
means "the most beautiful," and
aside from her beauty the queen
owes her fame to her important
political role, opening diplomatic relations with the queen
of the Hittites, Puduhepa.

A model of the tomb of
Nefertari is displayed in the
halls of Turin's museum. Made
on a scale of 1:10, it shows the
splendid wall paintings; restored
at the end of the 1980s, they
have been returned to their
lively polychromy.

Fragments of Nefertari's sarcophagus were found
in the tomb, along with several shabti statuettes
and elements of furnishings in the queen's name;
the attribution of other objects is less certain,
including a pair of mummified knees, which may
belong to an intrusive burial of a later epoch.

▲ Portrait of Queen Nefertari, tomb
of Nefertari in the Valley of the
Queens, Western Thebes.

The portico of the tomb of Iti was decorated with lively paintings depicting scenes of agricultural life, hunting, offerings, and funerary worship. The painted plaster scenes were removed from their original setting and brought to Turin, where they are preserved and represent an important example of the provincial art of Upper Egypt.

Excavations at Gebelein provided information primarily on the First Intermediate Period and the Middle Kingdom. To this period dates the tomb of the "chancellor of the king and leader of troops" Iti, buried with his wife, Neferu, in a tomb with a pillared portico opening onto barrel-vaulted shrines.

During the 1920s, Schiaparelli explored one of the richest necropolises in Egypt at Gebelein, a short distance from Luxor. The site has traces of occupation dating from predynastic times to the Greco-Roman age.

▲ Painting in the tomb of Iti and Neferu, from Gebelein, First Intermediate Period, painted plaster, h circa 160 cm, Fondazione Museo Antichità Egizie, Turin, S. 14354.

In 1903, Schiaparelli began excavations in the workers' village at Deir el-Medina, an important source of archaeological documentation of daily life in an ancient Egyptian town. The excavations were resumed in the 1920s by an expedition led by Bernard Bruyère, who wrote a detailed account.

The Italian mission's principal discovery was the tomb of the architect Kha, buried with his wife, Merit. The funerary stele from the shrine had already arrived in Turin, part of the collection assembled by Drovetti; the burial site was quite a distance from the site of the funerary worship, hidden by a heap of detritus.

The excavators found the tomb intact, still sealed by a wooden door closed off by a wall. In it were the bodies of the spouses, complete with their funerary goods and furnishings.

In terms of their variety and the quality of the objects, the tomb furnishings of Kha constitute one of the most important windows on the private life of a well-do-do family roughly 3,500 years ago. The furnishings, clothes, food, and tools present an image that is both vivid and at the same time surprisingly modern.

▲ Statuette depicting the architect Kha, from the tomb of Kha at Deir el-Medina, Western Thebes, 18th dynasty, painted wood, h 43 cm, Fondazione Museo Antichità Egizie, Turin, S. 8335.

"Can you see anything?" "Yes, wonderful things." (Lord Carnarvon and Howard Carter at the opening of the tomb of Tutankhamen)

Tutankhamen's tomb

Tombs with splendid decorations had been brought to light in the Valley of the Kings at Thebes since the beginning of the 20th century; also found was the hiding place to which the mummies of several pharaohs from the preceding epoch had been moved during the Third Intermediate Period. No one, however, had yet found a royal tomb intact, complete with mummy and furnishings. Many archaeologists continued to dig, always hoping to succeed. Among these was the Englishman Howard Carter, who, with financing from Lord Carnarvon from 1917 on, had concentrated his work in the area around the tomb of Ramses VI. The discovery of the remains of huts that had housed workers in ancient times gave hope of another tomb in the area. After five seasons of somewhat disappointing results, on November 5, 1922, the diggers found a step cut in the rock: this was the top of a stairway leading down to a door bearing intact seals from the authorities of the royal necropolis. The hallway behind the door was full of stone and also jewels and amulets spread on the floor, indicating that the tomb had been visited by thieves and then closed up again. Behind a second door Carter found four small rooms stuffed full of an immense treasure: four shrines in gilt wood mounted one inside the other contained the four sarcophagi of the mummy of King Tutankhamen, and the furnishings included regal objects, royal emblems, statues, alabaster vases, jewels of every kind, clothes, furniture, carts, weapons, musical instruments, and funeral furnishings.

◄ Photograph of Carter, kneeling, opening the casket holding the sarcophagus of Tutankhamen; behind him is his assistant A. Callender.

Chronology
Howard Carter
(London, 1874–
London, 1939)
At the end of the 20th century, various objects from the excavation of the tomb were found in Lord Carnarvon's castle.

Principal works
1904: *The Tomb of Thoutmosis IV* (with P. Newberry)
1906: *The Tomb of Iouiya and Touiyou* (with G. Maspero and P. Newberry)
1923–33: *The Tomb of Tutankh-Amen* (with A.C. Mace)

Bibliography
James 1991.

Related entries
Tutankhamen, Tomb furnishings, Valley of the Kings, Theban necropolis

During excavation of the antechamber of the tomb, Howard Carter, himself a painter and artist, found his attention drawn to a chest that he himself described as "A chest in painted wood that most probably should be ranked among the most precious objects in the tomb . . . it bore decorations of exquisite workmanship in lively colors, with scenes of hunting on the curved panels of its lid, scenes of battle on the sides."

After the robberies that took place in the tomb of Tutankhamen, the priests of the necropolis cleaned up the furnishings and again closed the tomb. Like other containers, this chest probably originally held objects of the royal wardrobe. Carter described its contents: "Inside the chest there was a lively jumble of things, a pair of reed and papyrus sandals, a royal robe . . . and three pairs of court sandals skillfully worked in gold, a gilt headrest, and other objects of various kinds."

▲ Chest with scenes of hunting and war, from the tomb of Tutankhamen in the Valley of the Kings, Western Thebes, 18th dynasty, painted wood, h 44.5 cm, Egyptian Museum, Cairo, JE 61467.

The paintings emphasize the courage and warrior skills of the king. This is stereotypical Egyptian propaganda, celebrating the exploits and victories of the ruler in his role as triumphant leader. Egypt's enemies are here personified by a group of Africans being routed by the courageous pharaoh. It is most likely, however, that the young Tutankhamen never led a military expedition.

*The embattled pharaoh wears the blue war crown (*khepresh*) and a kind of breastplate; he stands on a chariot drawn by two richly caparisoned horses and is about to let loose an arrow. Behind him are attendants with long fans and a group of nobles on other chariots. Many of the objects depicted in the scene were found among the tomb furnishings.*

During antiquity, looters broke into the tomb of Tutankhamen. They managed to make their way into the tomb, opening breaches in the walls of the internal rooms. Perhaps surprised by guards, they fled, dropping to the floor the few jewels they had managed to grab.

When Carter opened the tomb he found the unbroken seals of the guards of the necropolis still in place. The vestibule of the tomb and a side room were full of objects of every type, as was an annex to the side of the burial chamber.

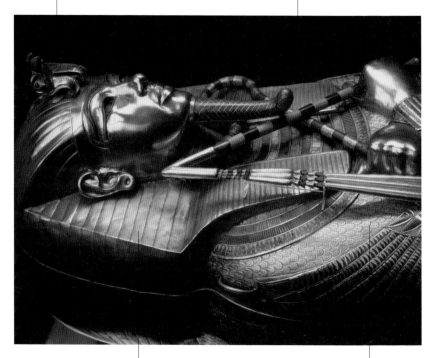

The inner sarcophagus of Tutankhamen, a notable piece of goldworking with a weight of 110 kg, is the most spectacular such work ever found.

▲ Inner sarcophagus of Tutankhamen, from the tomb of Tutankhamen in the Valley of the Kings, Western Thebes, 18th dynasty, gold, precious stones, and vitreous paste, h 51 cm, Egyptian Museum, Cairo, JE 60671.

The mummy of the king was closed inside three sarcophagi. The outermost in gilt wood is still in the Valley of the Kings and contains the body of Tutankhamen; the middle one in gilt wood is in the Cairo Museum together with the innermost one, in solid gold.

Inside the shrine was the container for the canopic jars made of a block of calcite with four spaces and a cover; each cavity had as cover a portrait of the pharaoh and contained a canopic jar in the shape of a miniature sarcophagus.

The shrine is in the form of a small temple topped by a baldachin; both are set atop a sledge and decorated with friezes of uraei.

With their oval, pointed faces, elongated eyes, and large ears, the features of the goddesses still reveal the influence of the Amarna style.

Each side of the container is protected by the embrace of a goddess: Isis, Nephthys, Selket, and Neith. Each goddess in turn holds the hand of one of the four sons of Horus, protectors of the embalmed viscera, depicted on the walls of the tabernacle.

▲ Container for the canopic jars of Tutankhamen, from the tomb of Tutankhamen in the Valley of the Kings, Western Thebes, 18th dynasty, wood and gold, h 198 cm, Egyptian Museum, Cairo, JE 60686.

The back is surrounded by a frame topped by uraei and dominated by a vulture with spread wings. The side cartouches bear the name of the king in its original form, Tutankhaten, which also appears on the central panels.

The deeply curved seat is inlaid to imitate the skin of a leopard, with other animal skins worked in the central rectangle; the precious skins are created with intarsia in ebony, ivory, and gold.

The seat folds by way of a hinge located halfway along the length of the legs; it has a rigid upright piece to which the high curved back is attached; the legs are carved to form the necks and heads of ducks; their eyes are visible, as are their beaks, which open to hold the bar of the horizontal supports for the chair. In the empty space is the sema-tawy, symbol of the union of the Two Lands.

In front of the throne is a foot rest decorated with nine figures of imprisoned enemies: the king could thus tread upon the "Nine Bows," meaning all foreign peoples.

▲ Throne of Tutankhamen, from the tomb of Tutankhamen in the Valley of the Kings, Western Thebes, 18th dynasty, wood and gold, h 120 cm, Egyptian Museum, Cairo, JE 62030.

"Tell el-Amarna is one of those sites that are of enormous importance to the history of Egyptian civilization. It had a shorter life than any other city in the country" (Sir Flinders Petrie)

Amarna excavations

Although it had already been visited during the Napoleonic expedition, some parts of the city of Akhetaten (Tell el-Amarna) were explored by the English Egyptologist John Gardner Wilkinson in 1824, followed by work by Lepsius, Petrie, and the Egypt Exploration Fund. Beginning in 1911, the German Institute, under the direction of Ludwig Borchardt, carried out systematic excavations and established the topographical arrangement of the city; the work was later carried ahead by British missions. The finds provided a great deal of information concerning the layout of the inhabited area and its territory and also threw light on historical aspects of the New Kingdom. The Amarna Letters, an archive of clay tablets bearing cuneiform writing, preserve correspondence between 18th-dynasty pharaohs and rulers in the Near East, allies of Egypt. The discovery of the workshop of the chief sculptor Thutmose, credited with the famous portrait of Queen Nefertiti today in Berlin, provided new information on artistic trends of the period. With the end of the reign of Akhenaten, the city too ended its life, and its structures were dismantled and reused as building materials. So it was that irregularly cut blocks that originally belonged to buildings in the city of Amarna were discovered when emptying the pylons built by Horemheb in the temple of Karnak.

Chronology
Ludwig Borchardt
(Berlin, 1863–
Paris, 1938).

Principal works
1908: *Works of Art from the Egyptian Museum at Cairo*
1911–36: *Statuen und Statuetten von Königen und Privatleuten im Museum von Kairo*
1923: *Porträts der Königen Nofret-ete aus den Grabungen 1912/13 In Tell el-Amarna*
1938: *Ägyptische Tempel mit Umgang*

Bibliography
Aldred 1988

Related entries
Amenhotep
IV/Akhenaten

◄ Two princesses, daughters of Akhenaten, from Amarna, 18th dynasty, painted plaster, h 40 cm, Ashmolean Museum, Oxford, 1–41 (267).

The queen wears a high blue crown decorated with colored ribbons and embellished by a uraeus serpent.

The portrait of Nefertiti presents balanced proportions; the face is thin, the nose narrow, the lips are fleshy. The image maintains much of its original vitality because of the almost perfect preservation of its polychrome decoration, leaving visible its subtle shadings of colors.

The fact that the pupil of the left eye is missing has led to speculation: was it lost, or was the bust never completed?

Thutmose created this splendid bust in painted limestone. It is possible that the bust was used as a model for making other images of the queen.

▲ Bust of Nefertiti, from Amarna, 18th dynasty, painted limestone, h 50 cm, Ägypisches Museum, Berlin, 21 300.

Excavations of the northern area of the city of Amarna brought to light the remains of a large palace that might have been the opet, *or royal harem, where the court's women and princes lived. Numerous objects bearing the name Nefertiti have been found in this building, indicating that this was probably the queen's private residence.*

The queen is believed to have withdrawn to a private existence during the last years of her life, although the reasons for that decision remain unknown. According to some, the fact that she had given birth to six princesses but no princes may have diminished her power and influence at court.

Tutankhamen is the only member of the Amarna royal family whose body has been identified. The identity of several mummies found in very poor condition in the Valley of the Kings has been the subject of dispute; some believe they could include Nefertiti herself, her daughters, or Smenkhkare.

Nefertiti's genealogical tree cannot be established with certainty. Her original family is not known (she may have been related to the powerful priest Ay), and there is question of whether she was the mother of Smenkhkare, successor to Akhenaten, or even of Tutankhamen himself.

▲ The so-called palace of Nefertiti at Amarna.

"Having removed the slabs, I slipped into the opening . . . and found myself in a small room half-filled with mud . . . We were standing in front of . . . Osorkon II" (Pierre Montet)

Royal tombs of Tanis

Chronology
Pierre-Marie Montet
(Villefranche-sur Saône,
1885–Paris, 1966)
The tombs of Tanis were
protected by a system of
pits that filled with sand
as quickly as sand was
dug out of them.

Principal works
1928–29: *Byblos et l'Égypte*
1947–51: *La nécropole royale de Tanis*
1952: *Les énigmes de Tanis*
1957, 1961: *Géographie de l'Égypte ancienne*
post-1985: *Vies des Pharaons illustres*

Bibliography
Stierlin, Ziegler 1988.

Related entries
Sheshonk I, Tanis

The site of San el-Hagar in the eastern Delta, known as Tanis to the Greeks, had already been excavated around the middle of the 19th century by Mariette, who found numerous statues dating to the Middle Kingdom and the Ramessid period; he thought the site was either Tanis or Per-Ramesse, the capital Ramses II built as an alternative to Thebes, which is also mentioned in the Bible. Later excavations by Petrie at the end of the century led him to conclude that Tanis, capital of the 21st dynasty, had been built reusing material from Heliopolis, from Memphis, and from Per-Ramesse itself. Only in 1929 did regular excavations begin at Tanis, conducted by Pierre Montet, who had the firm intention of proving the identity of Tanis with Per-Ramesse and also with Avaris, the capital of the Hyksos. After ten years of work, digging in the outer wall of the great temple of Amon, Montet found the burials of six kings and nobles from the 11th and 12th dynasties, including Psusennes I, Amenemope, Osorkon II, and Sheshonk III. The burial chambers, built reusing blocks from elsewhere, were located in the structure of the sanctuary, probably for reasons of security. In fact, the royal burials held splendid furnishings, including silver sarcophi, gold funerary masks, jewels, and gold plates. The tombs of Tanis are the only royal burials, along with that of Tutankhamen, to be found practically intact.

◄ View of the excavations of Tanis (modern-day San el-Hagar).

The archaeologist Pierre Montet did everything he could to obtain permission to excavate at San el-Hagar and to find financing for the work in the inhospitable site. It took him eleven years of excavations before finding the royal tombs in 1939.

Some of the tombs at Tanis had been looted (Osorkon II and Sheshonk III), while that of Amenemope was intact and that of Psusennes I was also wonderfully rich.

The outbreak of World War II forced Montet to end his work in Tanis, on May 3, 1940. By 1943, however, he was back on the site, because news of the spectacular discovery had driven thieves to try to steal the royal treasures. Fortunately, the most important objects had been sent to the Cairo museum

▲ Pierre Montet examining the sarcophagus of Psusennes I.

The precious objects among the king's furnishings included bracelets and anklets, necklaces, rings, and weapons. There were also gold and stone amulets as well as shabti statuettes, servants for the afterlife.

The furnishings included gold plates and a ritual brazier that had previously belonged to Ramses II, one of the frequent instances at Tanis of the reuse of objects and building materials from earlier epochs.

The sepulcher of Psusennes I was composed of an outer sarcophagus in pink granite, a middle one in black granite, and an inner one in silver.

The silver coffin is the mummiform image of the king with the heqa crook and nekhakha flail in his hands, the nemes headdress, and the uraeus serpent on his forehead. Inside, the mummy of Psusennes I was covered with a golden mask and a gilt robe.

▲ Upper part of the sarcophagus of Psusennes I, from Tanis, 21st dynasty, silver and gold, 185 cm long, Egyptian Museum, Cairo, JE 85917.

"It was the fate of the two temples at Abu Simbel . . . that still weighed. On paper, the two rock temples had alternatively been saved or given up as lost" (Georg Gerster)

Nubian temples

The largest undertaking of Egyptian archaeology was the emergency salvation of twenty-odd temples in the Nubian region, to the south of the First Cataract. The region was scheduled to become an enormous artificial lake in 1960, a result of construction of the Aswan High Dam. The needs of a population in continuous growth had forced the Egyptian government to undertake the construction, and the needs of archaeology required an immediate response. A similar event had already happened in the area at the end of the 19th century with construction of a lock in the same area. In response to an appeal from several leading Egyptologists, the United Nations involved more than fifty countries in the project. The idea was to relocate the principal archaeological sites to safe areas. For many temples, the only practical solution was to dismantle them in blocks and then reconstruct them. From 1960 to 1980, sixteen temples were dismantled and reassembled. Some of these, such as those of Abu Simbel, had been cut into rock, and others were large, freestanding temples, such as that of Kalabsha; the Isis sanctuary was moved from the island of Philae to a nearby island, adapted to accept it. In a sign of thanks to the technical and financial assistance provided, Egypt made gifts to the countries that had contributed the most, giving them structures that are today preserved in New York, Leiden, Madrid, Berlin, and Turin.

In depth
The saved temples:
Amada and Ellesiya
(Thutmose III and
Ramses II)
Wadi es-Sebu'a
(Amenhotep III and
Ramses II)
Beit el-Wali, Derr,
Gerf Hussein, and
Abu Simbel
(Ramses II)
Philae, Kalabsha,
Kertassi, Debod,
Tafa, Dendur, Dakka,
and Maharraqa
(Greco-Roman age).

Bibliography
Christophe 1977.

Related entries
Nubia and Abu Simbel

◄ View of the dam
built at the First
Cataract between the
end of the 19th century
and the early 20th.

The idea to contain the waters of the Nile floods with a dam at the First Cataract dates back to ancient times. The idea was given urgency in the 19th century with the increasing problem of irrigating Egypt's fields so as to satisfy the food needs of a nation in enormous demographic growth.

The first dam at Aswan went into construction in 1890, but it had to be rebuilt several times and raised several times. In 1960, the High Dam (Saad el-Ali, in Arabic) was built farther upstream and is functioning today.

The temples of the sanctuary on the island of Philae had been greatly damaged; the blocks were eroded by prolonged immersion in water, and the painted decorations on the reliefs had almost dissolved. Alarm warnings were sounded, including one from the French writer and traveler Pierre Loti in the book La Mort de Philae.

A 19th-century lock blocked the flow of water during the Nile floods, making the level of the river rise in the area of the First Cataract. The monuments in this area spent several months submerged in muddy water.

▲ Trajan's kiosk in the sanctuary at Philae was nearly submerged early in the 20th century.

The structures were completely dismantled, literally cut into blocks; each block was inventoried and stored. The buildings were rebuilt upriver from the original site on a specially prepared area.

An immense dome in reinforced cement had to be built to support the weight of the artificial hill behind the larger temple.

The two rock temples of Abu Simbel, built by Ramses II, are symbolic of the effort made by all of humanity to preserve the important evidence of its cultural heritage.

The construction of the High Dam at Aswan represented a threat not only to the temples in the region of the First Cataract but also to all the monuments of Lower Nubia, all the way to the Second Cataract.

Near the site of Abu Simbel a village was built for the technicians and workers with their families with room for two thousand people. The settlement was furnished with structures made necessary by the work and with services (shops, hospitals, recreational areas) essential for the daily life of a large number of people belonging to different nations and cultures.

▲ The temples of Abu Simbel during the phase of reconstruction.

References

◄Louis Armstrong playing his
trumpet for his wife and the
Sphinx at Giza, 1961.

Delta and Middle Egypt

Legend

1. Alexandria
2. Buto
3. Xoïs
4. Mendes
5. Tanis
6. Pelusium
7. Sais
8. Sebennytus
9. Naukratis
10. Avaris
11. Athribis
12. Bubastis
13. Wadi al-Natrun
14. Heliopolis
15. Cairo
16. Abu Roash
17. Giza
18. Abusir
19. Saqqara
20. Memphis
21. Dahshur
22. Lisht
23. Meidum
24. Hawara
25. El-Lahun
26. Heracleopolis
27. Beni Hasan
28. Speos Artemidos
29. Hermopolis
30. Amarna
31. Asyut
32. Akhmim
33. Abydos
34. Dendera
35. Thebes
36. Hermonthis
37. El-Kab
38. Hierakonpolis
39. Edfu
40. Kom Ombo
41. Aswan
42. First Cataract
43. Island of Philae
44. Amada
45. Abu Simbel
46. Buhen
47. Second Cataract
48. Semna
49. Kumma

0   100 km

Upper Egypt and Lower Nubia

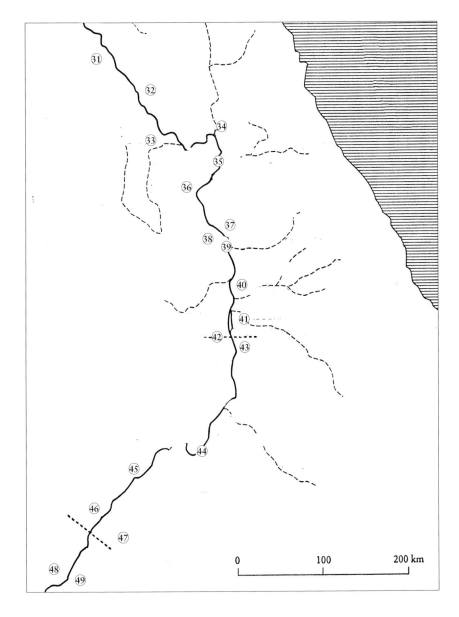

Chronology

All the dates are BC; to avoid weighing down the entries, we have limited the definition to the dates given in parenthesis beside each period or dynasty. Chronological repetitions or inconsistencies are the result of periods of more than one regent or of political instability. Some rulers are listed without dates for the simple reason that historians have not yet established solid dates for their reigns. Some reigns were brief, which explains the appearance of only one year beside a ruler's name.

Predynastic Period (4500–3300 BC)
Pre-Thinite Period (3300–3150 BC)
Thinite Period (3150–2700 BC)
1st dynasty (3150–2925 BC)
"Scorpion"
Narmer, 3150–3125
Aha, 3125–3100
Djer, 3100–3055
Uadji, 3055–3050
Den, 3050–2995
Adjib, 2995–?
Semerkhet, ?–2960
Qaa, 2960–2925

2nd dynasty (2925–2700 BC)
Hetepsekhemwy
Nebra
Nynetjer
Weneg
Sened
Peribsen
Khasekhemuy

Ancient Kingdom
(2700–2200 BC)
3rd dynasty (2700–2625 BC)
Nebka
Djoser (Netjerikhet)
Khaba

Sekhemkhet
Neferkara
Huni

4th dynasty (2625–2510 BC)
Snefru
Khufu
Djedefra
Khafre
Baefra
Menkure
Shepseskaf

5th dynasty (2510–2460 BC)
Userkaf
Sahura
Neferirkara
Shepseskara
Raneferef
Nyuserra
Menkauhor
Djedkara Isesi
Unas

6th dynasty (2460–2200 BC)
Teti
Userkara
Pepi I
Merenre
Pepi II
Merenre II
Nitocris

First Intermediate Period
(2200–2061 BC)
7th and 8th dynasty
(ca. 2200–2160 BC)
9th and 10th dynasty
(ca. 2160–2040 BC)
11th dynasty, 1st part
(2160–2061 BC)
Mentuhotep I
Intef I
Intef II
Intef III

Middle Kingdom
(2061–1785 BC)
11th dynasty, 2nd part
(2061–1991 BC)

Mentuhotep II, 2061–2009
Mentuhotep III, 2009–1998
Mentuhotep IV, 1998–1991

12th dynasty (1991–1785 BC)
Amenemhet I, 1991–1962
Sesostris I, 1962–1928
Amenemhet II, 1928–1895
Sesostris II, 1895–1878
Sesostris III, 1878–1842
Amenemhet III, 1842–1797
Amenemhet IV, 1797–1790
Neferusobek, 1790–1785

Second Intermediate Period
(1785–1552 BC)
13th and 14th dynasty
(1785–1633 BC)
15th and 16th dynasty
(ca. 1730–1530 BC)
17th dynasty (1650–1552 BC)
principal Theban rulers:
Rahotep
Intef V
Sobekemsaf II
Gehuty
Mentuhotep VII
Nebiryau I
Intef VII
Taa I
Taa II
Kamose

New Kingdom
(1552–1069 BC)
18th dynasty (1552–1295 BC)
Ahmose, 1552–1526
Amenhotep I, 1526–1506
Thutmose I, 1506–1493
Thutmose II, 1493–1478
Hatshepsut, 1478–1458
Thutmose III, 1458–1425
Amenhotep II, 1425–1401
Thutmose IV, 1401–1390
Amenhotep III, 1390–1352
Amenhotep IV/Akhenaten,
1352–1338
Smenkhkara, 1338–1336
Tutankhamen, 1336–1327
Ay, 1327–1323

Horemheb, 1323–1295
19th dynasty (1295–1188 BC)
Ramses I, 1295–1294
Seti I, 1294–1279
Ramses II, 1279–1213
Merenptah, 1213–1202
Amenemes, 1202–1199
Seti II, 1202–1196
Saptah, 1196–1190
Tausret, 1196–1188

20th dynasty (1188–1069 BC)
Sethnakht, 1188–1186
Ramses III, 1186–1154
Ramses IV, 1154–1148
Ramses V, 1148–1144
Ramses VI, 1144–1136
Ramses VII, 1136–1128
Ramses VIII, 1128–1125
Ramses IX, 1125–1107
Ramses X, 1107–1098
Ramses XI, 1098–1069

Third Intermediate Period
(1069–664 BC)
21st dynasty (1069–945 BC)
Smendes I, 1069–1043
Amenemnisu, 1043–1040
Psusennes I, 1040–993
Amenemope, 993–984
Osorkon the Elder, 984–978
Siamun, 978–959
Psusennes II, 959–945

22nd dynasty (945–715 BC)
Sheshonk I, 945–924
Osorkon I, 924–890
Sheshonk II, 890–889
Takelot I, 889–874
Harsiesis, 870–860
Osorkon II, 874–850
Takelot II, 850–825
Sheshonk III, 825–773
Pimay, 773–767
Sheshonk V, 767–730
Osorkon IV, 730–715

23rd dynasty (818–715 BC)
Petubasti, 818–793
Sheshonk IV, 793–787)

Osorkon III, 787–759
Takelot III, 764–757
Rudamon, 757–754
Iuput II, 754–729
24th dynasty (727–715 BC)
Tefnakht, 727–716
Bakenrenef, 716–715

25th dynasty (ca. 774–656 BC)
Alara
Kashta
Piankhi, 747–716
Shabaka, 716–702
Shabataka, 702–690
Taharqa, 690–664
Tanutamani, 664–656

Late Period
(672–332 BC)
26th dynasty (672–525 BC)
Necho I, 672–664
Psamtik I, 664–610
Necho, 610–595
Psamtik II, 595–589
Apries, 589–570
Ahmose II, 570–526
Psamtik III, 526–525

*27th dynasty, 1st Persian Period
(525–404 BC)*
Cambyses, 525–522
Darius I, 522–486
Xerxes I, 486–465
Artaxerxes I, 465–424
Darius II, 424–404
Artaxerxes II, 404

28th dynasty (404–399 BC)
Amyrtaeus, 404–399

29th dynasty (399–380 BC)
Nepherites I, 399–394
Psammuthis, 394–393
Achoris, 393–380
Nepherites II, 380

30th dynasty (380–342 BC)
Nectanebo I, 380–362
Tachos, 362–360
Nectanebo II, 360–343

2nd Persian Period (343–332 BC)
Artaxerxes III Ochus, 343–338
Arses, 338–336
Darius III, 336–332

Last indigenous dynasty
Khababash, 333

Glossary

Ankh: hieroglyphic sign denoting the concept of "life"; it is shaped like a cross ending in a loop.

Canopic jar: containers used to hold the internal organs (liver, lungs, stomach, intestines) removed during the process of mummification; each jar was protected by a different divinity.

Cartouche: oval or oblong outline that encloses the name of a pharaoh or elements of his name.

Cataract: rocky area of rapids along the course of the Nile; there are six cataracts.

Cenotaph: funerary tomb or monument that does not contain the body of the deceased.

Cosmogony: an explanation, as with myths, of the creation or origin of the world.

Cubit: unit of measure equal to the distance between the elbow (*cubitum* in Latin) and the tip of the middle finger.

Djed: hieroglyphic sign denoting the concept of "stability"; it is shaped like a pillar topped by four capitals.

False door: rectangular architectural element resembling a door that serves as the "entrance" to the tomb; in front of this stands the table or slab on which offerings are placed.

Heqa: crook-shaped scepter, one of the Egyptian symbols of sovereignty.

Hypogeum: an underground burial chamber.

Hypostyle hall: hall or courtyard in a temple with a roof resting on rows of columns.

Mastaba: from an Arabic word for "bench," a tomb typical of the Thinite Period and the Old Kingdom with a superstructure shaped like a tumulus with sloping sides and a flat top.

Menat: necklace associated with the cult of the goddess Hathor.

Necropolis: "city of the dead"; a cemetery with structures for worship of the deceased.

Nekhakha: flail-shaped scepter, one of the Egyptian symbols of sovereignty.

Nemes: typical striped headcloth worn by pharaohs, sometimes with a uraeus at the forehead.

Nomarch: "overlord of a nome," hence the ruler of a province.

Nome: province or administrative district of ancient Egypt; there were forty-two such divisions.

Obelisk: monument in the form of a tall shaft of stone; an elongated, usually four-sided column ending in a pyramidal point (from a Greek word for "spit").

Ostracon, ostraca: fragment of pottery bearing an inscription.

Peristyle: courtyard surrounded by a colonnade.

Predynastic: relating to the period before Egypt's dynastic rulers.

Prenomen: one of a pharaoh's royal titles; his throne name.

Prostyle: building with one or more rows of columns in front of it.

Pylon: monumental gateway or portal, as to the temple, usually composed of two towers linked by a bridge and surmounted by a cornice.

Sem: title used for priests involved in certain funerary rites and rituals. They wear a leopard skin and are often depicted in association with the Opening of the Mouth ceremony.

Serdab: from an Arabic word for "cellar," a closed-off room in a burial chamber used to house a statue of the deceased or his *ka*.

Serekh: rectangular motif, perhaps representing a palace façade, in which the pharaoh's Horus name is written.

Shen: hieroglyphic sign denoting the concepts of "eternity" and "protection"; it is shaped like a knotted cord.

Shendyt: characteristic skirt made of pleated linen.

Sistrum: musical instrument, similar to a wire rattle, associated with the worship of various Egyptian divinities, most especially Hathor and Isis.

Sphinx: representation of the sun god and the king in a composite form, with a lion's body and a human, hawk, or ram's head.

Theocracy: form of government in which rule is attributed to the gods or to a ruler who is divinely guided or possesses divine characteristics.

Tiara: decorative headband or semicircle.

Titulary: group of names associated with an Egyptian ruler; a pharaoh usually had five names in his titulary.

Udjat: the left eye of Horus, lost during a battle against Set and later found by Thoth; it is a symbol of recovery from illness.

Uraeus, uraei: representation of the sacred asp that appears above the forehead on royal crowns and headdresses.

Usekh: wide necklace composed of several strands of beads.

Vizier: Turkish term used to indicate the chief minister of a pharaoh.

Museums

Berlin: Ägyptisches Museum und Papyrussammlung

This collection assumed great importance after the acquisition of several masterpieces of Egyptian art following the German excavations at Tell el-Amarna. Among the works here is the famous bust of Nefertiti and the head of Queen Tiy.

Bologna: Museo Archeologico, Collezione Egizia

This collection began with the works the artist Palagio Palagi left the city on his death in 1860. The collection's importance was increased by research conducted in Egypt by teams from the city's university. The collection is currently displayed in Palazzo Galvani.

Boston: Museum of Fine Arts

This museum has roughly 45,000 works representing the history of Egypt from the Predynastic Period to the Byzantine. Of particular interest are the objects related to the museum's excavation work at Giza, including the statues of Menkure.

Cairo: Egyptian Museum

This museum, which currently hosts the world's largest collection of Egyptian antiquities, was formed to preserve the finds from archaeological excavations conducted under the guidance of the Antiquities Service, instituted in 1835. The main building in Midan Tahrir in the center of Cairo was built in 1900 by the French architect Marcel Dourgnon. The 120,000 pieces displayed date from the Predynastic Period to the Roman era. Of particular interest are the objects from the tombs of Hetepheres (mother of Khufu), princesses of the Middle Kingdom, Thutmoses III and IV, Yuya and Tuya (sisters of Amen-hotep III), pharaohs of the 22nd dynasty of Tanis, and Tutankhamen, which occupy most of the second floor. A separate hall is dedicated to the numerous mummies of kings, queens, and nobles found in the Theban cachettes.

Florence: Museo Archeologico, Sezione Egizia

The original nucleus of this collection was composed of objects that belonged to the Medici family during the 18th century; further works were added to the collection following the archaeological expeditions sponsored by Archduke Leopold II and directed by Champollion and Rosellini in the period 1828 to 1829. Ernesto Schiaparelli reorganized the collection in the 19th century, and in the 20th the works in the Papyrological Institute were added. The museum's holdings document the history of Egypt from prehistory to the Coptic period.

London: British Museum, Department of Ancient Egypt and Sudan

There have been Egyptian antiquities in the British Museum virtually since the formation of the museum; in 1753, the museum acquired the collection of Sir Hans Sloane, and following Nelson's defeat of the French fleet, the antiquities the French had collected in Egypt (among them the enormously important Rosetta Stone) were added. The museum's collection came to number 10,000 objects through the acquisition of the important collection assembled by British Consul Henry Salt, in part with the assistance of his agent G.B. Belzoni. The archaeological activities of the Egypt Exploration Society further enriched the museum, and there were also acquisitions made in Egypt by the archaeologist Wallis Budge early in the 20th century. The collection illustrates the history of the Nile Valley from Neolithic times to the Christian age.

Luxor: Museum of Ancient Egyptian Art

In a modern structure that opened in 1975, this museum displays important archaeological finds from the area of Thebes. Among these works are several statues of Amenhotep III; there are also several objects from the tomb of Tutankhamen. An 18-meter-long wall has been reconstructed using blocks that were originally from the city of Akhetaten (Amarna) and were then reused by Horemheb in the temple of Karnak after the dismantling of Akhetaten. Also among the museum's holdings are several splendid sculptures found in 1989 in a cachette in the temple of Luxor.

New York: Brooklyn Museum of Art

This collection includes several masterpieces of Egyptian art dating to the period between the New Kingdom and the end of the Ptolemaic Period, in particular statues, reliefs, jewels, tomb furnishings, and papyri.

New York: Metropolitan Museum of Art

This museum's collection of Egyptian art is among the most prestigious in the world. It consists of roughly 36,000 objects of artistic, historic, and cultural importance from the Paleolithic to the Roman era. More than half of the collection was assembled during the museum's archaeological campaigns, which began in 1906 and continued for almost thirty-five years. The objects are organized chronologically and reflect the aesthetic values, history, religious beliefs, and daily life of ancient Egypt.

Oxford: Ashmolean Museum of Art and Archaeology

This collection is composed in large part of gifts from Elias Ashmole to the university and presents a long period in the history of humanity, from the Paleolithic to the Victorian Age; there are many objects from the Near East and Egypt.

Paris: Louvre, Musée du, Département des Antiquités Égyptiennes

The first conservator of the Louvre's Egyptian collection was Jean-François Champollion, the decipherer of hieroglyphics. The collection includes both objects acquired by private citizens and antiquities collected by various European diplomats (among them Henry Salt and Bernardino Drovetti). Beginning in the middle of the 19th century, when Mariette founded the Antiquities Service, the museum's collection came to include finds from important archaeological excavations at Saqqara, Tod, Medamud, Bawit, and Deir el-Medina. Following the reorganization of the museum, the Egyptian collection was arranged to form a thematic route on the ground floor and a historical presentation on the second floor.

Turin: Fondazione per il Museo delle Antichità Egizie

The origin of this museum dates back to 1824 and the acquisition of the collection of Consul Drovetti by Charles Albert of Savoy, although the Savoy family had owned several Egyptian objects in the 18th century. There are extraordinarily important statues—including the basalt statue of the enthroned Ramses II—and papyri; beginning in 1904, the collection came to include objects from excavations conducted in Egypt by Ernesto Schiaparelli (in the Memphite and Theban necropolises and in Middle Egypt). The most recent acquisition was the rock temple of Ellesiya, saved from the water of Lake Nasser during the 1960s. Displayed on three floors, the 6,000 objects chronologically illustrate the phases of pharaonic history.

Vatican City: Museo Gregoriano Egizio

In halls decorated with Egyptian-style motifs are displayed the Egyptian antiquities from archaeological excavations performed in the center of Rome and at Tivoli, along with acquisitions made in Egypt by private collectors; the collection also includes objects donated to the Holy See by the government of the republic of Egypt. Among the most outstanding works are several brought to Rome by emperors as well as Egyptian-style Roman works.

Vienna: Kunsthistorisches Museum

Along with precious objects from the Near East and southern Arabia, this collection includes important works from the pharaonic period; acquisitions made following important archaeological excavations were added to the collection of antiquities originally assembled in the 19th century.

General index

Bibliography

Aldred C. 1980, *Egyptian Art in the Days of the Pharaohs. 3100-320 BC*, Thames and Hudson, London.

Aldred C. 1988, *Akhenaten, King of Egypt*, London and New York.

Allen James P. 2000, *Middle Egyptian. An Introduction to the Language and Culture of Hieroglyphs*, New York.

Arnold D. 1979, *The Temple of Mentuhotep at Deir el-Bahari*, New York.

Arnold D. 1994, *Lexicon der agyptischen Baukunst*, Werlag. (in eng. *The Encyclopaedia of Ancient Egyptian Architecture*, Cairo 2003).

Assmann J. 1989, *Maât. L'Égypte pharaonique et l'idée de justice sociale*, Paris.

Assmann J. 2000, *Images et rites de la mort dans l'Égypte ancienne*, Paris.

Assmann J. 2005, *Death and Salvation in Ancient Egypt*, New York.

Aufrere S., Golvin J.C., Goyon J.-C. 1991, *L'Égypte restituée. Sites et temples de Haute Égypte (1650 av. J.-C. - 300 ap. J.-C.)*, Paris.

Aufrere S., Golvin J.C., Goyon J.-C. 1994, *Sites et temples des déserts: de la naissance de la civilisation pharaonique à l'époque gréco-romaine*, Paris.

Baines J., Lesko H.L., Silvermann D.P. 1991, *Religion in Ancient Egypt: Gods, Myths and Personal Practice*, New York.

Baines J., Malek J. 1982, *Atlas of Ancient Egypt*, Oxford.

Belzoni G.B. 1988, *Viaggi in Egitto e in Nubia contenenti il racconto delle scoperte archeologiche fatte nelle piramidi, nei templi, nelle rovine e nelle tombe di que' paesi, seguiti da un altro viaggio lungo la costa del Mar Rosso e l'Oasi di Giove Ammone*, ed. A. Siliotti, Verona.

Berman L.M., Bryan B.M., Delange E., Kozloff A.P. 1993, *Aménophis III, le Pharaon-Soleil*, Paris.

Boessneck J. 1988, *Die Tierwelt des Alten Ägypten untersucht anhand kulturgeschichtlicher und zoologischer Quellen*, München.

Chadefaud C. 1993, *L'écrit dans l'É-*gypte ancienne, Hachette Livre, Paris.

Champollion J-F. 1970, *Monuments de l'Égypte et de la Nubie. Vol. I, Éditions de Belles-Lettres*, Genève.

Christophe L.A. 1977, *Campagne internationale de l'UNESCO pour la sauvegarde des sites et monuments de Nubie. Bibliographie préparée, Unesco*, Paris.

Christophe L.A. 1979 (a cura di), G. B. Belzoni, «*Voyages en Egypte et en Nubie*», Paris.

Ciampini E. 2004, *Gli obelischi iscritti di Roma*, Roma.

Clayton P.A. 1982, *The Rediscovery of Ancient Egypt. Artists and Travellers in the 19th Century*, London.

David A.R. 1986, *The Pyramid Builders of Ancient Egypt. A Modern Investigation of Pharaoh's Workforce*, London - Boston.

Dawson W.D., Uphill E.P. 1995, *Who was who in Egyptology*, London.

Decker W., Herb M. 1994, *Bildatlas zum Sport im Alten Ägypten. Corpus der bildlichen Quellen zu Leibesübungen, Spiel, Jagd, Tanz und verwandten Themes*, Leiden.

Della Monica M. 1980, *La classe ouvrière sous les Pharaons*, Paris.

Della Monica M. 1991, *Thoutmosis III. Le plus grand des pharaons. Son époque, sa vie, sa tombe*, Paris.

Depuydt L. 1997, *Civil Calendar and Lunar Calendar in Ancient Egypt*, Leuven.

Dorman P.F. 1991, *The Tombs of Senenmut*, New York.

Drower M.S. 1985, *Flinders Petrie. A Life in Archaeology*, London.

Dunand F., Zivie Ch. 1991, *Dieux et hommes en Egypt*, Paris.

El-Saghir M., Hegazy E.S., Goyon J.-C., Golvin J.-C. 1989, *Guide de Karnak*, Paris.

Faulkner R.O. 1953, "*Egyptian Military Organisation*", in *Journal of Egyptian Archaeology 39*, London.

Faulkner, R.O. 1972, *A Concise Dictionary of Middle Egyptian. Addenda and Corrigenda*, Oxford.

Fiechter J-J. 1994, *La moisson des dieux. La constitution des grandes collections égyptiennes 1815-1830*, Paris.

Frankfort H. 1948, *Kingship and the Gods. A Study of Ancient Near Eastern Religion as the Integration of Society and Nature*, Chicago.

Friedman R. (editor) 2002, *Egypt and Nubia: gifts of the desert.*, British Museum, London.

Gallo P. 1997, "*Luoghi di culto e santuari isiaci in Italia*", in Arslan E. (editor), *Iside. Il mito Il mistero La magia.*, Milano, pp. 290-296

Goedicke H. 1986, *The Quarrel of Apophis and Seqenenre'*, San Antonio.

Goyon, J.-Cl. 1972, *Rituels funéraires de l'ancienne Égypte. Introduction, traduction et commentaire*, Paris.

Grandet P. 1993, *Ramsès III. Histoire d'un règne*, Paris.

Grandet P., Mathieu B. 1997, *Cours d'égyptien hiéroglyphique*, Paris.

Griffiths, J.G. 1960, *The Conflict of Horus and Seth from Egyptian and Classical Sources*, Liverpool.

Griffiths, J.G. 1970, *Plutarch's De Iside et Osiride*, Cardiff.

Grimal N. 1988, *Histoire de l'Égypte ancienne*, Paris. (in eng., *A History of ancient Egypt*, Blackwell Publishing 1994.)

Habachi L. 1972, *The Second Stela of Kamose and his Struggle against the Hyksos Ruler and his Capital*, Glückstadt.

Hartmann F. 1923, *L'agriculture dans l'ancienne Egypte*, Paris.

Herold J-Ch. 1962, *Bonaparte in Egypt*, New York.

Hornung N. 1999, *The Ancient Egyptian Books of the Afterlife*, Ithaca.

Ikram S., Dodson A. 1998, *The Mummy in Ancient Egypt. Equipping the Dead for Eternity*, London.

James, T.G.H. 1972, *The Archaeology of Ancient Egypt*, London-Sydney-Toronto.

James T.G.H. 1991, *Howard Carter and the Discovery of the Tomb of Tu-*

tankhamun, London-New York.

James, T.G.H. 1992, *Howard Carter, The path to Tutankhamun*, New York and London.

James, T.G.H. 2000, *Tutankhamun. The Eternal Splendour of the Boy Pharaoh*, London - New York.

Janssen, J.J. 1997, *Village Varia. Ten Studies on the History and Administration of Deir el-Medina*, Leiden.

Janssen R.M., Janssen J.J. 1990, *Growing up in Ancient Egypt*, London.

Janssen R.M., Janssen J.J. 1996, *Getting old in Ancient Egypt*, London.

Kitchen, K.A. 1972 (rev.ed., 2004), *The Third Intermediate Period in Egypt (1100-650 BC)*, Warminster.

Kitchen, K.A. 1982, *Pharaoh Triumphant. The Life and Times of Ramesses II, King of Egypt*, Warminster.

Koenig Y. 1994, *Magie et magiciens dans l'Égypte ancienne*, Paris.

Krupp, E.C. 1983, *Echoes of the Ancient Skies. The Astronomy of Lost Civilizations*, New York.

Lachaud R. 1995, *Magie et initiation en Égypte pharaonique*, St-Jean-de-Braye.

Lauer J-Ph. 1977, *Saqqarah. La nécropole royale de Memphis: quarante siècles d'histoire, cent vingt-cinq ans de recherche*, Tallandier.

Leblanc Ch. 1989, *Ta Set Neferou. Une nécropole de Thèbes-Ouest et son histoire. I: Géographie - Toponymie historique de l'exploration scientifique du site*, Le Caire.

Lehner M. 1997, *The Complete Pyramids*, London.

Lichtheim M. 1973-1976-1980, *Ancient Egyptian Literature. A Book of Readings. Volume I-III*, Berkeley.

Lollio Barberi O., Parola G., Toti M.P. 1995, *Le Antichità Egiziane di Roma Imperiale, Istituto Poligrafico e Zecca dello Stato*, Roma.

Lucas A., Harris J. 1962, *Ancient Egyptian Materials and Industries*, London.

Lurker M. 1994, *An Illustrated Dictio-nary of The Gods and Symbols of Ancient Egypt*, London.

Malek J. 1986, *In the Shadow of the Pyramids. Egypt during the Old Kingdom*, London.

Manniche L. 1989, *An Ancient Egyptian Herbal*, British Museum Press, London.

Manniche L. 1991, *Music and Musicians in Ancient Egypt*, British Museum Press, London.

Manniche L. 1997, *Sexual Life in Ancient Egypt*, London-New York.

Manniche L. 1999, *Sacred Luxuries*, London.

Manuelian der P., Allen J.P. 2005, *The Ancient Pyramid Texts*, Atlanta.

McDowell A.G. 1999, *Village Life in Ancient Egypt*, Oxford.

Meeks D., Favard-Meeks C. 1997, *Daily Life of the Egyptian Gods*, London.

Midant-Reynes B. 1992, *Préhistoire de l'Égypte. Des premiers hommes aux premiers pharaons*, Paris.

Möller A. 2000, *Naukratis: trade in archaic Greece*, New York.

Montet P. 1952, *Les énigmes de Tanis*, Paris.

Moran, W.L. 1987, *Les lettres d'El-Amarna*, Paris. (in eng. *The Amarna Letters*, Baltimore 1992.)

Nicholson P.T. 1993, *Egyptian Faience and Glass.*, Aylesbury.

Nunn, J.F. 1996, *Ancient Egyptian Medicine*, Cairo.

Oren E. 1997, *The Hyksos: New Historical and Archaeological Perspective*, Philadelphia.

Partridge P. 1996, *Transport in Ancient Egypt*, London.

Petrie W.M.F. 1931, *Seventy Years in Archeology*, London.

Portman I. 1989, *Luxor. A Guide to the Temples & Tombs of Ancient Thebes*, Cairo.

Quirke S. 2001, *The cult of Ra*, London.

Rachet G. 1996, *Le Livre des Morts des anciens Égyptiens*, Monaco.

Reeves N. 1990, *The Complete Tu-tankhamun: The King, the Tomb, the Royal Treasure*, London.

Reeves N. 2000, *Ancient Egypt. The Great Discoveries*, London.

Reeves N., Wilkinson R.H. 1996, *The Complete Valley of the Kings. Tombs and Treasures of Egypt's Greatest Pharaohs*, London.

Robins G. 1993, *Women in Ancient Egypt*, London.

Roehrig C.H. 2005 (edited by), *Hatshepsut from queen to pharaoh*, New York.

Rosellini I. 1977, *Monumenti dell' Egitto e della Nubia. Vol. I: Monumenti storici. Vol. II: Monumenti civili. Vol. III: Monumenti del culto*, Genève.

Sauneron S. 1988, *Les prêtres de l'ancienne Égypte*, Paris. (in eng. *The Priests of Ancient Egypt*, London 2000.)

Shaw I. 2000, *The Oxford History of Ancient Egypt*, Oxford.

Stierlin H., Ziegler Ch. 1988, *Tanis. I tesori dei Faraoni*, Milano.

Valbelle D. 1990, *Les Neuf Arcs*, Paris.

Vandersleyen C. 1971, *Les guerres d'Amosis. Fondateur de la XVIIIe dynastie*, Bruxelles.

Verges F.L. 1992, *Bleus égyptiens*, Leuven.

Verner M. 1999, *Die Pyramiden*, Hamburg (in eng. *The Pyramids*, New York 2002.)

Vernus P., Yoyotte J. 2005, *Le bestiaire des Pharaons*, Paris.

Weeks K.R. 2001, *Valley of the Kings*, New York.

Wildung D. 1984, *L'âge d'or de l'Égypte. Le Moyen Empire*, Paris.

Wilkinson T.A.H. 2000a, *Royal Annals of Ancient Egypt. The Palermo Stone and its associated fragments*, London - New York.

Wilkinson T.A.H. 2000b, *The complete temple of ancient Egypt*, London.

Wilson H. 1988, *Egyptian Food and Drink*, Aylesbury.

Ziegler Ch. 2002, *Les Pharaons*, Paris.

Photographic references

Ägyptisches Museum, Berlin, 87, 143, 200

AKG Images, Berlin, 25, 27, 28, 29, 30, 40 (above), 43, 49, 51, 54, 57, 62, 68, 70, 71, 79, 100, 114, 118, 124, 129, 135, 146, 147 (bottom), 148, 149, 151, 154, 155, 157, 158, 168, 177, 178, 192, 202–203, 204, 222, 234, 250, 259, 262, 263, 266, 269, 304–305, 307, 310, 312, 316–317, 318, 345, 348, 350 (above), 372

Ancient Art & Architecture Collection, Ltd., London, 99, 144, 170, 346

Archivio Enrico Ferraris, Turin, 123, 126

Archivio Mondadori Electa, Milan, 13, 20, 32, 34, 36, 38, 44, 53, 60, 61, 63, 66, 67, 69, 78, 80–81, 82, 83, 84, 105, 106, 109, 110, 113, 115, 119, 128, 141, 145, 179, 195, 196, 199 (above), 221, 223, 224, 225, 228, 230, 231, 252, 260, 286, 289, 293, 294, 295, 298, 301, 302, 303, 309, 311, 313, 320, 331, 337, 352, 353, 354, 355, 356, 361, 363; photo G. Lovera, Turin, 36, 37, 95, 98, 103, 108, 134, 150, 163, 184, 191, 194, 198, 201, 214, 226 (below), 227, 229, 242, 243, 248–249, 254, 274, 281, 292, 308

Art Archive, London, 8, 12, 15, 16, 21, 33, 40 (bottom), 47 (bottom), 64, 65, 76, 91, 104, 116, 122, 125, 140, 152, 171, 212, 239, 253, 258, 261 (bottom), 270–271, 276, 287

Ashmolean Museum, Oxford, 11

Bridgeman Art Library, London, 101, 107, 167, 206, 220, 327, 329, 330, 334, 339

British Museum, London, 247

© Corbis, Milan, 18, 23, 24, 41, 45, 50, 74–75, 86, 132, 142, 153, 156, 164, 218, 219, 232, 236, 237, 238, 257, 275, 277, 280, 285, 296–297, 321, 329, 332, 242, 243, 250 (bottom), 351, 359, 366, 367, 368, 369, 370, 371

Egyptian Museum, Cairo, 14, 77, 136–137, 166, 180, 185

Giacomo Lovera, Turin, 10, 35, 169, 226 (above), 299, 306, 322, 323

Heritage Image, London, 90, 199, 233 (above)

Kestner-Museum, Hannover, 130

Leemage, Paris, 22, 55, 92, 111, 112, 197, 210, 213, 217, 233 (bottom), 244, 246, 338, 349, 358, 360–361, 362, 364

© Lessing/Agenzia Contrasto, Milan, cover photo, 31, 48, 58, 94, 97, 102, 117, 127, 133, 138, 139, 147 (above), 163, 165, 176, 182, 189, 190, 209, 211, 215, 217, 241, 255, 256, 272, 289, 314, 333, 336, 340

Luca Mozzati, Milan, 279, 282–283, 315

Metropolitan Museum of Art, New York, 39

Museo Archeologico Regionale, Palermo, 347

Museo Egizio Gregoriano, Vatican City, 88

Scala Group, Florence, 85, 96, 120, 131, 187, 208, 209, 245, 290, 326